The American South

The American South

SEVEN BOOKS SUGGESTED
FOR REPRINTING BY
C. VANN WOODWARD

G. W. Dyer
Democracy in the South Before the Civil War. 1905

D. R. Hundley
Social Relations in Our Southern States. 1860

Charles H. Otken
*The Ills of the South, Or, Related Causes Hostile
to the General Prosperity of the Southern People.*
1894

Robert Royal Russel
Economic Aspects of Southern Sectionalism, 1840–1861.
1923

Robert Somers
The Southern States Since the War, 1870–1. 1871

D. Augustus Straker
The New South Investigated. 1888

Richard Taylor
*Destruction and Reconstruction: Personal Experiences
of the Late War.* 1879

THE

ILLS OF THE SOUTH

OR

RELATED CAUSES HOSTILE TO THE
GENERAL PROSPERITY OF THE
SOUTHERN PEOPLE

BY

CHARLES H. OTKEN

99365

ARNO PRESS

A NEW YORK TIMES COMPANY

New York ☆ 1973

Reprint Edition 1973 by Arno Press Inc.

Reprinted from a copy in
  The State Historical Society of Wisconsin Library

The American South
ISBN for complete set: 0-405-05058-5

Manufactured in the United States of America

———◆———

Library of Congress Cataloging in Publication Data

Otken, Charles H   b. 1839.
    The ills of the South.

    (The American South)
    Reprint of the 1894 ed. published by Putnam,
New York.
    1. Southern states--Economic conditions.
    2. Southern states--Social conditions. I. Title.
    II. Series.
    HC107.A13.08 1973b   330.9'75'04   72-11345
    ISBN 0-405-05061-5

THE

ILLS OF THE SOUTH

OR

RELATED CAUSES HOSTILE TO THE
GENERAL PROSPERITY OF THE
SOUTHERN PEOPLE

BY

CHARLES H. OTKEN, LL.D.

G. P. PUTNAM'S SONS

NEW YORK   LONDON
27 WEST TWENTY-THIRD STREET   24 BEDFORD STREET, STRAND

The Knickerbocker Press

1894

PREFACE

MY purpose in writing this book is found in the book itself. Some seventeen years ago the governor of a Southern State asked the author " what the sentiment of the people in his part of the State was concerning the lien laws." After inquiry of quite a number of furnishing merchants, the fact was revealed that all these merchants except one were opposed to the repeal of these laws. This inquiry led to investigation not only of the business system, but of related subjects. The result of this inquiry is now given to the public.

The book was written in no hostile spirit to any class of men. Its generous intent will disarm criticism. A condition of affairs exists that can not continue without serious hurt to all the people. General prosperity there is none. To call attention to the causes that underlie this condition, is the aim of the book.

I am indebted for valuable information concerning the education of the colored people in the States of Georgia, North Carolina, Florida, Arkansas, and Texas, to Hon. S. D. Bradwell, John C. Scarborough, W. N. Sheats, J. H. Shinn, and J. M. Carlisle, Superintendents of Public Instruction in these States; also to Hon. W. T. Harris, Commissioner of Education, for the latest educational statistics.

v

My acknowledgments are due Governors J. S. Hogg of Texas, Thos. G. Jones of Alabama, Murphy J. Foster of Louisiana, Henry L. Mitchell of Florida, J. M. Stone of Mississippi, and Hon. L. A. Whatley, Superintendent of Penitentiaries in Texas, and Hon. L. B. Wombwell, Commissioner of Agriculture in Florida, for crime statistics in their respective States.

I desire, also, to acknowledge my obligations to Judge J. B. Chrisman and Judge Wm. P. Cassedy, both of Mississippi, for reading portions of the manuscript.

C. H. O.

SUMMIT, MISS., *March*, 1894

CONTENTS.

CHAPTER I.

PAGE

THE CONDITION OF THE SOUTH IN 1865 . . .   1

Widespread desolation—Disadvantages—The new relation of former slaves—Whims and ignorance—Use of
freedom—Attitude of the Southern people to the old
relation—Encouragement—The negroes' fears easily excited—Consequences—The spell broken—Poverty of the
South—Shylocks—Debts and distress—The credit system
introduced.

CHAPTER II.

THE CREDIT SYSTEM   12

Usefulness of credit—Basal elements—Wealth and capital
—Value and production—Features of the credit system—
Opinion of Samuel Smiles—The debtor bound—Ignorance
—Carelessness—Infidelity and dishonesty—First step to
bankruptcy—A bad crop year—Lost all in ten years—The
covenant—Merchant Harlem's view of bad debts—General
effects—Millwell—Gains on a cash basis—Remedy—A
prosperous cash merchant—No general prosperity—Invest-
ments—No hostility—A serious condition.

CHAPTER III.

THE LIEN LAW MACHINE   33

Slow progress—Worth makes the man—Deeds of trust—
Their intent—Effect on labor—Merchants became large
landowners—Their grip on tenant labor—Resident farmers
without labor—Decoy ducks—A big screw loose—Bitter

vii

PAGE

memories—Patrick and Black John—Depredations—Cause
of violence—Credit system and cash—Lien laws, the backbone of the system—" Prettiest business in the world "—
Five hundred men tied up—" Eight hundred do my bidding"—Honesty relegated to an inferior position—The
galling yoke—Unscrupulous transactions—Lien laws have
not benefited the negro nor the white people—Lien laws
have placed a discount on all services—Strike the laws from
the statutes—A large class has the experience, a small
class the gold, as the fruit of these laws.

CHAPTER IV.

COTTON PRODUCTION 54

" We never do "—Our business system—Henry W. Grady
—Comments by the *New Orleans Picayune*—Debts and
cotton production—" His line of credit "—The chances—
Hon. B. H. Hill—Wade Sherman's experience—Canons
of commerce perverted—The difference—More cotton—
From Maryland, through Texas—" Superb estates "—A
million bales in excess—Corn acreage, short—Live at
home.

CHAPTER V.

TESTIMONY 65

Farmer Haygood and Merchant Caperton—Credit, cash,
and discount—Who pay the bad debts ?—Ninety million
bales could have been saved—Samuel Drew—Alexandre
Dumas—Farmers handicapped—Does not know—Need of
sympathy—Fifty to one hundred and twenty-five per cent.
—Credit, the money-making business—High prices—Testimony in Alabama—Senator Irby—The true cancer—*Raymond Gazette* of Mississippi—The *Selma Times* of Alabama—Louisiana — Mississippi—Tennessee — Arkansas—
Texas—Five million dollars lost per annum—Elements
of high prices.

CHAPTER VI.

PAGE

TESTIMONY CONTINUED 81

The first step—What Alabama reports—Florida—Georgia
—South Carolina—Over thirty thousand liens in eleven
counties—North Carolina—The situation unchanged in
1893—Groping in the dark—Local disturbances—The
Clarion Ledger of Mississippi on the lien laws—A practical example—Cost to record liens—Gains on cash basis at
various rates—Gains on cash basis to ten men—Gains on
cash basis to 2,005 men on 10,000 bales of cotton for
twenty years—Not a local condition—Joseph Baxendale.

CHAPTER VII.

AGRICULTURAL PRODUCTS 97

Arrearage in food crop—Cereals in 1860—Cereals in 1889
—After twenty-nine years, seven States had less grain than
in 1860—Cotton absorbed—The lesson of Table III.—
Increase of the acreage and population—Increase of white
and black—Persons engaged in agriculture in ten States—
Cause of deficiency in grain—Shortsighted political econo-
mists—The labor cause—Laborers on farms classified—
Value of negro labor in Table VIII.—Deterioration—What
they do not raise—Productions of Hayti—" The people
make the country "—Productions in Jamaica—The situation in the English West Indies—The proof from three
lands—Value of Southern farms—Value of ten Northern
States—The experience from 1870 to 1879.

CHAPTER VIII.

THE FARM LEAKS. 121

Little things—Value of method—The live stock cause—
Deficiency—Live stock in 1860 and in 1890—Balance sheet
of losses—Statement of a Mississippi merchant—A long
step toward independence—Food products of 1860, 1870,

PAGE

1880, 1890, and 1892—Fertilizers and fences—Fruit of twenty-seven commercial crops—Thirty years' experience—The dawn of a better day.

CHAPTER IX.

OUR BROAD ACRES 134

Our vast domain—The ten States—Comparisons—Farm land—Ownership—European and railroad ownership—Americans—Locality of alien lands—Railroad land and the German Empire compared—Land owned by syndicates in the South—The land movement—Size of farms in 1860 and in 1880—Number cultivated by owners—Cultivated on the rental plan—Cultivated on the share plan—Total of these, per Table VI.—Tenure of farms—Difference in twenty years—Large plantations on the increase—Owner-ship in 1860 and in 1880—Who own these farms?—Shy-lock's plan—Effect of our business methods on the land question—The statement by the *St. Louis Republican*—England's farm tenantry, by Senator D. W. Voorhees—The patent and passport of the Anglo-Saxon race—Salaries of England's clergy—England's landlords—Opinion by Ruskin—Peril to the American estate—Opinion by the *World*—*Galveston News*—The Panhandle of Texas—Land corporations and Governor Hogg of Texas.

CHAPTER X.

THE PERVERSIONS IN BUSINESS 165

Business, an honorable term—Moral distinctions defaced—The science of exchange—The service of the merchant class—American farmers—Bad men—Crookedness in busi-ness—The situation of the South, an invitation—The gall-ing yoke—Ruin and riches—Might is right—Honest Mr. Hacker—The epitaph—Another pernicious doctrine—The retaliatory idea—Unscrupulous failures in business—Honest failures—Perjury—The Cretians—The Bengalee—A catalogue of lies—Negative goodness—The lack of indi-

PAGE

vidual responsibility—Public opinion—Its power—The value of prudence—The demand of duty—Dr. J. G. Holland—The true man—William Temple—Value of moral forces—Sentiments of a Southern statesman—The nation's wealth—Fairness—Millionaire condition—Causes.

CHAPTER XI.

Towns—Their Influence 187

Object of towns—Chief employment—The boast—Townships that lost population—Effect on towns—Indifference —What can be done?—Six square miles—The town's workshop—Education—High-sounding names—Too much and too little—Effects—High schools—Confusion—The counterfeit and the true—Moral influence of towns—Value of the influential class—The subordination of moral considerations to business—Responsibility of prominent men— No life isolated—The town a political centre—The government of a dozen.

CHAPTER XII.

The Progress of the Negroes 201

Their passive nature—What have they done for themselves?—Kinds of negroes—Classes on American soil— Pure and mixed—Kind in each section—Movement—Leaders—Progress—Racial qualities—Rev. Dr. E. T. Winkler —Negroes in the West Indies—The South's endeavor to educate compared—Organized benevolence—State contributions—Crime—In six Northern States—In six Southern States—The difference between white and black—Increase of crime—Burden in the South—Mr. Everett's statement in 1833—The Legislature of Connecticut in 1834—Vermont—Resolution by the Legislature of Ohio in 1835— Transformation in the South—Rev. Dr. MacVicar—Alabama—Mississippi—Pike County—Idleness and vices— Court expense—Effect of education—Fruitage of churches and schools—Relation of the whites to the blacks.

CHAPTER XIII.

PAGE

THE NEGROES AS FARM LABORERS 236

Result of the incentives to work—Degrees in the work of the old and new generation—Condition now and then—Not self-sustaining—Non-productive classes—Workers—Prospect of the educated Hamite—A pauper race—White labor increasing—Difference between white and black labor—Without supervision, black labor is a failure—Cotton production by white labor, and the Commissioner of Agriculture for 1876—The *Century Magazine*—Gain of white labor per annum—Mr. Edward Atkinson—" The old nonsense " in reference to white labor—Attention to the race question demanded.

CHAPTER XIV.

NEGRO COLONIZATION 248

The historic record—The common opinion—The outlook of the English West Indies—Judgment of United States Senator Hammond in 1845—Thomas Jefferson—Senator J. J. Ingalls—Mr. Lincoln—The even chance to the negroes, North and South—The veto of history—Hemmed in by a Chinese wall—The path of safety—Opinions of prominent colored men—Colonization ends the strife—Dr. M. R. Delany, a negro of pure blood—The colored Cleveland Convention in 1854—The Great Congo Basin of Africa—A feasible deportation plan—Advantages —Deal justly with the black man.

THE ILLS OF THE SOUTH.

CHAPTER I.

THE CONDITION OF THE SOUTH IN 1865.

The Past but lives in words; a thousand ages were blank if books had not evoked their ghosts and kept the pale embodied shades to warn us from fleshless lips.—BULWER.

WIDESPREAD desolation reigned in every portion of the South in 1865. The war of the States was ended. The South had staked all— lives and fortunes—upon a principle, and lost. The four years' struggle, with its hopes and its fears, was behind them; defeat, with all its vast significance, was before them. The Southern soldiers returned to their homes. It is not too much to say, that a large majority of the soldiers of the Confederate armies had homes. But these homes of comfort and plenty in 1861 were not those to which they returned after the surrender. A great change had swept over them. Four years' ruthless war had left indelible marks. Time with its ravages, the mismanagement of farms and plantations left largely in charge of the negroes, the vandalism of armies in the destruction of property, had made hideous alterations in the condition of the country. Dilapi-

dated dwellings, fences out of repair and in many
instances burned, sugar-houses and gin-houses damaged or in ruins, were seen everywhere. Farms once
producing profitable crops were now grown up in
broom-sage. The chimneys of hundreds of comfortable dwellings furnished the only evidence that these
places were once the abodes of human habitation.
Cattle and live-stock of every description were largely
diminished. Everywhere devastation met the eye.

The Southern farmers commenced life anew under
many and disheartening disadvantages. Not a few
were well advanced in years, and had large families.
There was mourning throughout the Southland.
Many husbands, fathers, and sons slept on distant
battlefields, never to return. Thousands of widows
were left penniless. The gloom was appalling, and
the people were poor. Those that had something
left were ill-prepared to help their poorer neighbors.
Hundreds returned maimed in body. There was
nothing to relieve these scenes of ruin, save the
brave, resolute determination to commence the hard
struggle for existence.

Their former slaves were freedmen. Four million
negroes were not only free, but were invested with
civil rights. What a novel condition! What a
tremendous experiment! Nearly a million negro
families commenced the business of housekeeping
without a dollar in their possession. Their masters
were poor. The negro was ignorant; he could
neither read nor write. In all knowledge pertain-
ing to the management of business, or relating to
political matters, he was a child. He was made the

victim of cruel impositions on the part of designing men. His truest friends found it impossible to reason with him. He was shy of his old master. The stranger who made him large promises and fulfilled none, had influence with him. The dishonest man, playing upon the negro's ignorance, could secure his work for one-fifth of the crop made. The old master's offer of one-third was rejected. This ignorance of the negro complicated matters seriously. The immediate effect was, that the farmer who had worked twenty-five hands, commenced his year's work with five or ten croppers, and they inferior laborers, while men who had never owned a slave had twenty. Negro labor was a gambling commodity. In a majority of these latter cases nothing was made, and in a few years these men, who expected to work freedmen as they had seen them work when slaves, found themselves hopelessly involved in debt. The negro was emancipated from servitude and from wholesome restraints. He enjoyed his newborn freedom in full measure. Saturday was a holiday. To visit the towns on this day was paradise on earth.

His whims were marvelous. To attend a negro funeral, ten miles distant, was a duty; to help the sick man in distress was another matter. Political meetings had a peculiar fascination for him. Carpetbaggers arranged these gatherings during the reconstruction period. The time for such meetings was usually at night, when the political office seeker, generally a stranger to the Southern people, made preposterous promises to his dusky hearers. The

division of the white folks' property was a charming
theme. " Forty acres and a mule " was not a myth,
but a genuine promise made by a genuine impostor.
A solid negro vote for such a friend was as certain
as the negro's credulity in the delusion. It widened
the gulf between the negro and his former master.
He became thoroughly estranged from his old
master. Neither kindness nor reason could control
him. Suspicion misconstrued the fairest acts and the
most disinterested motives of his friends. Behind
these motives the negro saw some fell purpose to
re-enslave him. A hint to this effect from his
political boss was sufficient to awaken his worst fears.
His alarm took fire. The dreadful intimation of
such a possibility—a return to slavery—spread like
wildfire. In twenty-four hours the horrible news
was conveyed from cabin to cabin, and whispered
with bated breath. On election day he came to
vote, not as an individual, but in companies of fifty,
one hundred, two hundred strong, provided with
tickets ; and without breaking ranks, each man waited
with patience for the time to deposit a vote for his
friend. Such was the travesty for years on the
high privilege of an American citizen. The despotism of fear, secretly and artfully fanned by this class
of adventurers, was stronger than the purest endeavors of honest men to serve the credulous freedmen.

Attendance on religious meetings, protracted for
a week at a time, was a species of mania with the
negro. The large crowd, the exciting harangue of
the preacher, the singing of several hundred voices,

the shouts of the most impressible natures, made
these gatherings irresistible in their attractions.
The wild, weird scene captivated his fancy. He
felt good. His feelings were deeply stirred. Here
he was conscious, too, of freedom. He could stay
till midnight, and this was a common occurrence.
No authority could command: "It is time to go
home." If husband and wife and children trudged
through rain and mud, and reached home by two
o'clock in the morning, it was all right. Wasn't
Dick a freedman? Wasn't his family free? Freedom made him a fool during these early years after
the war. What else could be expected? The negro
could not appreciate its meaning. To him it was
license. It meant to do as he pleased. He could
rise no higher in his conception. If he stretched
his freedom to the robbing of a hen-roost, the kill-
ing of a shote or a yearling that did not belong to
him, he felt no shame; he knew no compunction of
conscience. If, after a sleepless night, he went sulk-
ily to work, and did his work generally wrong, and
then in a fit of passion knocked his employer's mule
in the head, and that employer asserted his authority
in the use of the cane argument across Dick's back,
promptly the case was reported to the carpet-bag
sheriff. The sheriff was the boss of the county—the
friend of the negro. A fine of ten dollars by the
justice of the peace, the loss of a hundred and fifty
dollar mule, and the decamping of Dick and his
family, made up the finale of the protracted meeting or of the nocturnal political gathering. Such
was the earliest fruit of freedom. That amid these

perplexities, forced to deal with the negro incapable
of understanding his own interest, the white people
should occasionally resort to extreme measures, was
but the natural outgrowth of this relationship.

Let it be stated here that the Southern people
are a unit in their cheerful approval of the accomplished fact—the freedom of the negro. Negro
slavery is dead forever.

The Christian people of the South offered every
encouragement to the negroes for regular religious
worship. They counseled them, and in every way
cultivated friendly relations. When they desired
men of their own color as preachers, and houses of
worship of their own, the white people aided them.
That these gatherings soon after the war were often
abused, and the hours of service extended to unreasonable length, are well-known facts.

The negro was excited by every bauble. This
racial quality made him the dupe of the political
adventurer; the victim of every unscrupulous man
who wished to use him. He was easily affected by
his hopes and fears. Any absurd story to re-enslave
him placed him at the disposal of his informer, to
do his bidding. Fearful where there was nothing
to fear, unable to detect the imposition, spurning
the advice of Southern men, the situation during
the first ten years after the war was full of turmoil.
The negroes, destitute of the rudiments of political
knowledge, controlled the affairs of the Southern
States. Ignorance governed intelligence. Black
and tan legislatures imposed heavy burdens upon
the people. Taxes were high. A summons to the

negroes to attend a political club, at night or in the
day, must be obeyed. Protestations were vain.
No matter how urgent the work was on the farm,
even if the cotton and corn were in the grass, their
presence at the club was imperative. During an
approaching election, to lose two days in a week at
political meetings, besides Saturday, no matter how
much the growing crop suffered, did not concern
the negroes. To meet a crowd of two or three
hundred negroes, all mounted on mules and horses
the property of their employers, was not an uncom-
mon sight. Such crowds, led by a single white man,
were often met riding through the country. These
negroes were in many instances instructed to oppose
the white people—their old masters—by men who
had no interest in the welfare of the country.
They used the negroes for their own selfish purposes, burdened the country with heavy taxes,
played upon the groundless fears of this ignorant
people, and each year sunk the farming community
deeper in debt. As long as the negroes could be
influenced by the great bugbear re-enslavement,
they voted solidly for this class of men. They
believed the adventurer omnipotent to save them.
But this state of affairs could not continue. The
condition of the Southern States was desperate.
A crisis was approaching. The South could not
then, can not now, be made a Hayti. Ten years'
woe-begone experience of iniquitous misrule had
tested the patience of the Southern people to the
utmost. The hour of deliverance must come. The
white people determined to rid the land of these

bad men. The majority of these men had one ambition—to fatten upon the country. They cared nothing for the negro, and in the welfare of the people they had neither part nor lot. The inexorable law of self-preservation demanded their expulsion. Necessity urged it every day. They were nearly to a man, with some noble exceptions, firebrands to society, haters of social order, and their misrule was augmenting the debts of the farmer every year. With this riddance, the negro's bugbear of re-enslavement soon died the death. He was disenchanted. The illusion which bound him so long, vanished. Since then, thousands have entered the Democratic fold, and a vast number care nothing for politics. They have discovered that "forty acres and a mule" is a hoax. Another discovery has been made, that the Anglo-Saxon race must rule this country. The superior race must dominate. All the high interests of the South demand it. Such domination is mercy to the negro in his present condition. The affairs of government cannot be intrusted with any degree of safety into the hands of an ignorant and inferior race. It can not be done in the South. It is not done in the North. To do so, means anarchy and ruin to the negro.

It should be observed that the situation of the Southern States, here described, was the retrograde and ruinous movement of the country, immediately after the close of hostilities. That condition in 1865 was unique. In all these Southern States there was not an inland village or town containing a single store that could furnish a barrel of flour or sugar, a sack of coffee or salt, a pair of shoes or boots, a yard of calico or a yard of domestic; a hat, a cap, or a suit of clothes. Not a knife, a spade, a garden rake, a hoe, or a plow could be found. The destitution of every needful domestic article was general, and the people were in need of everything. But if the stores had been full of every variety of merchandise to supply every want, the people had no money. Confederate money was plentiful, but current money there was none. Here and there a little gold may have been found. The great body of the people had no money. Neither had a large percentage of the people anything with which to procure money. Those who had cotton sold it at a high price, and were able to provide their home wants. Speculators in cotton who were able to remain at home during the war on account of their age, or the ability to secure substitutes, fared well. This class of men, who in 1861 were worth nothing, or at best a few thousand dollars, were in 1866 rich. A hundred bales of cotton represented forty thousand dollars. Men who were poor at the beginning of the struggle, were wealthy at its termination, representing fifty, a hundred, and two hundred thousand dollars in cash. They became the money lenders of the country. Some few were moderate and reasonable in their terms in aiding their unfortunate neighbors. Others were hard and exacting—veritable Shylocks. Their opportunity had come, and they proposed to use it in full measure. It was the feast day for moneyed tyranny. The situation was deplorable to the poor and the unfortunate. The times were out of joint.

Add to these troubles the fact that quite a number of men whose solvency was unquestioned in 1861, had old debts to pay, and they had nothing with which to pay them. Some of these claims were security debts; others were for negroes bought when the war commenced. Hard, relentless creditors demanded payment with an urgency and a teasing persistency that drove the debtor to borrow money at exorbitant rates, and secured the same by a mortgage on his land. The foreclosure of such mortgage was in many instances a foreseen fact. A place worth ten thousand dollars was sold for half, and even one-fourth, of that sum. Hundreds of families that had never known what poverty meant, and unaccustomed to its pinching and humiliating distress, were homeless and beggars in the land of their birth. Many families nurtured in all the elegant refinements of life, were reduced to the hard necessity of doing the drudgery which a few short years ago was the work of slaves. The distress was bitter and keen. Others shifted their debts from one creditor to another, and, after years of hard toil, paid the principal and twice and three times that sum in interest. What a hard struggle it was! The milk of charity--the humane feelings —had soured in many a bosom.

This condition of affairs in the South introduced a vast credit system whose tremendous evils and exorbitant exactions have brought poverty and bankruptcy to thousands of families. As a policy, it is vindictive in its subtile sophistry ; as a system, it has crushed out all independence and reduced its victims to a coarse species of servile slavery ; as a relief measure, it is cruel in its deception and in its demands.

It is proposed, in these pages, to portray the evils not of credit, but of the credit system, with such other concomitant evils as menace many vital interests of the Southern people. A crisis is approaching. The future is dark with storm-clouds.

CHAPTER II.

THE CREDIT SYSTEM.

"Of what a hideous progeny is debt the father! What lies, what meanness, what invasions on self-respect, what cares, what double dealing! How, in due season, it will carve the frank, open face into wrinkles! How, like a knife, it will stab the honest heart."— D. JERROLD.

CREDIT is useful in an eminent degree. The business system prevailing with such hurtful and dangerous tendencies in the Southern States, is enslaving the people, and, by its insidious operations, concentrating productive wealth in the hands of the few. It reduces a large body of people to a state of beggary, fosters a discontented spirit, checks consumption, produces recklessness on the part of the consumer, places a discount on honesty, and converts commerce into a vast pawning shop where farmers pledge their lands for hominy and bacon upon ruinous terms in harmony with the pawning system.

The doctrine of credit is, that it is confidence in the integrity and truthfulness of our fellow-men. These qualities form a strong basis of trust. Where they exist, doubt as to the fulfillment of a promise loses its sickly hue. Ability to perform the promise made is the foundation upon which confidence must rest. These three basal elements—*ability, integrity,* and *truthfulness*—are the strong ribs of genuine credit.

When they are impaired by whatever circumstances, misfortunes and providential dispensations excepted, confidence is damaged. Where these qualities exist, trust is their normal outgrowth. It is natural to trust when all the conditions upon which it depends are favorable. Trust in our fellowmen must be measured by the essential elements that give it birth.

The basis of confidence is wealth, and wealth is composed of all those objects which can be used and exchanged for other useful things. Food, clothing, houses, land, and whatever object can gratify human desire and that can be appropriated, constitute wealth. Money in itself is not wealth. It has nothing to gratify human desires. It can satisfy no human want. The money of the civilized world could not have kept Robinson Crusoe from starvation. The silver of Peru, had it been coined into money, could not procure for Pizarro a pound of bread or a pound of iron. Money measures wealth; this is its function. Neither does wealth consist in mortgages, bonds, and stocks. They are mere title-deeds to wealth. A mortgage upon a farm divides the ownership. These commercial instruments are the mere symbols of genuine wealth. A five-thousand-dollar United States bond is a lien on the wealth of the whole country. Should production cease, the bond would be worth less than the paper upon which it is written. None of these

things can in themselves gratify human desires, and
unless there is wealth, which they are supposed to
symbolize, they can not be exchanged.

Neither is all wealth capital; but all capital is
wealth. So much of wealth as is used in production
is capital. Five hundred dollars invested in machinery to be used is capital. It is employed to produce
wealth. If the five hundred dollars is locked up,
the wealth it represents is idle. It produces nothing,
serves no good purpose to mankind in procuring
objects of desire or comfort.

Production creates value; it develops wealth.
It multiplies those various objects that minister to
human wants and enjoyment. The farmer, by whose
exertion a crop of cotton, corn, or wheat is created,
under the laws of God is a wealth producer. The
tree of the forest, transformed into lumber, has
value conferred upon it by human industry. The
lumber is useful and desirable for many purposes.
The same is true of iron changed into horseshoes.
All industries that confer value upon the material
provided by the bounty of God are wealth producers. Some of these industries confer value by
direct methods; others by indirect. The ax, the
hatchet, the saw, the spade, the plow, are all instruments of value; but other persons than those that
made them must use them in the production of
those things that shall minister to our desires.

Wealth developed by production is the foundation
of confidence. Such a foundation is necessary to
commerce—necessary in the manifold forms of exchange. The employer trusts the truthfulness and

integrity of the employee to do the work proposed. The merchant reposes confidence in those with whom he has business relations. In all the various forms of trade, occupations, and industries, this confidence is a very important factor. Without it, human industries would halt; exchanges would be burdened with needless work. In commerce this element performs a larger and more useful function than money itself. Why should A of New Orleans send a thousand dollars to B of New York, when C of New York owes this sum to A of New Orleans? A's draft on C in favor of B will adjust the claim. Destroy the basis of this confidence, and this method of settlement is at an end. All healthy credit must be sustained by ability, integrity, and truthfulness.

The features of the credit system in vogue in the Southern States during the last twenty-five years, differ widely from those of credit. It operates upon a different basis. The credit mode of doing business and the plan of the credit system are far apart. While credit is helpful, stimulating in the development of wealth, the credit system is depressing, discouraging—destroying hope. The one is rational, an aid to progress; the other is irrational, and clogs the forward movement of the people.

(1) This system is responsible for an indefiniteness as it respects the debtor, which amounts to tyranny. When A borrows a hundred dollars from B, he knows definitely the rate of interest he has agreed to pay B. The rate of interest is determined

before the money is taken. By this method there is no such understanding. All the satisfaction the debtor can get is, he must pay certain prices. If the merchant has agreed to furnish him, it is sufficient for the farmer to know that he must pay these prices. Whether the prices are moderate, reasonable, unreasonable, exorbitant, or ruinous, does not concern the purchaser. It is a financial transaction which is as clear as the noonday sun to one party, the creditor, and as dark as a starless night to the other party, the debtor. Would that this statement were fiction instead of a hard, ugly fact! The purchaser is enveloped in mists. He travels in the dark twelve months in the year. He does not know whether he pays forty or a hundred per cent. profit. This is a secret not to be divulged. Human nature is weak. The power is all on one side, and the necessity for supplies, real or imaginary, on the other. The history of nineteen centuries has certainly taught the world one impressive lesson, that power, wherever found, has seldom been sparing in its exercise. It is not in the nature of power, generally speaking, to be merciful. It has not a tender heart. The milk of human charity comes not from this source. The power of this system is a subtle, expensive, crushing machinery.

" Regard for ' Number One,' " says Samuel Smiles, " is the prevailing maxim. High profits are regarded as the *summum bonum*—no matter how obtained, or at what sacrifice. Money is our god; ' Devil take the hindmost,' our motto. The spirits of darkness rule supreme."

> " Mammon has led them on,
> Mammon, the least erect of all the spirits
> That fell from heaven."

(2) The debtor is bound to the creditor when once he has commenced to make a purchase. If he has incurred a debt with one merchant, he can not readily get credit from another merchant. The reason is obvious. The risk under the system is great. No merchant cares to take a customer who is already in debt to another. If there is a mortgage the transfer is attended with difficulties. The purchaser, as a rule, has no option. He is tied up under this peculiar plan. He may be dissatisfied with his merchant, whose prices may seem exorbitant ; he may have found a merchant whose terms are fairer, but if he is in debt, he is in no condition to make the change. The debt chains the farmer to the firm with whom he is trading. He can not buy where it suits him. The price asked is the only chance to get what he wants, even if that price amounts to confiscation. Blindly he must buy, if he buys at all. " Competition " is a word not found in the debtor's dictionary. " What power in civilized society," says Macaulay, " is so great as that of the creditor over the debtor ? "

(3) Those who buy supplies under this system can not tell how much they have bought during the year until the cotton crop is delivered. It is believed to be true of 75 per cent. The only check to the making of purchases is upon the class of poor farmers whose property is small, and whose crop consists in a half-dozen bales of cotton. The limit is fixed at

2

$50, $75, or $100. When merchandise to the amount
agreed upon has been bought, a halt to further
advances is called. The merchant may not be
blamed for refusing to extend the credit beyond
the value of the expectant crop. No such limit is
fixed for the man whose real estate is large, and
whose personal property in the form of horses,
mules, and cattle is ample. If the purchaser has a
family of somewhat expensive tendencies, the account at the end of the year will generally be larger
than he expected. Upon what did the good, easy,
careless man base his expectation? He kept no
account of his purchases. In a vast number of
cases, the bill, as it is commonly known, is called
for in November and December of the year. The
wail of merchants in January is generally, "We
have large balances to carry over for next year."
The size of the crop, the price of cotton, and the
purchases made, determine the size and the number
of balances. Few are the years that from 50 per
cent. to 75 per cent. of the farmers who thus bought
supplies did not come out in debt to their merchants at the close of the year. These facts are
gathered from conversations with many merchants
and a large number of farmers. A slight improvement one year is reversed by an unfavorable crop
year the next. The indefinite plan of purchasing,
and ignorance of the amount bought until the cotton has been sold, is a fruitful source of disaster to
the country. "Fifty per cent. of the people," said
a prominent merchant in 1891, "in my section are
in debt, and from 25 to 35 per cent. are not in an

easy condition." This incubus still tyrannizes the people. This method is ruinous to any people. It is called business in the sense of trade and transactions. It is all certainty and definiteness so far as the items bought, and the footing up of the merchant's ledger are concerned, and it is all uncertainty and indefiniteness so far as the farmer is concerned.

(4) The mode of doing business is the wicked foster-mother of much carelessness, and carelessness is not the basis of prosperity. It may be business to some people, but it has a greedy heart. "I haven't had a settlement," said a farmer of ordinary intelligence, " in six years." "Do you ask your merchant to make out your account at the end of the year?" "No! I sometimes ask him how we stand; and when he says, 'You are all right,' I'm satisfied. I have done business with him for twenty years, and have never asked him for a bill." Confidence is on the rack! "Are there many in your neighborhood who never call for an account?" "A right smart of them. The niggers never ask for a bill, and don't get it if they ask for it." Granting that all merchants are honest, the poor, ignorant negro, as well as the careless white farmer, in the absence of a written statement, has no opportunity to examine his year's transactions for himself. That honest merchant may be an infidel as respects the Bible, but his faith in keeping accounts is extraordinary; there is no flaw in this confidence. The amount of blind trusting he demands of these careless, ignorant people, is immense. Infidelity here would impose a good deal of labor. Such manage-

ment bodes no good to the country. Not one merchant in ten thousand would be willing to do business with other merchants in this way. Dishonesty has the power to cheat and defraud in prices, in weights, and in measures, under such circumstances, with impunity. That the spirit of discontent should show itself, and the cry of "hard times" should be heard, ought not to surprise any one. "There is no money in farming," says the planter. Certainly not, under such wild management. There is a big screw loose here, no matter how honest all parties may be. It is time to examine foundations. Silent and imperceptible are the causes that undermine the prosperity of a country. A magazine of explosives lies hid beneath this highly favored mode of business.

(5) When all the cotton made during the year has been delivered and sold, and the farmer comes out in debt on the 31st of December, that farmer has taken the first step toward bankruptcy. If he is a small farmer, $25, $50, or $75 is a heavy burden to carry. Take these cases: Hezekiah Drawbridge owes $25 at the close of the year; his credit limit was $75. Stephen Goff owes $50; his credit limit was $150. Buff Tafton owes $75; his credit limit was $250. The year during which these debts were made was fairly good, the purchases were moderate, there was no sickness in these families. The following year similar credit arrangements are made, and they purchase the full amount agreed upon between them and their merchants. From some unaccountable or accountable cause, the cotton crop is a little worse, or the price of cotton is a little less. The

winding up of the second year's farm operations finds Drawbridge, Goff, and Tafton with the following debts confronting them, respectively: $65, $115, $155. The outlook is blue for these farmers, and they feel blue. Thus, or nearly thus, this system operates in thousands of cases. Each year the plunge into debt is deeper; each year the burden is heavier. The struggle is woe-begone. Cares are many, smiles are few, and the comforts of life are scantier. This is the bitter fruit of a method of doing business which comes to the farmer in the guise of friendship, but rules him with despotic power. To a large class of men, the inscription printed in large, bold characters over the door of the credit system is: "The man who enters here leaves hope behind," and it tells a sad and sorrowful history. Anxious days, sleepless nights, deep wrinkles, gray hairs, wan faces, cheerless old age, and perhaps abject poverty make up, in part, the melancholy story. The bitter reflection about the whole matter is, that, as a general rule, there was no substantial cause for this result.

(6) "A bad crop year, Mr. Tafton." "Mighty bad, mighty bad," replies Mr. Goff. "We are ruined. I reckon our merchants won't furnish us another year unless we give a mortgage on our land. I used to think that I would see any man in Halifax before I'd do that. It's come to that now, or starvation." The end of these men as freeholders is near at hand. Drawbridge, Goff, and Tafton, and their companions in misery, wear sad and long faces. On some dreary, cold day in December, when nothing can well be

done on the farm, these men ride to town, each to execute that hard instrument called a mortgage, which in so many cases means ruin to themselves and their families. These ugly handcuffs are on, and they are hard to get off. This business method has peculiar attractions for these iron tools that chafe the flesh, but more the spirit. Independence! It is gone. Humiliation and dependence bow the head of the proud spirit. It is a rugged, thorny path these men must travel. A little earnest self-denial faithfully practiced for a few years, would have assured them ease, comfort, and competence.

(7) Thus it is that not a few farmers in the South who held a fee-simple title to their property, lost all in ten years. They worshipped Moloch. Their adoration destroyed their independence, their self-respect, their lands, and their chattels. There are men who made an average of fifteen to twenty-five bales of cotton a year, owned from five to ten head of mules, and from five hundred to one thousand acres of land, with comfortable residences and all necessary out-houses, who found themselves homeless and poor at the end of ten years. There is a cause. It sleeps within the womb of this business arrangement. There must be an enormous abuse lurking some-where in these operations; it involves well-meaning and innocent men who keep no accounts, and, as a rule, apply no business principles to their farm work or their expenses, in hopeless poverty. Neither the merchants alone, as a class, nor the farmers alone, as a class, are to blame for this state of things; but the commercial contract, under whose articles they

formed a joint copartnership to do business, deserves full and signal justice. It is a covenant to which the parties of the first part are thoroughly organized, thoroughly systematic in keeping accounts, thoroughly acquainted with the cost and selling price of merchandise, and thoroughly informed as to their expenses. The parties of the second part are thoroughly unorganized, thoroughly unsystematic, thoroughly uninformed as to prices and as to their ability to pay them, thoroughly in the dark as to what their product will be or its price, and thoroughly in the dark as to their expense account. The parties to the covenant are unequally matched. System, exactness, power, and risks—risks, however, provided for by high prices, and often secured by liens—are on the one side; general inexactness, weakness, and heavy burdens in the form of prices are on the other side. The most certain thing about the covenant is, that the parties of the second part must pay the parties of the first part a definite sum. The price of cotton, sugar, molasses, rice, tobacco, and all other merchandise may fluctuate, but the debit side of the ledger maintains its figures with stubborn and relentless regularity. Hard times do not affect them. Storms and inundations do not change them. These figures remain unscathed amid social and political convulsions. Sickness and death can not discount them. Certainty and uncertainty have gone into copartnership as a basis for the country's prosperity.

(8) The many risks incident to this business involve many bad debts. The honest man must

pay the debts of the dishonest man. Merchant Harlem does a $100,000 credit business per year. He has 600 customers, who make 3,000 bales of cotton. Twenty per cent. of the customers are first-class men; 150 men are in fair condition—they are somewhat in debt. A reverse in their farm work, a bad crop year, or serious sickness in their families, will bring them at once to the dead-line where hope puts on its sickly hue. The remaining 250 obtain credit under a variety of conditions. That there should not be some rascals in this whole number, is as probable as that a cornfield should be without weeds. These bad debts, which ultimately may be charged up to profit and loss, will range from $1,000 to $5,000 per annum. This anticipated loss is considered when the selling price of the merchandise is marked. Were there no loss, the price would be less. Risk always raises the price of commodities. Every honest man must help to pay his *pro rata* of the bad man's debts. There is not a merchant in the South, selling goods on credit, whose losses from this source have not amounted to thousands of dollars. This burden must be borne by the purchaser.

These are some of the ugly features of this business method. It has done much to debauch public sentiment. It has enslaved thousands of good people. It has brought about a state of dependence that reduces the great body of agricultural people to a condition of serfs, the name excepted. It deserves serious consideration. The situation is alarming to free men. It is no small matter that

3,000,000 farmers should be dependent upon 10,000 men. We blame not the merchant class. They have drifted into this channel, and have concluded there is no other way. Some like it, because, to them, it is a feast. This method of trading has lowered the tone of public morals. It is not a secret that perjury often walks the streets, unwhipped of justice. False swearing is common. Wealth obtained by dishonest means is respectable, and occupies a front seat on the dais—the seat of honor in the great temple of public sentiment; and that public sentiment, like a cracked bell, jangles out of tune. Robust honesty is still in the land, but it is timid and passive. It is shackled by environments. About 300 farmers are, on an average, at the mercy of one man. Year in and year out, for a quarter of a century, this submission has been endured. There is no money in the country, save during the winter months. All those who have dealings with the farming class, rendering to them valuable and necessary service, are involved in these impoverished circumstances. Enterprise is stunted. Progress is choked. Whatever is of the highest value to the country, relating to its material advancement, its intellectual and moral elevation, is depreciated and throttled by this ruinous method. A young merchant, who had amassed in five years some $8,000, expressed his interest in the country in terms quite in consonance with his belief and practice. Farmer Haygood explained that he had not been able to bring more cotton to market on account of the impassable condition of the roads. Millwell,

the young merchant, replied: "I don't care a damn
for the roads! I don't care a damn for the whole
country, so you bring me the cotton and the
coon-skins."

The following table shows the property of thirteen
Southern States in 1880. It will furnish food for
reflection, and may throw light upon the circumstances that have hampered the progress of the
people:

VALUATION OF PROPERTY IN 1880.*

	REAL ESTATE.	PERSONAL PROPERTY.	TOTAL.
Virginia	$233,601,599	$74,853,536	$308,455,135
West Virginia	105,000,306	34,622,399	139,622,705
North Carolina	101,709,326	54,390,876	156,100,202
South Carolina	77,461,670	56,098,465	133,560,135
Georgia	139,983,941	99,488,658	239,472,599
Florida	18,885,151	12,053,158	30,938,309
Alabama....................	77,374,008	45,493,220	122,867,228
Mississippi.................	79,469,530	31,158,599	110,628,129
Louisiana..................	122,362,297	37,800,142	160,162,439
Texas	205,508,924	114,855,591	320,364,515
Arkansas	55,760,388	30,648,976	86,409,364
Kentucky	265,085,908	85,478,063	350,563,971
Tennessee	195,644,200	16,134,338	211,778,538
Total	$1,677,847,248	$693,076,021	$2,370,923,269

In 1860 West Virginia was a part of Virginia.
The valuation of property, real and personal, including slaves of these States in 1860, was $5,868,209,-
219.

Suppose that the annual store accounts in these
States from 1865 to 1890 were equal to $300,000,000.
Let this sum represent the credit price, and that
sum is 25 per cent. in advance on the cash price.

* Compendium, Tenth Census, Part II., p. 1508.

Let this 25 per cent. cover not only the advance on cash prices, but all needless and extravagant purchases and all tricky transactions. This is a moderate average advance on the cash basis.

Had the Southern people, by economy and self-denial, brought their business to a cash basis at the close of the year 1868, they would have saved annually this 25 per cent. The people in these thirteen States would have saved in one year, $75,000,000 ; in ten years, $750,000,000 ; in twenty-five years, $1,775,000,000. This sum added to the property in 1890 would bring the valuation of all property in the thirteen States to within less than $2,000,000,000 of the status in 1860.

If these facts and figures do not convince the people of the pernicious and ruinous tendency of the business plan, what will?

On the basis of this advance of 25 per cent. on the cash price, $500 worth of cotton pays $400 worth of supplies bought on credit. The supplies are worth $400 cash, but, as they were bought on credit, $100 must be added to secure these supplies on credit.

The prosperity of the Southern people is very largely contingent on cash transactions and competition in business.

As late as 1893 we found these prices still ruling the market on a necessary article of consumption, flour. From February to September the average price of flour in the city of St. Louis was, for Patent, sold under three fancy names, $3.35 ; for Majestic, sold under five fancy names, $3.09 ;

for Extra Fancy Grade, sold under three fancy
names, $3.00; for Fancy Grade, sold under three
fancy names, $2.65; for Choice Grade, sold under
three fancy names, $2.40; for Plantation Grade,
sold under three fancy names, $2.30. These fancy
names, such as Challenge, Capitol, and Lillian,
represent the same grade of flour. Each merchant
adopts the brand that suits his taste. As will be
noticed, for six grades of flour there are twenty
different names or brands.

These quotations, a merchant assured us, were
those of grocers. At the mills any grade of this
flour can be bought at ten cents less, and perhaps
fifteen cents less per barrel. Adding railroad freight,
after deducting ten cents per barrel, to the last five
grades, we have the following cost price at the point
of delivery: Majestic, $3.91; Extra Fancy, $3.82;
Fancy, $3.47; Choice, $3.22; Plantation, $3.12.

This flour was sold *on credit* at $6.00 and $7.00
per barrel. We will suppose that one of the first
three grades was sold at this price. In this case
the profit on the Majestic was 53 per cent.; on the
Extra Fancy, 57 per cent.; on the Fancy, 72 per
cent. Others paid $7.50 as per bill seen, credit
price. The average cost of Patent flour was $4.17.
According to this price the profit on Patent flour
was 79 per cent. If this was the price on any of the
other grades, the profit on Majestic was 91 per cent.;
on the Extra Fancy, 94 per cent.; and on the Fancy,
116.

A cash merchant informed us that he had sold a
grade of flour equal to the Majestic, from January

to October, for $4.50 cash on an average, at a net profit of 12½ per cent. ; and that a farmer who bought his yearly supplies on a credit had paid for flour a grade below this at $6.00 per barrel. Had he bought for cash his flour would have cost him $4.29¾. He would have saved 44½ per cent. This is the difference between cash and credit prices. On 10,000 barrels of flour of this grade the farmers would save on a cash basis $17,025.

It is probable that the same difference between cash and credit prices rules the market in regard to dry goods, domestics, sheeting, prints, shoes, hats, hardware, agricultural implements, ready-made clothing, and all the commodities usually bought by farmers at a general supply store. A friend informed the writer that he bought floor matting at a strictly cash store for 16 cents per yard ; for the same grade of matting, the price was, in a town where credit prices prevail, in one store, 25 cents, and in another, 30 cents per yard. These were cash prices in a place where the bulk of business is transacted on a credit basis. This means that the cash price of this article in the credit town was 56¼ per cent. in one store, and 87½ per cent in the other store, in advance of the cash price of this article in the cash town. A lady informed the writer that she bought flannel for 12½ cents per yard, and a friend of hers bought the same flannel for 35 cents per yard on credit. On this article the credit price is 180 per cent. in advance of the cash price. If each of one hundred persons buys eight yards of flannel at 12½ cents per yard, cash, the cost to the one hundred persons will be $100. If the same number of persons purchase the same number of yards of this article on a credit, the cost will be $280.

The remedy for this state of things is severe economy, earnest self-denial, and a fixed determination to buy for cash. Two years of self-denial and economy will enable the majority of the Southern white people to buy on a cash basis.

Mr. —— of Mississippi, a merchant, commenced business with $500. He sold all goods at an advance of ten per cent. on the cost price, freight added. When we formed his acquaintance, and were his guest for two days, he was the owner of five stores. In 1878 he sold in one of these stores, during the months of January, February, March, and April, $20,000 for cash. This town had no factory, no special industry on a large scale, that distributed money among the people. Mr. —— was eminently successful as a merchant. He was a thoroughly conscientious Christian gentleman. His pastor—a gentleman widely known in the South as a Christian minister and as an author—said to us: " Mr. —— never advertises in the usual style in the town newspaper, but every few weeks he publishes a price list, cash, of various commodities—as much as will fill a column in the paper. His representations are true, and no clerk is permitted to deviate from these prices for that week." He prospered, and benefited the people.

I asked a prominent lawyer how many first-class lawyers—men standing at the head of their profession in the State—had been able to lay aside, during

twenty-five years of toil, ten thousand dollars?
" They can be easily counted," was the reply. The
great majority make a moderate living. The same
is true of physicians, and of professors in institutions
of learning. The governor of the State, the justices
of the supreme court, judges of circuit and chan-
cery courts, and other officers of trust and responsibility, make a bare living. Ministers of the gospel,
no matter what their talents or their service may
be, are proverbially poorly paid. Yet all these
exalted vocations in life not only demand talents of
a high order and superior aptitude, but require
years of expensive literary and technical education.

The skilled mechanic, after serving an apprentice-
ship of four years, and in some instances longer, makes
a living. Be the industry what it may, be the vocation in life, however exalted, however responsible,
however great the preparation essential to fill it
worthily, outside of the charmed circle of trade
the compensation rarely exceeds a modest living.
Often it means a miserably pinched living. Of the
farming class this is the sum : a few are out of
debt, and struggle to keep their heads above water,
and live fairly well, but on an economical basis ; the
majority are in debt, and the prospect is, that a large
number are hopelessly involved.

Five thousand dollars invested in trade, even if
half is borrowed money, has a far better chance to
make in a few years twenty-five thousand, fifty
thousand, and a hundred thousand dollars, than has
five thousand dollars in preparing for any of the
learned professions, or invested in a farm, to make a

meagre living. Survey the field of human industry in the Southern States, and the fact is everywhere patent, emphasized in every vocation and calling of life, that there is no general prosperity. In large cities there are no doubt some prosperous physicians and lawyers, and prosperous men in other callings of life. It is not so in the country at large.

There should be no hostility between the merchant class, the farming class, and all other classes. But this business method is not only bringing bankruptcy to the farmers, but practically and really it is damaging the just and reasonable interest of all other classes, since, in a great agricultural community, the professions and mechanics are largely the servants of the farming class.

An alarming state of affairs has impressed its die in recent months upon the attention of the country. When people are prosperous, they have neither the time nor the disposition to engage in lawlessness. Men who can not see afar off, moving in a narrow circle, toiling hard, discouraged, despondent, in debt, the farm under mortgage, ruin and poverty staring them in the face, are easily led into desperate measures, and that to their own undoing. But little sunshine streams into their lives. The situation of the country, view it as we may, is serious.

CHAPTER III.

THE LIEN LAW MACHINE.

" Worth makes the man, and want of it the fellow;
The rest is all but leather or prunello."—POPE.

THE progress of Southern farmers to secure an ordinary competency is very slow. We refer to that class who own their land, from 100 to 2,000 or 3,000 acres. These landowners, provided with necessary live stock, are struggling to make a living. Capital amounting to $500 and $5,000, with personal labor added, is not remunerative on the farm. It pays no interest in a majority of instances. The investment itself is in danger. The product on thousands of farms has not been sufficient to pay the annual expense account. What then? A part of the property, real or personal, or both, must make up the difference between the income of the farm and its expenses. A good crop may cancel this balance, but this is a rare occurrence. The general rule is, the balance is increased until a part of the land, or all of it, adjusts the claim. It is history to-day, that farms of every dimension, all over the South, and the live stock, with the products raised on these farms, have barely enabled the occupants to live. In other words, in many instances the farms, horses, mules, and cattle,

3

personal labor of the owners, and the general products raised, were required to pay the expense bill.
Ten years made these men homeless.

A still larger number, whose condition is not so
bad, are toiling year after year, but can not reach the
point to buy supplies for cash. They are always a
year behind. Every year they are contending with
risks. Storms, a drought, a rainy season, a bad crop
year generally, inefficient labor, low price of cotton,
high prices incident to this method of doing business, extravagance in buying, are all ugly contin-
gencies. Many a sorrowful experience will recognize
these elements in the business problem. To secure
supplies next year, security may be demanded in
view of the risk to be taken. The following year,
affairs on the farm may be worse still.

It is certain the farming community of the South
is not in a prosperous condition. What are the
causes? Is it extravagant living? Are the prices
too high? Is the cotton crop too large—the supply
greater than the world's demand? Is it the labor
system? These, and other elements, enter the
problem. Some of them are generic, affecting the
common condition of the people; others are individual in their nature. Spending more than the
income is not a common fault, but it has brought
disaster to thousands. "I can not afford it," is
easily said; but it takes courage and wisdom to act
upon it.

It is proposed to consider one of the general
causes that have led to this impoverished condition
of the Southern farmers. We believe there is no

substantial consideration why affairs should remain as they are. There is a cause which underlies the evil. If it be real, remove it. We believe, with Pope: "Worth makes the man, and want of it the fellow." A higher value placed on integrity, a healthier moral sentiment in reference to right-doing, and the bestowal of confidence where it is deserved, would bring us back to the natural chan-nels of trade. Cash business is, in the main, a neces-sity for the great body of the people. They can not conduct business on principles whose operations they do not understand, and which make success to secure a decent living well-nigh hopeless.

Deeds of trust have largely retarded the progress of the people. In one way or another they have hindered financial prosperity. The man who thus involved himself, whether he gave a lien on his land, his live stock, his prospective crop, or on all com-bined, was bolted to a hard condition. In not a few cases, economy in buying was not the rule. The prices paid for his supplies were high—so high that he could not afford to make the purchases. Had cash trade been the rule, many articles which he bought on credit would not have been bought on a cash basis, unless the price was far different. Both considerations, the absence of economy and the high prices generally, made the expense account of this class greater than the income.

The inefficient and unmanageable negro labor, soon after the war, involved Southern farmers deeper in debt than they were involved in 1865. Lien laws were enacted in all the Southern States to help this class of men, as well as the negroes. The humane intent of these laws was to furnish a basis of credit. The man who had land could give a lien on that. Those who had live stock only could get their year's supplies on this security. Those who had neither land nor live stock could rent land and a mule, and could give a lien on the prospective crop to secure the landowner, and the merchant for the goods bought. This last lien enabled the negroes to be independent of the white man's supervision.

No legislator could foresee the practical operations of these laws. One of the first effects was to derange negro labor. He was desirous to be to himself; to get away from his former master; to feel that all the old relations of a former condition were destroyed forever. This was natural. Whether it was wise in the negro to be his own manager, and act upon his own responsibility, is another question. The negroes had everything to learn, and the disposition to learn and be directed was wanting. The truth is, the old master was the negro's best friend and safest adviser. Unfortunately, the negroes as a class were far more disposed to listen to the stranger than to the old master.

Prior to the enactment of these laws, some negroes worked on the wage plan. The number that worked in this way, as far as our observations and inquiries extend, was small at any time since the war. It never met with much favor among the negroes. It involved too much regularity as to the hours of work, and too much direction on the part of the employer as to how to do the work. It was irksome. The semblance of the old slavery regime was in this plan. The negroes thought so. The wages were graded according to general efficiency and industry. It was difficult to make them understand why one negro's work was worth eight dollars a month, and another's ten dollars. The employer furnished everything under this plan, and assumed all responsibility for supplies bought of the merchant.

The share plan was a favorite with the negroes. They were their own managers. The employer furnished the land, the mule, and necessary farm tools. He was responsible to the merchant for the supplies furnished the share worker. He generally received half the cotton and corn made by the negro. The corn was in many cases less than the quantity furnished by the employer and consumed by the plow animal during the year.

How did this plan work? Generally speaking, it neither benefited the negro nor the white farmer. The reason is plain. As soon as the negro became his own manager, his industrial qualities declined in value. Besides, he generally managed affairs badly. We speak of them as a class, and not of the exceptional good and successful negro farmers—a small number at best. The negro under this plan gave little attention to the corn crop. He raised no meat. The result of the year's work proved that his half of the cotton was not sufficient to pay the store account. The balance due the merchant was paid by the employer. The employer, already in debt, and unable to pay his annual store account, in time lost part or all his land.

In various localities in every State, merchants came into possession of many farms. Some merchants had a strong hankering to become large landowners. It exalted them in the estimation of the world to be the possessors of 50,000, 100,000, and 500,000 acres of land. By indirect means, the aim was to get possession of land. What revelations this policy has to make, is in the future. Some merchants took land because they could not help themselves. Other merchants so conducted their business that the necessity to take land was firmly resisted.

Before the lien laws were enacted, and before they were used as a basis of credit, thousands of farmers in every Southern State had already largely increased their debt obligations to merchants. At that period in Southern history, had no lien laws been enacted, and had all credit business been reduced to one-tenth of what it was annually, the whole South would now be solvent and prosperous. It would have entailed some suffering, but no one would have starved. Such an economic policy would have been of untold value to the negroes.

Under the operations of this system of business and these laws, merchants in various localities became large landowners. It was quite natural that they should desire to utilize these lands. What they did, other men similarly situated would have done. These merchants became competitors with the farmer. Each desired to make the industry a success. There can be no question that the merchant, or any other class of men, had just as much right to own land and to cultivate that land, and to employ negro labor or white labor, as the farmer. On general principles it was a mistake. Wherever this was done, bitter rivalry between the resident farmer and the merchant farmer of the town ensued. All things in love and war are fair, is a falsehood. Modes of procedure may be legally right, yet they are not always expedient. They may, in this instance, damage the common interest of the seller and the buyer.

The practical working of this new plan may be profitably illustrated. Mr. A., a merchant, owns one hundred farms. He proposes to cultivate these places on the share or rent plan. In no case, under these circumstances, does he employ hands for wages. The risk is too great, and supervision is impossible. In some instances land is sold, mostly to negroes; here and there to white men. He does a furnishing business. He provides them with plow stock and farming implements, if necessary; also with bread and meat and clothing. This will be severely allowanced by the crop prospect. And this bread and meat supply, it is claimed by those who have the opportunity to know the facts, is less, in many instances, than the necessity of hunger demanded. The merchant is not to be blamed for refusing to furnish a man more than he is able to pay. The method of working farms in certain localities is under consideration, and not men. The purposes of men may be fair, yet the principles upon which they act may prove disastrous to the general welfare. These men—the one hundred—are the customers of this merchant. Liens of one sort or another bind these people to him. What they make on these farms is practically his.

Where these one hundred farms of the merchant are located are two hundred places owned by resident white farmers. Some of them are in debt to the same merchant, with no prospect of getting out of debt. The demand for security, if other supplies are asked for, is only a question of time. Some are already under mortgage. Others are in debt, but it is held in bounds. It is manageable. They are not in easy circumstances—somewhat pinched in home comforts. They jog along as best they can. They are hampered, restless, and dissatisfied when work goes generally awry. They know there is a screw loose somewhere, but what screw is it? They know that they are not prosperous—they are barely keeping their own. A few of the two hundred are free. They are out of debt. The number is exceeding small. The circumstances of some of these are very favorable, and the others live hard, save every dime, and are chiefly concerned with hoarding their money for the sake of hoarding. The miserly disposition of this very small class is the warp and woof of their lives.

With this location of the tenants of the merchant farmer, and the resident white farmers, we are prepared to consider some of the fruitage resulting from this condition. It is a condition made possible by the lien laws of the country. Without them, the merchant farmer would lose his grip on his tenants. Neither he, nor any other man in his senses, would attempt to operate farms in this way, unless lien laws placed property, real and personal, and the crop, under his control. It is a common opinion, that the tenants on the places of the merchant farmers fare worse, upon the whole, than those working for resident farmers. The attraction of the negro tenant for these places is, that he is lord of all he surveys on his farm. He is the sole master of his time, work, and management.

The results of these peculiar local circumstances born of lien laws may be briefly summed up:

1. One of the first effects of the attempt of merchant farmers entering into competition with resident farmers in the farming industry, is the difficulty on the part of the latter to secure labor. The merchant with a big store appeared, in the estimation of the negro, a rich man. The white farmer by comparison was poor, and himself dependent upon this rich merchant for supplies. The negro prefers the rich man to the poor man. The negro never had much regard for "poor white trash." The merchant had the vantage ground in securing labor. Practically, the merchant embarrassed the debt-ridden farmer. It was not so intended, but it operated in this way.

Then there was a charm in being his own boss on the merchant's place. This was a large inducement to the negro. One landowner lived in town, the other in the country. Supervision of work gave the tenant no annoyance on a place whose owner lived in town.   Poor farming and poor products followed.

Another incident of this plan was the occasional unfair means used to get labor. " Decoy ducks " were used. The "boss idea" always pleased the negro. Other plausible considerations, such as becoming a freeholder, were employed; so that it happened, here and there, that a negro would leave the place of the resident farmer, when his labor was most needed, giving no other reason than that he wanted to leave, or that a "spell had been put on him by some other negro, making him dissatisfied." His contract, and the loss sustained by his leaving, had no effect to change his purpose. All this was galling to the country people.

2. The labor on merchant farms demoralized the labor on places of resident farmers.   Discipline and regular industry among the negroes are, at best, declining in value. This plan introduced a new element of danger and confusion. The negroes on the merchants' places enjoyed and took great privileges. They worked when they pleased; they visited when they pleased; they rode to meetings and everywhere else, by day and by night, when they pleased ; and they enjoyed this lazy, slipshod mode of life to their hearts' content. It had the spice of Africa in it. It did not stop here. They taunted the negroes on places of resident farmers, who did not follow their idle and vagrant example, as "black niggers that didn't have sense enough to be free," and other expressions of scurrilous import.   This conduct did the damage to the farming people in these localities.

The resident farmer saw in this state of things a big screw loose. Not a few had less than half the number of negroes that they could provide with land. The worst feature was, those they had were demoralized by the labor on merchant places. To control them was a difficult thing. To get work out of them was a task. The danger of losing even these inferior laborers was great. Patience was worn threadbare. Other resident farmers, with land and live stock sufficient for twenty and more hands, could not secure a single negro laborer. They folded their arms in black despair. The situation of these men, burdened with debt, the property of not a few covered with mortgages, with an insufficient complement of labor, and that not controllable, and in some cases no labor at all, was as blue as indigo. They were crippled in their work and their prospects by the very men into whose coffers they poured every dollar made on the farm. It is not charged that this was done intentionally. What was the remedy? Men were at sea without a compass. Ruin never before looked so much like ruin as these circumstances plainly prophesied to the farmers thus situated.

3. This purpose on the part of merchants to cultivate farms obtained under the credit system, and the lien laws of the country, waked up bitter memories. The application is to individuals. The effect refers to many. To illustrate: Mr. Henry, a farmer, was in debt to his merchant $3,000. This debt was the result of balances carried over for years. The farm owned by Henry was cheap at

$5,000. After much discussion and hard feeling, the merchant bought the place for $3,500. The old account and a small place valued at $400 and $100 cash closed the transaction. Thus ends this matter, but not so the consequences in the years to come.

Time passed on. The parents were dead, and the children were scattered in various parts of the country. Patrick, the youngest son, occupied the little place received in exchange with the merchant's account for the old homestead. Mr. ——, a near neighbor, incidentally remarked one day to a group of friends, that the Henry place cost in actual cash $1,000. Be this as it may, Patrick, now a married man, heard of the report. He was desirous to rent the place, and, if possible, buy it.

His father's merchant was still doing business in the same town. Patrick offered to rent it, so did Black John, one of the old Henry negroes. Eight bales of cotton was the rental. Patrick offered nine bales, but Black John got it for eight. Patrick was an energetic, intelligent young farmer. Such, in substance, was the information imparted to us.

The old homestead was on the same road, and a few miles distant from the little farm where Patrick lived. Here was material for thought. The legal aspect of the transaction cannot be questioned. But something is due to circumstances, to associations, to those tender ties that give aroma to life. " My mother's bedroom," said the young man, " is now occupied by father's carriage-driver. Had he but rented the place to any other man, white or black, I would not feel so outraged. I have good feeling for our old servant Black John; but I can not separate myself from the endearing associations of my parental home. The very mention of father, mother, brothers, and sisters calls up sacred memories, and these cluster about my birthplace. Why was my offer to rent the homestead so rudely rejected?" It is hoped that such cases are rare. The sympathy of the community was with that young man. The feelings of the people were smouldering. These are bitter memories.

4. Another effect showed itself in many depredations. These tenants fared no better than other tenants in making a living—rather worse. As a class they were often hard pressed for food. In such case " mine and thine " were ignored. Shoats, sheep, young cattle, and poultry were common prey. The corncrib and the potato-bank, if accessible, were not sacred objects to a hungry stomach. Ten tenants, we were informed, representing 30 persons, made 30 bales of cotton and 500 bushels of corn. They raised no potatoes, or next to none, and no meat. Half of the cotton and corn belonged to the landowner. The remainder paid for the supplies furnished during the year. Fifty-two dollars will not suffice to buy food and clothing for three persons to each tenant on an average.

It is not meant that the condition of all tenants of this class was this bad, nor yet that that of the tenants with resident farmers was much better; but that this peculiar plan of renting land to negroes without supervision, means poor crops, especially food crops. And poor crops lead to stealing. Why should the people be deluded with the idea that this sort of management can promote the prosperity of the country? The poor negro is not benefited, and the foundation is laid for trouble.

5. Thievery among negroes, if not the cause, has been the occasion, of much violence. It is difficult to appreciate the situation. Honest men that work hard to make a living, and fail in so many instances to make ends meet, and then have the little they make, stolen, are certainly annoyed beyond endurance.

6. With these environments, the two hundred farmers have an uphill business, in these localities, at farming. If they were encouraged by sympathy and generous interest, unmixed with selfish considerations, it is firmly believed that the result would benefit them, the negroes, and the general trade. So much for the bad effects of lien laws in various localities.

It is our purpose now to examine some of the effects of these laws on the general condition of the farming class in the South. A level-headed man remarked in our presence, " Had I the money, and did I wish to enter the mercantile business, and wished to make money fast, I would choose the furnishing business on the credit plan ; but if I wanted to do an honest, straightforward business, I would sell for cash."

The credit system is a step generally toward lien laws. Either one enslaves ; the latter intensifies the condition. Whenever the danger point is reached, these laws are sure to be invoked. Were these laws repealed, the furnishing business would soon come to a dead halt in thousands of cases. Economy and freedom would in a few years take the place of extravagance, credit prices, and slavery. Whatever kindness may be in these methods, it is dearly bought. It certainly does look, from all the experience of the past, that this plan of buying on long time, secured by liens, is the very best means to remain poor all the days of one's life. This method as a whole keeps a man poor, wrecks his peace of mind, makes him old before his time, and destroys his independence. He can not trade where he pleases, if he has agreed to do business with a given merchant. Besides, in the course of years, he is bound to suffer more or less humiliation. If this is not a mean bondage, what is? When shall the delusion that this state of things is necessary, be broken?

"The furnishing business is the prettiest business in the world." This was said in our presence, and, we are sure, with no bad motive. It is repeated here to show how fascinating this method of selling merchandise is to some minds; what a hold it has on the life purpose. This liking to sell on credit is the strong fortress that must be stormed. There must be a cause for it. If the merchant likes to sell his wares in this way, the difficulty to induce a certain class of men to buy frequently what they don't need, and more frequently what they can not afford to buy, is not great. This way of buying needless things has made a big gash in the solvent condition of the farmer. The buyer must put on big brakes on his wants. This is one healthy step in the right direction. The heavier the load, the more important to put on brakes. So ought it to be with men in debt. A seedy coat is more honorable than a debt incurred by extravagance, high living, and heedless buying.

But what is it that is pretty about the furnishing business? Five hundred men tied up to do business with one man! So hampered that they can not do business with any other merchant during the year! Forced to pay long-time prices! Is this condition a beautiful and healthy state of affairs to these men? It may be beautiful to the merchant, but not to the men who dine on a crust, and, toiling hard through winter's cold and summer's heat, are poor. Let us call it, rather, the bondage business. In a certain company of gentlemen the remark was made, that slavery in the Southern States was dead forever. "It is a mistake," said Mr. ——. "I have eight hundred men who do my bidding; they can not do as they please. If I say, 'Plant cotton,' they plant cotton." It was an ungracious remark; it expressed a great deal too much. A business that imposes such conditions is indeed beautiful, but only to one class of men.

This mode of business relegates honesty to an inferior position. It is certainly true of all those whose property is under liens. Doubt as to their good faith, and perhaps their ability to pay for their year's supplies, inspired the requirement of a lien. If this fear is real, that this class of people will buy more than they can pay for, why deal with them?

Would not a refusal to sell them goods prove a blessing in the long run? Why help improvident men to rob themselves of their property? Is not this the sad route hundreds have taken? The fact that the act of assuming such obligations is voluntary does not shift the responsibility, in part, at least, of those who can foresee the usual disastrous result. But what about the honest customers who are not tied up in this way? Of what use is the well-tested honesty of any man, the moment he asserts his freedom? He trades with B a few months, buying, of course, on credit. Merchant C suits him better. Will C sell him on time, after he had begun to trade with B? Suppose C does furnish him, will not B complain, demand a settlement or security, or bring suit? The gravamen of such a transaction has nothing to do with the men concerned in it, but with this bondage business. The rights of the parties are not under consideration. The man that furnishes supplies may be in the right, and the buyer in the wrong. The point is not what each party ought to do when such a contract has been formed, but the object is to show results—fruitage. The man is not free, and the most robust honesty is often not worth the paper on which it is written. Honesty is relegated to the background. The credit obligations and the lien laws are everywhere pushed to the front.

The strange part about it is, that Anglo-Saxon freemen have for so many years, and so patiently, submitted to this galling yoke. The men who say this yearly debt system can not be reversed, forget

4

the period from 1861 to 1865. Half the self-denial then practiced, now applied for a few years, will assure a healthy, prosperous condition. Best of all, it will bring independence. Conquer this deadly, unseen foe to Southern prosperity.

> " By no means run in debt ; take thine own measure.
> Who can not live on twenty pound a year,
> Can not on forty; he's a man of pleasure,
> A kind of thing that's for itself too dear."

But it is fashionable to run in debt—to live beyond the income. Style must be kept up. To live economically, to lay up something for a wet day, and to pay as you go, are safe virtues, and very honorable. "But what will Mrs. Grundy say?" Her opinion is harmless. Is it fashionable to beg—to humble one's self in the dust, to submit to possible indignities, to cringe and fawn, to assume unbearable burdens, voluntarily to go into a copartnership with sorrow— and at last to leave the family in want and sore distress?

These lien laws have been the occasion of many unscrupulous transactions. Fair-minded, straight-forward dealers, in large number, have not abused these instruments ; but rascality has feasted on the opportunity. Signatures have been forged to notes ; figures altered. A pound avoirdupois, according to the black code, contains 12 ounces, and a yard, 25 inches. Poor nigger! Poor, ignorant white man! How you have suffered at the hands of the Philistines! Meanness, trickery, and fraud have had full sweep at many an unfortunate victim.

Have these laws done no good? Their original

intent was kind. There is too much arithmetic in these instruments. Most men are not well up in figures. They can not calculate the long, rough road to be travelled. They cannot see the end to which they lead. They start in a fog, and end in a fog. They levy a tax on idleness, on extravagance, and on rascality. They are generally in printed form. How many interlineations have been made between the lines, that were not agreed upon? They have not benefited the negroes, and what good have they done to the white people? Had they never been formulated in the Southern States, not a man would have starved to death. The canons of trade would not have been subverted. These laws have done "good by stealth; the rest is history."

They have placed a discount on all other services —services of the highest value to society. Do the blacksmith and wheelwright take a lien on the property of the farmer for work done? No! these men take their chances, or sell their account to the merchant that holds the lien at a discount of 10 or 20 per cent. But this depends upon circumstances. If this is done, the farmer pays the discount, and 10 per cent. on the face value of the account. The saddler and buggy-maker either take their chances, or dispose of their bills to the lien holder upon similar terms. The other industries fare no better. The preachers take their chances absolutely. With them it is all honor; no "deed and trust" for them. The physicians, riding through pelting rainstorms, by night and day, take even chances with the other unfortunates whose interests were not considered

when these so-called anaconda laws were enacted.
These classes have managed to get along without
these securities. Why make the distinction? Why
place every calling in life at a disadvantage? Why
not give the large farming class a lien on the property of merchants to secure fair dealing? The great
body of honest merchants would not do this, and the
great body of honest farmers would not ask it. There
ought to be some kind of protection. A lien implies
distrust. If distrust is honorable in the one case,
why should it be dishonorable in the other case?

But these are not parallel cases. What is the
difference, as a matter of simple justice, between
the dealer that furnishes fifty dollars' worth of provisions to a man, and the physician that renders
fifty dollars' worth of valuable service to the same
man? The lien holder, protected, covers the man
with distrust; the physician, by force of necessity,
exercises confidence, and takes his chances in hope.
Put all men on the same footing. Strike these laws
from the statutes of every State, or greatly modify
them. Make it difficult for a man to get off his
estate by this piece of machinery.

Under the treacherous operations of these laws,
farmers involved themselves in debt, gave security
on their estates when cotton was selling at 30, 25,
20, 15, and 10 cents per pound. They bought land,
horses, and merchandise when the great Southern
staple brought a high price. Everything else was
high. Interest accumulated year by year. A steady
pressure was kept on cotton production. Grain
growing and meat raising were neglected. The

increase of the cotton crop pressed down its price. Now, when cotton is down to 7 cents, the attempt to pay old debts incurred when the price of cotton ruled at 15, 12, and 10 cents, is an herculean task. Many farmers are hopelessly ruined. Who is responsible for this desperate state of affairs? Not the merchant nor the farmer, but this subtle relief device, the lien laws, and the annual credit supply business. This system brings sad experience to one class of men, and gold to another class.

CHAPTER IV.

COTTON PRODUCTION.

SOME years ago the Legislature of Massachusetts made a law requiring that children of a certain age, employed in the factories of that State, should be sent to school a certain number of weeks in the year. While visiting the factories to ascertain whether this wise provision of the State government was complied with, an officer of the State inquired of the agent of one of the principal factories at New Bedford, whether it was the custom to do anything for the physical, intellectual, or moral welfare of the work people. The answer would not have been out of place in the captain of a coolie ship : " *We never do ;* as for myself, I regard my work people as I regard *my machinery*. They must look out for *themselves*, as I do for *myself*."—WILLIAM MATHEWS, LL.D.

OUR business system has regarded the people very much the same way. Capital calls no halt in the race for gain. The general prosperity of the people—their welfare—is not the question. Progress is measured by the aggregate capital of the few. There are said to be fifty millionaires in the South. What about the 18,000,000? Comparisons may be odious, but they often convey alarming truths. It takes 360,000 people to make one millionaire.

Mr. Henry W. Grady in an address to the young men of a Southern university, in 1889, said : " Our great wealth has brought us profit and splendor, but the status itself is a menace. A home that costs

$3,000,0co, and a breakfast that costs $5,000, are disquieting facts to the millions who live in a hut and dine on a crust. The fact that a man ten years from poverty has an income of $20,000,000, and his two associates nearly as much, from the control and arbitrary pricing of an article of universal use, falls strangely on the ears of those who hear it, as they sit empty-handed, while children beg for bread. Economists have held that wheat grown everywhere could never be cornered by capital. And yet one man in Chicago tied the wheat crop in his handkerchief, and held it until a sewing woman in my city, working for 90 cents a week, had to pay him 20 cents tax on the sack of flour she bore home in her famished hands. Three men held the cotton crop until the English spindles were stopped, and the lights went out in 3,000,000 English homes. Last summer, one man cornered pork until he had levied a tax of $3 per barrel on every consumer, and pocketed a profit of millions. The Czar of Russia would not have dared do these things. And yet they are no secrets in this free government of ours! They are known of all men ; and my countrymen, *no argument can follow them, and no plea excuse them*, when they fall on the men who, toiling, yet suffer ; who hunger at their work, and who can not find food for their wives with which to feed the infants that hang famishing at their breasts."

These may be regarded as pessimistic views, but the hard facts of the condition of the two great factors, capital and labor, are alarm signals.

The New Orleans *Daily Picayune* of June 27, 1889,

in its comments on the address of Mr. Grady, shows clearly and tersely the end to which this condition is unmistakably tending :

" The prophet of evil is not a popular personage, but he is a wise one if his forecasts be well founded.

" Without doubt the greatest danger which to-day threatens the safety of our free American institutions is the rapid and enormous aggregation and concentration of wealth. This is the richest country in the world ; it will soon possess more citizens with greater fortunes than has ever before been known in the annals of civilization. This concentration of wealth in the hands of a few means a corresponding drawing away from the many of comfort, competence, and the just recompense of labor. The more rich men, the more paupers. One extreme necessitates the other.

" This concentration of wealth and corresponding concentration of poverty combine to produce the overthrow of democratic institutions, and to establish in their stead a powerful centralized government. For if the possessors of great wealth shall demand a strong government to protect them from the aggressions of the pauper masses, so also the indigent and improvident classes will call upon the government to seize upon all property and all industries, and administer them for the benefit of the whole people. These are the dangers which threaten, and they should alarm even the most enthusiastic optimist."

The debts of the people, incident to the credit system of the Southern States, have been no small factor in bringing about the over-production of the great staple crop. Men in debt, want money. Farmers know that cotton is the only crop that will bring money. In their opinion there is no time for anything else. They owe for land, for mules, for supplies of all sorts—bought at high prices. Cotton brings the money, and money pays debts.

What matters it if corn and meat raising is neglected, so a large cotton crop is made? This will deliver the man from his troubles. Thus reasons the average farmer.

For years a class of merchants encouraged their credit customers to raise cotton exclusively, or very largely. They reasoned very naturally and very logically, that, the more goods sold to farmers, the greater their sales and the greater their aggregate profits. Corn, bacon, and pickled pork are just as good commodities on which to make money as molasses, calico, and brogans. Mr. Henry W. Grady in his second article in the *New York Ledger*, 1889, writing on "The Era of Speculation in the South," states how this class of dealers viewed the matter of cotton raising: "When he (the farmer) saw the wisdom of raising his own corn, bacon, grasses, and stock, he WAS NOTIFIED that reducing his cotton acreage was reducing *his line of credit.* He was thus helpless. Carrying this *burden of usury,* and buying everything he needed, and having stocked his farm on credit, he made slow progress." What other progress could he make? Once in debt, he was forced to raise cotton to the neglect of corn and meat raising, no matter how ruinous. The debts of the farmer bound him to cotton. He was powerless.

He took *all the chances* as to price. If the cotton rose in price, the farmer was fortunate. He saw a rift in the dark cloud. His spirit rose in proportion to the price, and his purpose was soon formed to raise more cotton. He looked with wonder at the long-headed wisdom of his merchant who had ad-

vised him to raise a big cotton crop as the road out
of debt.   If the price fell, the farmer plunged
deeper in debt.   The fetters that bound him were
tightened.   During the first four years, after the
war, the price of cotton danced up and down, generally and alarmingly down.   In 1866, it was 65
cents; in 1867, it went down to 40 cents.   That
meant a loss of $117 per bale of 450 pounds.   It
was a loss of $5,850 on fifty bales in one year.
That farmer had all, or nearly all, his corn and meat
to buy.   No wonder he lost his breath, and a cold,
dreary doubt suggested itself as to the Solomonic
wisdom of the merchant.   That doubt was as cheer-
less and as benumbing as the lack of $5,850.
"What must I do?" said Farmer Jones to his
merchant.   "Plant more cotton; it is the only way
out of debt, and it is the backbone of credit."
More cotton was planted.   In 1868, the price of
cotton went down to 11¼ cents.   From 40 cents in
1867 to 11¼ cents in 1868 was a tremendous leap
downward.   In the mean time provisions kept up.
Bacon, 22 to 23 cents; molasses, from $1 to $1.25
per gallon; sugar, 15 to 22 cents per pound; coffee,
from 30 to 32 cents; a plow, $7; thread, 12½
cents a spool; flour, from $11 to $12 per barrel;
corn, $1.50 per bushel; calico, 20 cents per yard;
cottonade, from 40 to 50 cents per yard; lard, 28
cents per pound; nails, 10 cents per pound; can-
dles, 32 cents; Irish potatoes, $7 per barrel; russet
shoes, $2.75 per pair; Lowells, 28 cents; cotton
ties, 10 cents; and bagging, 35 cents; coal oil, $1
per gallon; matches, $5 per gross; brogans, $2.50

per pair ; tobacco, \$1 per pound. All these prices
had to be covered with cotton worth 11¼ cents per
pound. In 1868 the farmer realized on fifty bales
\$2,531, and lost, in consequence of the fall of price
from 40 cents in the preceding year to 11¼ cents in
1868, \$6,468.50. So that his losses for the years
1867 and 1868 amounted to \$12,318.50. Shortly
after this the price went up to 36 cents. It did not
benefit the farmer. Strange manipulation of prices!
This heartless, conscienceless gambling in cotton
prices ruined thousands. Hon. B. H. Hill, of
Georgia, was during this period hopelessly involved
to the amount of \$250,000. From that day to this
the method of business and the debts of farmers
have kept a firm pressure on the yield of cotton.
These causes have been main elements in the large
yield. The increase of population and the use of
fertilizers have added their per cent.

It was shown in a former chapter that the mercantile system of business had much to do in derang-
ing labor, and this condition had its effect on the
increase of the cotton crop, not so much by what
was done in raising cotton, as by what was left
undone—not raising meat, and often very little
corn. There is a bill lying before us on the table
which will illustrate this point. Wade Sherman, a
negro, made, in 1890, three bales of cotton valued
by his merchant at \$130.51. He bought corn, meal,
and grits, valued at \$34.05 ; the bacon bought cost
him \$38.55 ; the corn and bacon cost \$72.60. When
this was paid out of the cotton proceeds, he had
left \$57.91. More than half the cotton was spent

for corn and bacon; the merchant held a lien on all his live stock, valued at $225. The bill at the store, including the old debt, was $230. Wade was anxious to pay up, and for this reason raised mostly cotton, neglecting the cornfield and the hogpen. This folly impoverishes the poor negro, and not a few white men. But this is not all. The bill has another important food article—flour, costing $26.50, increasing his food bill to $99.05, leaving to Wade $31.46 for a year's work, after paying his provision account, consisting of flour, corn, and bacon.

If the demand is in excess of the supply the price rises. The demand for Southern cotton has made a constant gain in the markets of the world since 1872. Then "the American supply of cotton was 3,241,000 bales. The foreign supply was 3,036,000 bales. In the year 1888 the American supply was 8,000,000 bales, and the foreign supply 2,100,000 bales; both expressed in English bales. Since 1872 the population of Europe has increased 13 per cent.; cotton consumption in Europe has increased 50 per cent. Since 1880, cotton consumption in Europe has increased 28 per cent., the consumption of wool only 4 per cent., while the consumption of flax has decreased 11 per cent." *

The business monopoly has reversed and perverted the laws of trade and the canons of commerce. Healthy competition is dead. What there is, in the form of stimulating honest rivalry, is confined to small traders. Monopoly rules the farmer. "I

---

* Henry W. Grady.

have taken on twenty new customers—can't take any more," remarked merchant Windem. There it is. They are fast. Their trade belongs to Windem, and if Windem says cotton, cotton they are sure to raise.

There is no escape from the argument that the credit monopoly, controlled for twenty-five years by the merchants, has had much to do with the increase of the cotton crop. Debts and high prices can only be paid by this crop. Considerate merchants who advised farmers to raise corn, grasses, bacon, and stock were almost powerless. If they wanted the farmer's trade they must sell corn, bacon, and mules. But still there is a vast difference between the two merchants; one discouraged his customers from buying corn, bacon, and mules, the other was eager to sell to them whatever they wanted. This eagerness was rarely freely and frankly expressed, but rather adroitly concealed. The farmer's need was an open book. To make him cringe, and servile in his requests, was the thing wanted. The favor dearly bought was granted. Such men could hardly complain of prices. Such a man was Mr. Easygo. Mr. Windem bought for Mr. Easygo a mule costing $55, and charged him $115; took Mr. Easygo's note, drawing ten per cent. interest, and secured it by lien. He sold him flour for $15—cash price was $8; bacon for 15 cents—cash price, 7½ cents; and molasses at 75 cents per gallon. Mr. Easygo was advised to make a big cotton crop. Cotton only can pay for these big prices. All this huckstering business had but one end in view—to get a grip on the man's property and his trade for years to come. The trade was forced by a law of necessity into this merchant's hands. No matter what reasonable and lawful inducement conscientious merchants held out, the farmer's trade had to flow through one and only one channel. More cotton! *"From Maryland through Texas the merchants are prosperous."** From Maryland to Florida, and from the Atlantic seaboard to western Texas, the farmers are poor. Under the agency of these causes cotton increased and the price fell. Lands, live stock, chattels of every sort, and a half dozen cotton crops, went down to satisfy the claims of creditors.

"Superb estates, that had brought $200,000, dragged at $10,000; and estates that had sold for $65,000 went unhindered to the sheriff's hammer for taxes. Broader than these personal losses was the oppressive system entailed on the planting class. Having once mortgaged his crop for supplies to his merchant, the farmer was practically the slave of that merchant."*

If such was the fate of many lordly estates where intelligence and knowledge of business obtained, what could be expected of those humbler estates valued from $500 to $5,000, where income, gains, and losses are rarely calculated; where business and management are practically hap-hazard affairs? Who can doubt that the oppressive system was the strong inducement to increase the acreage in cotton?

The planter depending on this one crop, cotton,

---

* Henry W. Grady.

will remain poor so long as this one crop must pay
all his obligations and expenses. In 1892 the world's
requirement of American cotton was 8,500,000 bales,
and the increase of this demand is 1½ per cent per
annum.

If this be accurate, the world's demand for American cotton will be, for 1893, 8,600,000 bales; for
1894, 8,736,000 bales; for 1895, 8,867,000 bales; for
1896, 9,000,000 bales; for 1897, 9,135,000 bales; for
1898, 9,272,000 bales; for 1899, 9,412,000 bales. In
1890 the cotton crop was estimated at 9,000,000
bales. Had it been 7,000,000 bales, it would have
been too large under present canons of trade, though
the price, in this event, would have been enhanced.
Whenever this crop is a million bales in excess of
the world's need, it is ruinous to the farmer under
prevailing circumstances. Three related causes con-
spire to the serious disadvantage of the South:
over-production of cotton, under-production of grain
and meat, and buying on long time.

"The corn acreage in this country is 10,000,000
acres short." *   Whenever the corn acreage is short
in the West, and the raising of this grain is neglected in the South, the consequences to the South
are apparent.

The line of duty and of interest of Southern agri-
culturists is to live at home. Raise the necessaries
on the home farm. It is a safe rule. It is the road
out of trouble. There is no heart-ache in it. The
delusions of the past ought to satisfy any sensible
man of the wisdom of this policy. Reduce the cot-

---

* Mr. C. Wood Davis in *Atlanta Constitution,* 1892.

ton acreage. Every bale raised in excess of what the world needs, lowers the price. This is a plain proposition. The man who buys a plow not needed, will hardly pay for it the full price. The same common sense is applied to cotton.

CHAPTER V.

TESTIMONY.

The warp of the fabric is reality ; the woof, fiction ; the coloring domestic.—M. A. WILKINS.

FARMER HAYGOOD. "What difference do you make between cash and credit prices in supplying farmers who are solvent?"

MERCHANT JAMES CAPERTON. "I can make a reduction of 25 per cent. for the cash."

FARMER H. "Do I understand you to mean that a bill of goods costing $100 on credit, the same bill of goods will cost $75 cash?"

MERCHANT C. "Yes, sir! that is what I mean."

FARMER H. "But that makes a difference of 33⅓ per cent."

MERCHANT C. "Certainly, it makes a difference of $33⅓ on every $100. I multiply the face of the credit price, and call it 25 per cent. off. In reality, the purchaser saves $33⅓ on every $100. I treat the credit price just as I do school warrants. In 1875, I bought $2,200 worth school warrants at an average discount of 30 per cent. I paid $1,540 for these warrants, and made $660 on my money in one year, or nearly 43 per cent. You know Mr. Blakeley? He made $30,000 in four years during reconstruction times. He bought one warrant for

building a bridge costing $1,800, at a discount of 65
per cent. The bridge builder needed money. Mr.
Jones saw him buy that warrant for $630. Mr.
Blakeley made $1,170 on his money."

FARMER H. "Why do you make such a difference between your cash price and your credit price?"

MERCHANT C. "Mercantile business is a risky
and an expensive affair. I have 600 customers on
my ledger. Fifty are first-class men—they are solvent. Seventy-five are fairly good. Of the remainder, 275 are white men, and 200 are negroes. These
475 need careful attention. Some of them would
buy more in one year than they can pay for in three
years. Some of them don't do half work. They
will come to town for a pound of tobacco or a paper
of pins on a fine day when they ought to be at work.
I hold deeds of trust on many of their places, but
they don't seem to be uneasy. Every year some
cotton is run off to other markets. My annual
losses are heavy."

FARMER H. "That explains it. Your good customers must, in a measure, help to pay the losses
sustained by the bad ones."

MERCHANT C. "That's about it."

"The warp of the fabric is reality; the woof is
fiction; the coloring is domestic."

Nine million bales of cotton in 1890, at $35,
brought a gross income of $315,000,000. Out of
this must come the expense bill: for meat bought,
$45,000,000; for grain bought in the West, $20,000,-
000; for fertilizers, $11,134,784. Then, had supplies
been bought for cash, what would have been saved

on this account, and the useless and extravagant purchases that would have been prevented on a cash basis, would have put into the pockets of farmers, $100,000,000 more. Had meat and grain been raised on the farm, and everything been bought for cash, the saving would amount to $165,-000,000 yearly. Just think what this saving means for twenty years. Saved by this plan in twenty years, $3,300,000,000, or 90,000,000 bales of cotton valued at $35 each.

Samuel Drew said: "Economy and good management are excellent artists for the mending of hard times."

Alexandre Dumas gives a volume of good counsel in these pithy sayings: "All the world cries, Where is the man who will save us? We want a man! Don't look so far for this man; you have him at hand. This man—it is you, it is I, it is each one of us! How to constitute one's self a man? Nothing harder, if one knows not how to will it; nothing easier, if one wills it."

It is now proposed to introduce the general opinion of thoughtful people, and the evidence of the census report in relation to the business method or the credit system prevalent in the South. We believe this common and concurrent opinion is not only based upon facts, but is entitled to earnest consideration. The circumstantial evidence, to say nothing of positive knowledge of reliable men, shows that the farming community is tremendously handicapped. They are burden bearers. There is no doubt about the fact. They are down, and to get

on their feet is attended with almost insurmount-
able difficulties. We speak of them as a class.
Like the man in the quicksand, the more they
struggle the deeper they sink. Men down to the
armpits are advised to continue their efforts. But
every effort is fatal. The treacherous yielding sand
threatens to ingulf them. Our people stand on a
treacherous foundation.

The cause of their troubles is complex. One
form of it is the method of buying on time. The
great objection to it is, there are many things about
this credit plan, the average farmer can not compre-
hend. He does not know what obligations he is
trying to carry. A man can do so much work,
carry such a load, and no more. " Another straw
breaks the camel's back," is a true saying. What
is there mysterious about it? This is a fair question. In the first place, he does not understand
the terms of the plan—one feature of it in particular. If he had the money and could barely
afford to pay $4.25 for a barrel of flour, can he
afford to pay $7, the time price? Does he think
of this? Hardly. No one denies that prices on
nine months' time are high. He can not afford to
do business on these terms, and live. He eats up
his labor, his horse, and his land, without knowing
it. He is the man in the quicksand. Secondly,
he is all the time in danger of buying too much.
If the security is good, or if he has property, the
temptation is strong in this direction, and in this
event, he will not be denied the merchandise desired. Thirdly, he can not foresee what will happen

during the year. His crop may be short, and the general crop may be large. These and other causes may bring about a considerable balance due the merchant at the end of the year.

This way of trading is beyond the grasp of the average farmer. He can not calculate the disastrous consequences to himself. To ask a man to do business on this plan, is almost to invite him to enslave himself and his family. It has worked this way thus far.

What the country needs just now, to assure reasonable prosperity, is genuine sympathy between the merchant class and the farming class. Honest sympathy, transparent as God's daylight, is the need of the hour. "If I were to be asked," said Judge Talfourd, on whom Death was at that moment laying his hand, "what is the great want of English society—to mingle class with class; I would say in one word, the want is *the want of sympathy.*" * It is the need of the South. The greedy, selfish policy, by which a few are enriched, and many are impoverished, is a curse to any land in the long run. Men may call such a policy by the fairest name, and justify it by every specious argument at their command, yet such a policy is fundamentally wrong. To put the common welfare of millions on the rack, is neither humane nor just. "Righteousness exalteth a nation; but sin is a reproach to any people." There is no flaw or error in this great truth. The righteousness that elevates and prospers a nation, will do the same for the individuals composing the

---

* "Thrift," by Samuel Smiles.

nation. Oppression of every form, whether encouraged, stimulated, or invited by direct or indirect means, is in intent and in practice opposed to righteousness.

The cost of supplies on the time basis cripples the Southern farmer. Whatever else may be fiction, this is history from 1865 to 1893. What is this credit cost above the cash cost? The evidence shows that it is from *twenty-five* to *one hundred* per cent. above a fair cash valuation. Some of the most successful and competent business men in the South contend that merchandise in towns and country stores can not be sold for cash at a profit less than twenty-five per cent. The credit cost to the consumer ranges thus from fifty to one hundred and twenty-five per cent.

Prices, of course, have been subject to various fluctuations. When cotton was selling at thirty cents per pound, the margin of profit was larger than when cotton sells at seven cents a pound. Nor have these prices been uniform among all merchants. It is claimed that the general average prices, as stated, ruled the market for all men who bought on time.

The question is not whether merchants could do business of this nature on a less profit. It is presumed they could not, or they had no inclination to do so. If the first view be the just interpretation of these commercial transactions, then it is fair to conclude that the consumer, judged by the experience of the past, can not continue to be a partner to these transactions upon these terms and prosper.

These terms are denied by some. Catalogue prices are no criterion. The discount off to the trade is large. Articles of luxury are not under consideration, but the necessaries of life. If the terms are not as high as represented, why should this confessedly risky business be courted by so many men? Why should it be called the money-making business?

The direct information of individuals, various comparisons, the common judgment of reliable men and the testimony from ten Southern States, leaves no room for doubt as to the general average prices on the time basis. Besides, certain deductions, difficult to explain away, corroborate this common opinion.

Honorable business has no need for evasion or jugglery of any kind. It can stand all the light that may be let in upon it. The man that offers to sell a horse for two hundred dollars, and proposes to make by the sale one hundred dollars, has a perfect right to do as he pleases with his property. The price may be regarded as exorbitant, but that is his concern. The purchaser may decline to buy at this price, because it is too high, or because he can not afford it. In either event, the act is his own, and honorable. Neither the seller nor the purchaser is blameworthy. The price of the horse is under consideration, not men.

The credit price is the topic for investigation. Is it high?

A friend bought coffee for his family at 12 cents cash; a neighbor of his bought, on time, a similar article at 25 cents. A white farmer bought two articles of universal use on the farm for $9.80 cash ; another man bought similar articles on credit for $14. The cash price of a necessary article was $18 ; the credit price, $28.

These may be exceptional cases ; possibly are. If such transactions are made in one place, they may be made in another. The path of self-denial for twelve months is certainly the path of wisdom. Such an effort will bring its own reward in time.

"In Alabama 45 per cent. of the farmers, white and colored, are heavily in debt, without available means of liquidation ; and not less than 65 per cent. find it necessary to seek assistance from the county commissioners and the merchants. They pay over 50 per cent. more for their supplies than cash prices. Money is borrowed by mortgaging farms at interest rates ranging from 18 to 24 per cent. per annum. The negroes get about 35 per cent. of the cotton made in the State, but it is all pledged for supplies before it is gathered. On an average 90 per cent. of the whole crop is pledged before grown, for supplies and interest. All supplies on this basis cost upward of 75 per cent. above cash prices. The same thing is true of Mississippi. One-third of the farmers of Texas are hopelessly burdened with debt. They obtain from $2 to $5 advances from merchants on cultivated land secured by a crop lien. The annual rate of interest is 12 per cent. in Texas. Farmers pay from 15 to 25 per cent. ; the difference between cash and credit prices is from 25 to 50 per cent. In Arkansas 75 per cent. of the farmers in the cotton regions are in debt ; in the grass and grain region, 25 per cent. The tenant or share-hand farmer is scored at the rate of 50 to 100 per cent. In other words, it costs him two-thirds more labor to live than it would if he had the cash. The worst form of indebtedness is that contracted by securing advances on grown crops ; it throttles industry and breeds despair by reducing the borrower to slavery."*

"In my opinion, the true cause of the unrest which pervaded the State for some years before 1890 was a system of commercial extor-

* History of the Wheel.

tion or legalized robbery of the farming, and, in general, the poorer
class by the money owners and money lenders, in whatever form it
was loaned to the people, whether by bankers, private usurers, or
cotton factors. This system began as early as the close of the war,
when the Confederate soldier came home to find that all was lost,
both on the battlefield and his farm. In order to assist him in the
struggle to restore his fallen fortunes, to give him credit and standing in the commercial world, the lien law was enacted. It was
intended as a blessing, but became a curse so patent that in time the
farming classes cried out against it as *an infamous*, though *silent*,
oppressor. Merchants and bankers charged outrageous rates of
interest. With rates of 300 per cent. under the lien system, and 50
per cent. charged by bankers and merchants, the farmer was taxed
to death ; certainly to the point where forbearance ceased to be a
virtue, and where revolt was the remedy, both in law and equity."*

"Monopoly is the true cancer, but, like other cancers, its roots
penetrate the entire body on which it subsists ; in consequence of
which we challenge the world to produce the equal of some Arkansas
monopolists on a small scale. We know of a certain mercantile firm
who twenty-five years ago owned nothing comparatively, but to-day
own eighteen thousand acres of land, a great part of which is in
cultivation ; also mules, horses, cattle, and several stores. Perhaps
one person would be more correct than a firm, for one person owns
the greater part of the property. The inquiry arises, how did this
man, who had no capital to start with, amass that amount of property
in twenty-five years, while farmers who had capital grew poorer
every year? The answer is, monopoly and extortion ! These, in
the instance named, were managed through the 'anaconda' mortgage, which he succeeded in obtaining on crops and stock, and often
on lands. Then began the wholesale robbery by charging two and
three prices for the goods furnished, thereby reducing his victims to
extreme poverty ; yea, to financial skeletons. The poor victims,
unable to comply with the enormous demands, were '*sold out*' *at
shamefully low prices*, the mortgagee being the purchaser at two-
thirds the cash value placed on the property by appraisers chosen to
put the lowest valuation that decency would permit.

"The instant one of these anaconda mortgages is executed, the
maker becomes practically the slave of the mortgagee ; *he is deprived*

---

* Senator Irby from South Carolina.

of all means of obtaining credit elsewhere ; he is compelled to trade
with the holder of the mortgage; *he can not object to the quality or
quantity of the goods offered him, nor to the prices charged."* *

Competition is the life of trade, but this can have
no place under this system. Eight months before
the cotton is ready for market, the purchaser is
determined. Prices seeking equilibrium which wholesome competition would produce, is impossible.

The *Raymond Gazette*, a newspaper published in
the County of Hinds, State of Mississippi, had this
to say on the credit system, in one of its issues in
January, 1894:

" What tightness there may be in the money market in the South
is due more to reaction from the North than to the actual condition
of this section. It is a financial back-water setting in from a less
favored section than our own that we are suffering from. None the
less, there is an undisputed stringency in the money market. Merchants are afraid to make the usual advances until they see what the
banks are going to do. As for the banks, they are reported to be
flush with money, and yet holding on to it, until they can see their
way more clearly.

" But be the cause of the stringency what it may, our farmers may
as well make up their minds at once that they will have to buy less
on credit this year than they have been accustomed to do. It is a
good thing for all concerned that such is the case. The credit system has been so abused that it has become a curse rather than a
blessing, and the sooner it can be abolished the better it will be for
all classes of our people.

" It is bankrupting many merchants, and to outsiders the wonder
is that all are not bankrupted. There is a scramble among them for
custom that is simply amazing, and in the eagerness to get a darky's
trade all sound business principles seem to be thrown to the winds.
The writer has known a leading merchant in this county to make
advances to a penniless negro on no other security than an old pot-
iron, double-barreled gun, that was pretty badly off in the matter of

---

* History of the Wheel.

lock, stock, and barrel. That is an extreme case, but nearly all advances are much on similar lines. Raw-boned horses and hollow-horned cows make up much of the security on which advances are often made to the tune of four and five hundred dollars on a single darky. And these enormous bills are not made legitimately. There are tenant farmers who can show bills in which they were charged last year $9 to $11 for a barrel of flour that cost perhaps $3.50. And so with other goods. And not only are these iniquitous charges made on the necessaries of life, but the bills are swelled by charges for useless gewgaws, for corsets and bonnets and fancy shoes.

" While there are merchants who will fight for the possession of a darky with one hide-bound mule, nearly all will, naturally, demand all the security they can get. The shotgun merchant above mentioned had tried to get the negro's landlord to stand for him before the gun was taken. And so it happens that there are merchants who have become, by demanding security of landlords, the largest landowners in the country.

" So, after all, while many merchants have gone under, those who succeeded in business have succeeded on a large scale. They are men of great wealth, while their neighbors are poor ; and the poorest of all is the man who has a large body of land without the ready money to cultivate it. He has on his hands an unsalable elephant that is too good to give away and ruinous to keep. There are not many of the kind left. The merchants have swallowed them all. Such as are left would do well not to be tempted to go security for tenants. In nearly all cases where he does, he is left to ' hold the bag,' while the tenant has had victuals, clothes, and fancy articles, and the merchant has made his big profit.

"Volumes might be written on this subject. Enough has been said to make it plain that the sooner the credit system, as it now exists, is abolished, the better for all classes of the community."

The Selma (Alabama) *Times* says :

" The only way to get out of debt and get a good price for cotton, is for every farmer to raise his farm supplies. Then he can sell his cotton whenever the price suits him. That is the road that leads to agricultural independence."

This appeared in the *Times* in 1894.

But let us hear what is the general opinion from

ten Southern States concerning this mode of doing business, and its effect upon the prosperity of the tillers of the soil : *

LOUISIANA.

" The system prevails very generally throughout the State. RAPIDES: To a considerable extent, the merchants, the chief of which are Jews, have heretofore *got about all the negro made, whether that was one bale or ten.* CATAHOULA : Country merchants furnish small farmers or new beginners a reasonable amount of goods for themselves and families for the year, taking a mortgage on the crop. *Four-fifths* of the farmers deal in this way. DE SOTO : It is almost *universal;* very few planters pay cash for everything, and almost no laborers do. BOSSIER: It is *universal,* and *our greatest evil.* RED RIVER : To an *alarming extent* after a good season ; but a bad season checks the system.

MISSISSIPPI.†

" The habit of scattering the energies of the working force over large surfaces . . . *perpetuate the pernicious system of credit* and advances upon crops for provisions which could be more cheaply produced at home. MISSISSIPPI BOTTOM : It prevails *very generally* throughout the region and to the extent of the *whole* or *three-fourths* of the growing crop. In Holmes, it is *exceptional* that any one, white or black, pays cash for an article. *Deeds of trust are the rule.* In ISSAQUENA, frequently, the tenants (all negroes) when they have sufficient money and are able to pay cash as they go, prefer to keep their money and exhaust their credit. Upland Counties : The *system prevails generally* throughout the region and in most of the counties to the extent of *one-half* or *more* of the prospective value of the crop. ALCORN : Hands occasionally desert the crop after getting all the advances they can. MARSHALL : At least *one-half* of the crop is virtually raised on credit at *ruinous rates.* NOXUBEE, PIKE, and SIMPSON : But few laborers can get along without credit. HINDS : It is *due to this* that *land has no market value* and that labor is taken from the *landowners' control* and forced into cotton production exclusively. SCOTT : It is one of the *farmer's misfortunes* that he is in

---

* Tenth Census, Vol. V., Part I., p. 84.
† Ibid., pp. 78, 155.

debt and at the mercy of the merchant. SIMPSON : It is one great cause of the *laborer's extravagance* and wastefulness. LEAKE : Necessitates the exclusive production of cotton. AMITE : Especially among the negroes.

TENNESSEE.*

" It prevails to a *considerable extent* throughout the State, often to *three-fourths* the value of the crop.

ARKANSAS.†

" FULTON : ‡ It prevails to a *small extent;* none of the farmers are rich, and *they pay cash for what they buy.* MILLER and BOONE : The system is *quite general.* ARKANSAS, JEFFERSON, and GRANT : It prevails to a *very large extent.* COLUMBIA : To a *ruinous extent.* Nearly all the hired laborers are negroes, who obtain their supplies from the merchants, *the farmers having no control over their labor.* MARION : Farmers frequently have to mortgage to merchants at *very high rates of interest.* CONWAY : It prevails to *a large and ruinous extent,* and induces laborers to spend their year's wages in advance, and leads to lawsuits. WHITE, POPE, and FRANKLIN : To a *very serious extent,* so much so that in many cases the *credit given* is *equal* to the *full value of the crop.* DALLAS and GARLAND : To an *alarming extent;* in the latter county the condition of things is im- proving. BAXTER and DREW : *Largely,* and to *its fullest extent;* generally a planter is credited to the *full amount* of the crop, and in some instances to a greater amount. FAULKNER, SEVIER, LINCOLN, and UNION : The system is almost *universal.* SEBASTIAN : The poorer class of farmers secure the advances they need by mortgaging a few acres of the growing crop ; the better class obtain credit without mortgage. HOT SPRINGS : Farmers obtain credit to the extent of about *two-thirds* the value of the prospective crop. ASHLEY : *Three- fourths* of those renting and *one-half* of those owning land obtain advances from merchants. PULASKI : About *twenty per cent.* of the farmers obtain advances. SCOTT : About *thirty-five per cent.* CRAW- FORD : Probably *sixty per cent.* CLARK : *sixty-six and two-thirds per cent.* PRAIRIE : *Ninety per cent.* HOWARD : Credit is given to the amount of at least *one-half* of the bacon consumed ; breadstuffs are

* P. 104. † P. 106.
‡ Fulton's population is 6,684 whites and 36 negroes.

raised at home. CROSS and MISSISSIPPI : The system prevails to a *great extent.* CHICOT : The crop is made entirely on a *credit system*, as the negroes give a mortgage before the crop is planted for all supplies, to enable them to make and gather it. LEE : *Ninetenths* of the white and all the colored planters give mortgages to merchants for their supplies. CRITTENDEN : *Nine-tenths* of the crops are made by money advanced by merchants of Memphis and New Orleans. DESHA, WOODRUFF, and SAINT FRANCIS : The credit system *is almost universal.* CRAIGHEAD : Farmers *buy more* than they *can pay for*, but that don't *hurt their feelings* one particle.

TEXAS.*

"It is not prevalent in BURNET, GILLESPIE, CLAY, PALO PINTO, EASTLAND, FRIO, and LIVE OAK Counties ; to a very *small extent* in HOPKINS, VAN ZANDT, COOKE, DALLAS, GRAYSON, DENTON, JOHNSON, TARRANT, HILL, LAVACA, KARNES, GOLIAD, VICTORIA, ROCKWALL, TITUS, WILSON, COMAL, HARRIS, DE WITT, HARDIN, CHAMBERS, JEFFERSON, GUADALUPE, BLANCO, BEXAR, and ATASCOSA Counties. In other cotton counties of the State it prevails *very largely*, usually to *one-half* or *three-fourths*, and sometimes to the *full value* of a crop. In a few of the counties it is declining. As a rule, the landowner is made responsible for any supplies that merchants may advance to tenants or share-laborers. ROBERTSON County : Local or Galveston merchants advance supplies to about $30 *per bale* at 8 per cent. interest. GRIMES County : About *four-fifths* of the farmers obtain advances of goods ; planters pledge to merchants, who make advances as far as they feel safe, and at the close of the season generally *take all the crop.* Mortgages are sometimes given before the crop is planted, and *very few* can raise a crop without assistance. Merchants sell goods at cash rates, but *charge one per cent. per month on all credits.* COLORADO County : Besides obtaining supplies from merchants, the tenant also obtains *credit* on milch cows, corn, meat, etc., from the farm owners. The merchant always makes money, while the landowner suffers loss. It sometimes takes three years to pay for what was spent in eight months."

In 1886 the Commissioner of Agriculture thus sums up the situation in the Southern States :

"It appears that a large proportion of cotton

---

* P. 162.

planters are in debt for current supplies, and that the loss resulting amounts to $5,000,000 per annum in some States, and absorbs nearly or quite all the profits of production, while the soil is wearing away, with the lives of the cultivators, for the benefit of the commercial class." *

This sum paid for supplies in excess of the cash price would amount to nearly $70,000 yearly on an average for each county of the cotton-growing States. On this basis, each county sustained an average loss in twenty-five years of $1,750,000. It is not surprising that the Commissioner of Agriculture should say in reference to this situation, "This record makes a burden of interest that is unendurable."

Now, it is a noteworthy fact that such men as Mr. Henry W. Grady and Mr. Harry Hammond, the various State Agents of the Department of Agriculture, and observant men from every portion of the South, report the furnishing merchants everywhere prosperous. They are making money.

The contrast between their condition and that of the producer is very striking. Prosperity is the marked characteristic of the commercial class, as poverty and debts are the doleful features of the farming class. These are the features. How are they to be accounted for?

The contention is not with the merchant, nor with the farmer. Both have dropped into a groove. The system of business is mainly to be charged with the results that burden the South.

---

* Report of the Commissioner of Agriculture, 1886, p. 427.

The expensiveness of conducting this kind of business has necessitated high prices. It is well known that a vast majority of these furnishing merchants operated during all these years upon borrowed capital. The commission merchants generally charged the country and town merchants eight per cent. on the money to be furnished during the season, two and a half per cent. for acceptances, and the same per cent. for selling cotton. Storage and insurance of cotton formed items of expense. Often there was a loss on cotton of one and two dollars a bale. It is a general opinion that it takes ten per cent. on the sales to conduct business. The annual losses due to bad debts are never small. The theft of goods out of the store during the busy months of November and December must be added to the expense bill. Besides, in this business, balances are carried over every year. These items will run up a large per cent. that must be paid by the consumer. Add to this the net per cent. of profit. View it in whatever light we may, the business can not be conducted without a high rate of interest on the original cost.

That this is so, that the prices must be high, is confirmed by the evidence of prosperity of merchants. Everywhere are men engaged in the furnishing business whose capital ranged from $500 to $5,000. In a period of twenty-five years, when the Southern planters were struggling with poverty, debts, and the labor system, they managed to accumulate handsome fortunes, varying from $10,000 to $200,000.

CHAPTER VI.

TESTIMONY CONTINUED—ALABAMA, FLORIDA, GEORGIA, NORTH AND SOUTH CAROLINA.

ALL reformation must have its birth in thought. It implies changes, personal, social, religious, and political. The man who goes heedlessly on year after year with a plan whose disastrous results lie around him does not think. " I thought on my way," is the first step to a better life. Earnest thoughts about deranged and hurtful business affairs must be the first and essential step to a more prudent and a better management. The spendthrift, the sower of wild oats, the dreamer that sees "oceans of money" in every foolish scheme, and the man that makes no calculation in reference to his business, are not the men acquainted with effective thinking. This is the only kind of thought that has value. Mere vagrant thought that does not consider the means to an end is rubbish.

When reliable men from an extensive territory tell in plain words the damaging results traceable to the prevailing business system, the effect must be to stimulate thought; and effective thought will produce reform. The evidence concerning a long and eventful period of bad management should lead to earnest reform.

6

ALABAMA.*

" The system of advances, or *credit, so prevalent* throughout the *cotton-producing parts* of the State, is not without its *evil influence,* for the laborer and too often the *owners* of the land are obliged to get advances of provisions from their merchants, for the payment of which the crop is mortgaged ; and as cotton is the only crop which will always bring ready money, its planting is *usually insisted on* by the merchants making the advances. In this way cotton comes to be the *paramount crop,* and there is little chance for rotation with other things.

" The *system of credits* in the large *cotton-producing regions pre-vails to such an extent* that the *whole cotton crop* is *usually mortgaged* before it is gathered ; and when we consider that the *prices* charged for provisions, etc., thus advanced are at LEAST 50 PER CENT. HIGHER than regular market rates, and that the *cost of producing cotton* is given by our correspondents, *almost without exception,* at 8 *cents* a pound, it will need very little calculation to show that the laborer who makes a profit of only 2 or 3 cents a pound, or $12 to $15 a bale, on his cotton, *will have the chances too greatly against him ever to be out of debt to his merchants* when he relies solely upon this crop to provide the money ; and the *exorbitant interest* on the money advanced is not likely to be lessened so long as the *merchant's risks continue to be as great as they are.*"—PROF. EUGENE ALLEN SMITH, PH.D., *Special Census Agent for Alabama and Florida.*

Correspondents report for Alabama :

" In regions I., credits to the value of *one-half* the laborer's crop are often made by the landowner ; in regions II., credits are given *largely* in a few localities, but not as much as formerly ; in regions III., credits have only been recently asked and granted ; in regions IV., V., VI., and VII., credits *are almost universal,* and regularly consume the *entire crop* of the laborer."

FLORIDA.†

" In JACKSON, GADSDEN, LEON, JEFFERSON, HAMILTON, SUWAN-NEE, ALACHUA, and MARION, and where cotton is the chief crop, the

---

* Tenth Census, Vol. II., Part II., pp. 62, 63, 156.
† Ibid., p. 71.

credit system prevails, and often to a *ruinous extent*, as in many cases the farmers are *a year behind;* the merchants are willing to advance on growing crops and take *liens* for *heavy profits.* No remedy seems possible under the present system of planting cotton exclusively. In the lower counties, POLK, TAYLOR, and VOLUSIA,* the credit system does not prevail to any great extent, cotton not being the chief crop."

" The cotton production of Florida in 1860 was estimated at about 65,000 bales, in 1870 at about 39,000 bales, and in 1880 at about 55,000 bales. This decrease becomes all the more noticeable when we take into consideration the increase of the population during the same period." In 1860 the white population was 77,746 ; in 1880 it was 142,605. In 1860 the negro population was 62,677 ; in 1880 it was 126,690.

" The reason for this decrease in the cotton crop is thus stated by Hon. Dennis Eagen, former commissioner of immigration :

" ' The new conditions of labor have operated largely to reduce the acreage of this staple (cotton), and the attention of planters has been turned to the culture of other crops requiring the employment of a less number of hands.' " †

GEORGIA.‡

" Not to any extent in CATOOSA and GORDON.§ Provisions to tenants in MURRAY and CHATTOOGA, and *to a very great extent* in other counties. Since the late war, the great majority of the people have been in debt, and hence the system of credits and advances. To a small extent in UNION, HART, BANKS, HARALSON, and FULTON ; but in *all other* counties to the extent of *one-half* or *three-fourths* of the value of the crop. CENTRAL COTTON BELT : In all of the counties, but to a limited extent in MARION County. Advances are obtained by about *one-half* of the farmers to the extent of from *one-half* to *three-fourths* of the value of the crop for provisions, supplies, and clothing. LONG LEAF PINE and COAST REGION: To no extent in CAMDEN County ; limited in APPLING, COFFEE, BERRIEN, MONTGOMERY, WILCOX, CHATHAM, LIBERTY, WAYNE,

---

* White counties.
† Tenth Census, Vol. VI., Part II., p. 29.
‡ P. 174.
§ White counties.

CLINCH, and ECHOLS. In other counties it prevails to a *very great extent, one-half* or more of the farmers obtaining advances to the value of a large part of the crop. The system is declining in BROOKS, MONTGOMERY (liens only on live stock), and TELFAIR."

SOUTH CAROLINA.[*]

The statements concerning the economic conditions of this State are made by Harry Hammond, Esq., special agent of the census for South Carolina. He says:

"Purchasing supplies on a credit prevails to a *considerable extent,* especially among the small farmers. The exact rate at which these advances are made can not be given, as it is not charged as interest, but is included in an increased price asked for supplies purchased on a credit. It varies from *twenty to one hundred per cent. above the market value* of the goods, according to the amount of competition among the storekeepers, *who here, as elsewhere in the State, are by far the most prosperous class of the community, in proportion to the skill and capital employed.* The better class of farmers *do not approve of the credit system.* It furnishes facilities to small farmers, encouraging them to undertake operations they can not make *remunerative to themselves ;* it reduces the number of laborers, precludes high culture. The rental value of land is thus increased, and land which could not be sold for ten dollars may be rented for five dollars.

"The thriftless culture resulting from the small farm, unduly multiplied by this *unhealthy stimulus* of credit, causes many acres to be thrown yearly out of cultivation. Thus the increasing demand to rent land, in consequence of the *increasing facilities for credit* to small farmers, and the constantly diminishing area of arable land resulting from the very imperfect system of culture their lack of means forces them to adopt, create *high rents* injurious to the small farmer, and impoverish the landlord by deteriorating the quality of his land, as well as by *abstracting the labor* he would employ in remunerative culture.

"The system of credits and advances prevails to a *large extent,*

[*] Pp. 61, 65.

consuming from *one third* to *three-fifths* of the crop before it is harvested. The statement is general that this is on the decrease, and is correct in so far that a larger amount of supplies is being produced at home, and a larger number of purchases for cash are being made by farmers since 1875. On the other hand, the number of farmers having largely increased in the same period, the number working on advances, especially among the small farmers, has largely increased also. The records of the courts show that the *number of liens* on the growing crop is *greatly on the increase*, the rate of increase being *twenty-three per cent.* per annum for the last two years. The number of such liens on record in *eleven of the counties* under consideration is (there being no return from UNION) 30,205, a number nearly equal to the number of farms; but as two or more liens are not unfrequently recorded against the same crop, probably not more than half of the growing crops are under lien. The aggregate value of these liens is $2,354,956, an average to the lien of $77. It appears that the *five counties lowest* in the ratio of *farm productions* to *farm values* have a *larger amount* in liens by 13 per cent. than the *five counties* standing highest in this ratio. In the former, the recorded indebtedness is $4.28 for each acre in cotton, on which crop alone liens are taken. In the latter, it is $2.84 per acre in cotton. As may be inferred from the number and average amount of these liens, they are most taken from the smaller farmers, *usually renters*, for advances made by the landlord, or more frequently by the storekeeper."

NORTH CAROLINA.*

" Very little in COLUMBUS, GUILFORD, CHATHAM, and ALEXANDER. To a *considerable extent* in BRUNSWICK, ROWAN, ANSON, UNION, CLEAVELAND, CUMBERLAND, and DUPLIN. Not too much in PAMLICO. To value of *one-half of the crop* on an average in CARTERET, FRANKLIN, MECKLENBURG, and WAYNE. Only for fertilizers in ALAMANCO. In other counties, the system prevails to a *great extent,* and in several almost *universally.* † WAKE County : *Most farmers do not clear enough one year to enable them to grow the next year's crop.* The system is ' *blue ruin* ' to the farmer. CRAVEN County : The merchants and others take advantage by charging

---

* P. 77.
† Population : white, 24,289 ; negroes, 53,650.

extortionate prices. LINCOLN : Not much among those farmers *doing their own work*, but is almost universal among those who hire. EDGECOMBE, PITT, BEAUFORT: The practice is decreasing every year."

In 1893 the Southern situation remained practically unchanged. There may have been some slight improvement in various localities, but these few isolated and temporary cases can not be regarded as sure and permanent indications of an upward and forward movement toward a general progress in economic conditions. The average status during this year of the farming class of the South was unusually gloomy. There was general depression, and a strange feeling of unrest. An awakened feeble sense of wrong manifested itself. All is not well.

The unrest led to a search for the cause of their woes, and this, too, often when found, was not real, or vague and ill-defined, like other ill-defined and unsurveyed territory. Real hindrances against the farmer were clumsily managed. A dark, dangerous, zigzag course was taken, when the sunlit, straightforward method of calm, public protestations was sure of triumph. The right way of doing things is always the best. It may be a little slow, but it is the wisest. It has no train of pernicious consequences following doubtful and dangerous methods to correct evil. The air was full of pyrotechnics. A form of lawlessness arose, known as White Capism, in sections of various Southern States, striking terror to communities, placing the actors in the category of crime, adding to court expenses, and bringing grief and trouble to many families.

A vast deal charged to White Capism is not true ; perhaps nine-tenths of the outrages attributed to these men are not true. It became fashionable to charge them with every villainy. As long as a befogged and distorted public sentiment could see crime alone in the so-called White Caps, unscrupulous men saw the occasion, under the screen of this opinion, to gratify their spite or their revenge, or further their interest.

The end to be accomplished by this organization was not the same everywhere, nor were the causes that inspired the organization the same, if their acts form a safe criterion by which to judge them. In other words, the genus has a variety of species. The perpetrators of crime constituted a band of reckless, lawless men. Those whose one motive was to correct the labor system in certain localities, were another class. They harmed no man's person or property. Their great mistake was, they laid down the gap for the perpetration of crime by the other class. They established a mischievous precedent.

The end in view could have been secured by unobjectionable methods. The object was to free the lands belonging to merchants of negro tenants. The grievance was, that these tenants were a menace to live stock, and a demoralizing element to the labor of the neighboring farmers. It was, in substance, a war against uncontrolled, unsupervised, and, in not a few instances, poorly fed, labor. Supplies were furnished according to crop prospects.

These disturbances were local. The number of merchants who thus farmed was small. Had the fifty or one hundred thousand acres been divided into a number of large plantations, and occupied by negro tenants, it is doubtful whether any complaint would have been made. Supervision in this event would have been necessary, and the larder would have been kept full. But these tenants were scattered over a wide area of territory, on many farms, ranging from a hundred to a thousand acres, among four or five times that number of farms owned by white people. These tenants thus situated, thriftless, improvident, and poor; many with not a day's provisions on hand, and others with no provisions in their homes for days, were a constant source of anxiety to their neighbors.

This state of affairs could not last. Criticism was plentiful on the movement to break up this phase of tenant system. The press teemed with exaggerated stories, sometimes the product of mere idle rumor, and sometimes the product of prejudice or passion. One class of men condemned the movement with iron stoicism, because it was bad policy. Their view was correct, but this did not help the people in trouble. Their denunciatory gifts were large, but they were wanting in the gift to offer a remedy. They had no sympathetic interest in any of the three parties concerned : the merchants, the white farmers, and the negro tenants. Others disapproved the method, approved the object to be accomplished, and sympathized with the people. Wrong resulted to the merchants, but not through the men who gave orders to the tenants to leave these places after the crop was gathered. This is the common judgment of the people. The harm to the merchants was the result of the method. Had the merchants shown active sympathy for the people when they saw the storm coming, years before it darkened the horizon, or had the people adopted a frank, courageous policy, the class of merchants affected would have been the least sufferers. The men that approved the object, but not the plan, sympathized with the hard environment of the white farming class, and no less with the negro tenants in their unwise and dangerous position. If these tenants were a threat to peace, order, and property, their life was also the source of danger. Others condemned the relief measure, not as unwise in plan, but in itself. It was a hostile measure to them. For the suffering people, white and black, they had no particular interest. Their active concern for the people who had enriched them was of the same type as that of Surajah Dowlah when he shut up one hundred and forty-six Englishmen in the Black Hole of Calcutta. Had a conference been proposed, it would have been to their gain and to the benefit of all parties. Unfortunately, they saw the matter only in the light of a certain class of people at Philippi of ancient Macedonia—"The hope of their gain was gone." No good man favored wrong to them. Under all the circum·stances, and in perfect fairness, a motion from this merchant class for a better understanding and an amicable adjustment would have been most graceful and would have gone a long way to healing the grievances.

All these troubles had their root in the business system under review. The bulk of this land—over seventy-five thousand acres owned by one firm, and occupied largely by negro tenants—was lost by white farmers through the operation of the lien laws and the credit system.

These related evils are not dead. Early in February, 1893, the *Clarion Ledger*, one of the most influential newspapers of the State, published in the capital city of Mississippi, thus uttered its warning notes: "This lien-law device has wrought infinite evil. And it has but postponed the end. The effect of facility of credit on such a population destroyed the germ of the only practice—thrift and economy —which can save a farming community from ruin." The evidence is cumulative; the reasons for speedy reform are cogent.

The evil is not local; it is as widespread as the Southern States. What is the staple of conversation in every furnishing store of this territory during the closing days of December, 1893? "How are they paying up? Balances are many."

A few more samples out of many will close this feature of the chapter. The unchanged business policy has still its grip on the people. The information was furnished by responsible men. "A negro made ten bales of cotton in 1892, which brought him $427. After paying his rent, for land and two mules, $135, and $292 to his merchant, he closed the year's work with a balance due for supplies of $60."

The difference between cash and credit prices on three styles of vehicles was 42, 56, and 86 per cent. The difference on a number of articles of universal use on every farm was placed on an average at 33 per cent. by our informant. Add to this the fact that the government at Washington appropriated $250,000 to ascertain the mortgage indebtedness of the country, part of which is in the South. But what is even this sum in comparison with the expense of recording the various liens on property? The cost of recording the 30,000 liens in eleven counties of South Carolina in 1880 was $45,000. This burden had to be borne by the mortgageor.

It would be interesting to know the annual expense to record the liens of the South for the last twenty-eight years. If that sum was $250,000 for each year and for all the Southern States, and the cost of record for each lien $1.50, then the total cost for twenty-eight years was $8,000,000. This and other expenses formed a part of the general price on time.

It is now proposed to show the difference between cash and credit prices by three tabular statements. The first will exhibit a comparison between $100 credit price and the cash price, according to the rate per cent. opposite it, and which rate measures the advance of the credit above the cash price. The latter price is the valuation of merchandise on a cash basis. The same merchandise will cost $100, according to the rate per cent. this is above the cash valuation.

TABLE A.

CREDIT PRICE.	PER CENT. ABOVE CASH PRICE.	CASH PRICE.	GAIN ON CASH BASIS.
$100	.80	$55.55	$44.45
100	.70	58.82	41.18
100	.60	62.50	37.50
100	.50	66.66	33.34
100	.45	69.00	31.00
100	.40	71.42	28.58
100	.35	74.07	25.63
100	.30	76.92	23.08
100	.25	80.00	20.00
100	.20	83.33	16.67

The second table represents ten farmers, each of whom has bought annually merchandise on a credit basis to the value standing opposite his name. The second column shows the cash price, at a reduction of 25 per cent. on the face value of the credit price. This is the merchant's method of calculating percentage. The other three columns show the gains on a cash basis at this rate for different periods of time. According to this plan, any man could have reached a cash basis in three years by reducing his purchase one-fourth per annum for this period.

TABLE B.

GAINS ON A CASH BASIS AT 25 PER CENT. LESS THAN THE CREDIT
PRICE.

BUYERS.	CREDIT PRICE.	CASH PRICE.	GAINS ON CASH BASIS FOR		
			1 year.	10 years.	20 years.
John Wilkes	$100	$75	$25	$250	$500
Henry Glass	200	150	50	500	1,000
Peter Cooper......	300	225	75	750	1,500
Ralph Rowan	400	300	100	1,000	2,000
Sam. Watts	500	375	125	1,250	2,500
John Hicks	600	450	150	1.500	3,000
Dick Hoag........	700	525	175	1,750	3,500
Tom. Wells.......	800	600	200	2,000	4,000
Carl Upton........	900	675	225	2,225	4,500
Wm. Downs	1,000	750	250	2,500	5,000

The third form represents the business of 2,005
persons. Here too, it is supposed that the credit
price is 25 per cent. in advance of the cash price.
Should this be denied, notwithstanding the evidence
presented in this and preceding chapters, it is safe
to believe that the difference between the two
prices, and the purchases that would not have been
made on a cash basis, would fully save 25 per cent.
The first column shows the number of buyers;
the second, the sum bought by each on credit; the
third, the total credit price of the whole class in
column one; the fourth, the total cash price of the
whole class; the last three columns represent the
gains on a cash basis for three periods.

TABLE C.

Credit and Cash Prices compared for 2,005 Persons. Difference 25 per cent. Gains on a Cash Basis for one, ten, and twenty years.

NO. OF PERSONS.	CREDIT PRICE FOR ONE.	TOTAL CREDIT PRICE.	TOTAL CASH PRICE.	GAINS ON CASH BASIS		
				For 1 year.	For 10 years.	For 20 years.
1,000	$50	$50,000	$37,500	$12,500	$125,000	$250,000
200	100	20,000	15,000	5,000	50,000	100,000
200	200	40,000	30,000	10,000	100,000	200,000
150	300	45,000	33,750	11,250	112,500	225,000
125	400	50,000	37,500	12,500	112,500	225,000
100	500	50,000	37,500	12,50c	112,500	225,000
80	600	48,000	36,000	12,000	120,000	240,000
60	700	42,000	31,500	10,500	105,000	210,000
50	800	40,000	30,000	10,000	100,000	200,000
40	900	36,000	27,000	9,000	90,000	180,000
Total		$421,000	$315,750	$105,250	$1,052,500	$2,105,000

This calculation is based on an average sale of 10,000 bales of cotton, at an average price of ten cents per pound for a period of twenty years. The figures of this table deserve to be studied by thoughtful men. Calmly, and without bitterness, what lesson does this statement impress upon me, upon you, upon the merchant, upon the farmer, in its bearing upon the duty of to-day as seen by the sad experience of yesterday? Ten thousand bales of cotton at 10 cents a pound are worth $450,000. In these twenty years, cotton ranged in price from 18 to 7 cents. The average 10 cents will hardly be regarded as too large. Two years' self-denial to the value of one-third of the supplies bought, would have brought the people to a cash basis. In twenty years, 2,005 persons, farmers, would have saved on this basis $2,105,000. This is a large sum. This is more than the valuation of all the property, real and personal, of many a first-class county in the Southern States. What more? It is probable that these 2,005 farmers are in debt to the full value of $200,000 to-day. What more? Vast bodies of land have passed out of their possession.

Is this a local representation confined to some one section? Is it not typical of the various communities of the cotton-growing States? If there is any force in evidence, such is the case. Variations there may be, and no doubt there are; but the ruinous credit policy has depressed and burdened the farming people of all the Southern States.

Mr. Joseph Baxendale, of England, placed in his warehouses and places of business various maxims as instructive reminders of valuable truths in practical life. Being a humane and considerate man, he never lost sight of the interest and well-being of those in his employment. Some of these pithy sayings were "Never despair," "Time lost can not be regained," "Let industry, temperance, and economy be the habits of your lives," "He who spends all he gets is on the way to beggary."

If ever there was a cause urgently demanding the exemplification of the last maxim, it is to be found in the general financial status of the Southern farmers. Take the illustration of the 2,005 men. They have spent 28 cotton crops of 10,000 bales each, valued at $12,600,000. They have lost about

150,000 acres of land, and are pressed with an indebtedness of probably not less than $200,000.

Had the broad-minded, generous-hearted Baxendale been a merchant in our day, he would have advised *heroic self-denial* to those with whom he had dealings. One of his maxims was " Never to spend more than ninepence out of every shilling." Save one-fourth. There is hope in this plan. Again, he adds : "Upon industry and frugality our well-being depends." The counsel and disinterestedness of such a man would inspire confidence, and would soon bring about an era of good feeling and prosperity.

CHAPTER VII.

AGRICULTURAL PRODUCTS.

" Most men work for the present, a few for the future.
The wise work for both."

TEN Southern States are in arrears in food crops.
The ratio of supply between 1860 and 1880,
1860 and 1890, is not equal to the increase of population of these periods. In twenty years the whole
population in these States increased 53 per cent.;
in thirty years, 87 per cent. In the latter period the
whites increased 93 per cent.; the blacks, 77 per
cent. The negroes are laborers, and in 1860 they
were all agricultural laborers. Skilled workmen are
few. Their income comes under the heading of
wages. Whether they rent farm land, or work on
shares, or engage in other gainful pursuit, they are
laborers, and their moneyed income must correspond
to the kind of work they perform.

Whatever the grain product of these States was
in 1860, the increase in twenty years should be 53
per cent., and, in thirty years, 87 per cent.

Two circumstances only can adjust this arrearage.
First, that the excess of other than grain crops bal-
anced the deficiency in moneyed valuation. Second,
that a portion of the population of these States were
engaged in other gainful industries, and that their

7

pecuniary income was equivalent to the loss sustained in grain. Another circumstance may be suggested : that the consumption of grain was less than in former years.

In regard to the first circumstance, the evidence does not support any such conclusion. As to the second consideration, the manufacturing interests of the South displace but a comparatively small number from the farms. Railroads and sawmills, and industries of this kind may have displaced a few hundred thousand blacks. Whatever the displacement of negro labor from the farm may be from these causes, it has been more than offset by the large increase of white labor.

The inquiry deserving attention is, What are the facts in the arrearage of the grain crop in the South? The comparison is made with reference to Alabama, Arkansas, Florida, Georgia, Louisiana, Mississippi, North Carolina, South Carolina, Tennessee, and Texas. The status of these States will be a fair criterion by which to judge the South. In any event, the aggregate deficiency of these States in grain will not be denied.

The following tables will show this condition. They were compiled from the reports of the Department of Agriculture. The first shows the yield of six grain crops in the ten States in 1860; the second the yield of similar crops in 1889.

TABLE I.

CEREALS OF 1860.*

STATES.	WHEAT.	RYE.	INDIAN CORN.	OATS.	BARLEY.	BUCK-WHEAT.
	Bushels.	Bushels.	Bushels.	Bushels.	Bushels.	Bushels.
Alabama	1,218,444	72,457	33,226,282	682,179	15,135	1,347
Arkansas........	957,601	78,092	17,823,588	475,268	3,158	509
Florida	2,808	21,306	2,834,391	46,899	8,369	....
Georgia.........	2,544,913	115,532	30,776,293	1,231,817	14,682	2,023
Louisiana	32,208	36,065	16,853,745	89,377	224	160
Mississippi......	587,925	39,474	29,057,682	221,235	1,875	1,699
North Carolina..	4,743,706	436,856	30,078,564	2,781,860	3,445	35,924
South Carolina..	1,285.631	89,091	15,065,606	936,974	11,490	602
Tennessee..	5.459,268	257.989	52,089,926	2,267,814	25,144	14,481
Texas...........	1,478,345	111,860	16.500.702	985,889	67,562	1,349
Total	18,310,849	1,258,722	244,306,779	9,719,312	1,510,184	58,094

TOTAL CEREALS IN THE TEN STATES IN 1860.

Wheat....................	18,310,849	bushels.
Rye.............................	1,258,722	"
Indian corn	244,306,779	"
Oats.............................	9,719,312	"
Barley.......................	1,510,184	"
Buckwheat......................	58,094	"
Total........................	275,163,940	bushels.

* Tenth Census Report.

TABLE II.

CEREALS OF 1889.*

STATES.	WHEAT.	RYE.	INDIAN CORN.	OATS.	BARLEY.	BUCK-WHEAT.
	Bushels.	*Bushels.*	*Bushels.*	*Bushels.*	*Bushels.*	*Bushels.*
Alabama........	208,591	14,618	30,073,036	3,231,085	2,002	4,622
Arkansas	955,668	15,181	33,982,318	4,180,877	994	5,074
Florida.........	290	13,389	3,701,264	391,321	128	126
Georgia	1,096,312	87,021	29,261,422	4,767,456	6,053	3,527
Louisiana	257	374	13,081,954	297,271	598	....
Mississippi......	16,570	3,544	26,148,144	1,362,290	875	345
North Carolina .	4,292,035	276,609	25,783,623	4,512,762	3,521	12,621
South Carolina .	658,351	17,303	13,770,417	3,019,119	9,428	472
Tennessee	8,300,789	165,621	63,635,350	7,355,100	63,866	7,143
Texas...........	4,272,392	62,120	69,031,493	12,578,880	47,692	1,263
Total.......	19,901,255	655,780	318,469,021	41,696,161	135,157	35,193

TOTAL CEREALS IN THE TEN STATES IN 1889.

Wheat......	19,901,255	bushels.
Rye............................	655,780	"
Indian corn.....................	318,469,021	"
Oats	41,696,161	"
Barley	135,157	"
Buckwheat	35,193	"
Total......................	380,892,567	bushels.

* Production of cereals, Eleventh Census.

The grain crops increased 37 per cent. in twenty-nine years. Population increased during this period, 87 per cent. The gain in round numbers was 105,-000,000 bushels. The gain of Florida, Tennessee, and Texas was 106,000,000 bushels in round numbers. The aggregate grain in bushels of seven of these States was less in 1889 than in 1860.

In 1888, the cotton crop in the ten States was 6,898,020 bales, and brought $291,378,388.* This was a gain of a little over a million and a half bales, and this excess brought Southern farmers and planters nearly sixty-six million dollars; but the corn and oat crops were in arrears in seven of these States, based upon the increase of population, about 150,000,000 bushels, and these figures will about represent the valuation of the deficit of these two grain crops. Thus, it follows that the corn and oats absorbed the gain on cotton, with a large balance against the planter.

Table III. will show that the productive prosperity of Southern farmers, fifteen years after the war, gave no signs of an improved condition. Such food crops as potatoes, peas and beans, hay and corn, were less in 1880 than in 1860.

---

* Report of the Commissioner of Agriculture for 1889, p. 229.

TABLE III.

Statistics of Agriculture for Ten States—Alabama, Arkansas, Florida, Georgia, Louisiana, Mississippi, North Carolina, South Carolina, Tennessee, Texas.[*]

	1860.	1880.
Tobacco..................pounds	79,673,781	57,791,641
Cotton .... bales	5,331,439	5,697,079
Wool [†]....................pounds	7,357,252	13,950,094
Irish potatoes.............bushels	4,354,673	3,941,727
Sweet potatoes............. "	35,976,022	25,939,990
Peas and beans............. "	10,986,789	4,859,761
Orchard products................	$2,056,428	$6,116,840
Product of market-gardens........	$1,705,712	$1,415,891
Dairy products—butter......pounds	46,177,799	74,131,166
" " cheese...... "	527,545	304,410
Sugar-cane.............hogsheads	230,580	178,872
" maple............ ....pounds	151,065	4,103
Molasses, cane.............gallons	14,941,691	16,573,273
" sorghum.......... "	1,409,765	9,823,258
" maple............ "	92,275	4,270
Bees' wax.................pounds	625,902	507,803
Bees' honey.... .... "	7,582,422	8,511,088
Hay........................tons	641,731	410,497

The fact of this arrearage will be seen when we compare the total of these six grain crops with the population. In 1860, there were 36 bushels per capita; in 1890, 27 bushels per capita—a difference of 9 bushels. The aggregate deficiency at this latter period, in these ten States, was 133,664,000 bushels.

* Compendium, Tenth Census, Part I.

† Texas alone in 1880 clipped 6,928,019 pounds. On eleven of these products there was a loss in 1880, when population had increased 53 per cent. The corn was short in the ten States in 1880, as compared with 1860, nearly 21,000,000 bushels. Measured by the increase of population, it was nearly short 112,000,000 bushels.

The total deficiency in corn and oats alone was 114,864,478 bushels, and in corn alone 138,384,655 bushels. As there was a gain in the oat crop of 31,976,849 bushels over 1860, this must be deducted from the total loss of the corn crop, to make that estimate exact. The oat crop serves quite as well for the purpose of feeding live stock, as corn. The 133,664,000 bushels of the six grain food crops, expresses the exact loss in the productive prosperity of the States.

The correctness of this conclusion, measured by the increase of population, is reasonable. No industries in the South have withdrawn any perceptible portion of the population from agricultural pursuits. But even if this were the case, the food crops would still be necessary by the increased population. These food crops represent wealth just as much as cotton. The farm acreage for all crops in 1860 was 45,389,333 acres;* in 1880, the total acreage was 58,740,689—a gain of 29 per cent. in 20 years. If in the next ten years there should be a proportionate increase in acreage, then the whole enlarged farm area in the ten States will be 58 per cent. over 1860. But as population gained 87 per cent., the disparity is apparent. To illustrate: if three million farmers out of a population of fifteen million cultivate forty-five million acres, thirty million people, it would seem natural, ought to furnish six million farmers cultivating ninety million acres. Three reasons may account for the inequality between the augmentation of the farm area and population. First, dis-

* Report on Agriculture, Tenth Census, p. xii.

placement of labor from the farm. Second, intensive farming, and reducing the number of acres for field hands. Third, lazy and demoralized labor.

The gains of all the crops were neither 29 per cent. for 1880, nor 58 per cent. for 1890. Besides, 42 per cent. of the population contributed nothing to the farm products, or sought employment in other pursuits. The arrearage in the grain crops of the ten States is indisputable.

The following table exhibits the population of these States:

TABLE IV.

WHITE POPULATION.

STATES.	1860.	1880.	1890.
Alabama...............	526,271	662,185	830.796
Arkansas..............	324.143	591,531	816,517
Florida	77,746	142,605	224,416
Georgia...............	591,550	816,906	973,462
Louisiana.............	357,456	454,954	454,712
Mississippi...........	353,899	479,398	539.703
North Carolina	629,942	867,242	1,049,191
South Carolina........	291,300	391,105	458,454
Tennessee.............	826,723	1,138,831	1,332,971
Texas.....	420,891	1,197,237	1,741,190
Total	4,397,920	6,741,994	8,521,457

TABLE V.

COLORED POPULATION.

STATES.	1860.	1880.	1890.
Alabama................	437,770	600,103	681,431
Arkansas...............	111,259	210,666	311,227
Florida	62,677	126,690	166,678
Georgia................	465,698	725,133	863,716
Louisiana..............	350,373	483,655	562,893
Mississippi	437,404	650,291	747,720
North Carolina.........	361,522	531,277	561,170
South Carolina.........	412,320	604,332	692,503
Tennessee..............	283,019	403,151	434,300
Texas.................	182,921	393,384	492,837
Total.............	3,104,963	4,728,682	5,514,475

While the grain crops in these States have varied each year from 1860 to 1880, the aggregate deficiency during any one year can not be disputed. In 1886,* the corn crop was less in five of the ten States. In Georgia, there was a gain of 520,707 bushels. There was a large increase in the oat crop in all the ten States at this time. Yet, in the States of North Carolina, South Carolina, Georgia, Alabama, Mississippi, and Louisiana, there was only an aggregate gain in the combined corn and oat crops of a little over 4,250,000 bushels over 1860. This was the gain in twenty-six years, when the population had nearly doubled itself.

In considering the causes which have been mainly instrumental in producing the arrearage in food crops, a table will be given to show the human

* Report of the Commissioner of Agriculture, 1886, p. 368.

working forces on Southern farms in these States. A comparison between the table following, and the table on population, will show what proportion of the people are engaged in agricultural pursuits. It is to be regretted that no data are at hand by which the human labor force of 1860 could be compared with any subsequent period. It is hoped the twelfth census will give the country information as to the actual number of persons engaged in agricultural labor, of both races, white and black, male and female, of each race so engaged. It would be invaluable knowledge upon which to base conclusions for future action.

TABLE VI.

PERSONS ENGAGED IN AGRICULTURE IN 1880.* BY AGES, FROM 10 YEARS AND OVER.

STATES.	MALE.	FEMALE.	TOTAL.
Alabama..................	291,477	89,153	380,630
Arkansas.................	195,002	21,653	216,655
Florida..................	47,465	11,266	58,731
Georgia	329,856	102,358	432,204
Louisiana	147,538	57,768	205,306
Mississippi..............	252,324	87,614	339,938
North Carolina	314,228	46,709	360,937
South Carolina..........	208,672	85,930	294,602
Tennessee...............	275,620	18,533	294,153
Texas	330,125	29,192	359,317
Total................	2,392,307	550,166	2,942,473

The causes of this arrearage are, in the main, two-fold. One of these has been presented in a former

---

* Census Report, 1880.

chapter. It is referred to here to show its bearing upon food crops. If the lessons these pages are to impress shall have any value, it must be done by giving line upon line.

First, over-production of cotton has brought about the deficiency of grain crops in the South. The supply has been greater than the world's demand. Whatever other causes have operated against a remunerative price, this one cause has been chiefly instrumental in the result. Too much attention to cotton has reduced the crops of corn and oats. In 1860, the cotton acreage was 12,000,000 acres.* The increased acreage from that period to 1886 is 50 per cent. The American cotton is 57 per cent. of the world's product.

Had corn and oats in the six States mentioned on a former page received equal attention with cotton, the gain in these two food crops would have been 80,000,000 bushels. If we value these grains as worth to the farmer, one dollar a bushel, cotton seven cents a pound, and estimate a bale of cotton at 450 pounds, it will take 2,544,444 bales to balance the account in the deficiency of corn and oats.

"In June, 1870, when a large increase of cotton planting was reported, the declaration was made in the *Monthly* that the 'cotton growers seem determined to reduce the price to 15 cents,' which was accomplished within six months, by an increase of the cotton crop from a little more than three millions of bales to nearly four and a half millions; and

---

* Report of the Commissioner of Agriculture, 1886, pp. 382, 386.

in the report of June, 1870, it was stated that the penalty of growing four millions of bales instead of three, was a reduction of seven cents per pound, equivalent to $130,000,000 on the crop. Short-sighted political economists objected to that phase of presentation of the resulting loss, as incorrect; but when four millions of bales, at $76 per bale, produce but $304,000,000, while three millions of bales, at $109 per bale, bring $327,000,000, or $23,-000,000 more for the smaller crop than for the larger, there is the additional loss of the labor employed in making the extra million of bales, instead of producing food and forage supplies, now obtained at ruinous cost from the North; and all these losses, with their incidental results in thwarting systematic rotation and recuperative cropping, will far exceed the $130,000,000 of the above calculations.

"The crop of 1871, partly from diminution of area and partly from diminished yield, has probably fallen to the plane of that of 1869, and the price has advanced in almost equal proportion. While the recommendations of these reports, respecting the production of cotton, have been bitterly assailed by speculators and dealers, the positions taken are impregnable, viz.: that these fluctuations of productions and price are injurious alike to producers and manufacturers; that cotton in the Gulf States, while the prominent crop, should not be grown so exclusively as to run the price below a living profit and create a debt for provisions and supplies; that no one crop, which can scarcely average for years to come, however large it may be, a value of $300,000,-

ooo, . . . can alone make the South a wealthy or even thriving community."

This one thing the South has done. From 1865 to 1890, cotton planting has been a mania. The neglected corn field with all its consequences is a part of Southern history.

The second cause instrumental in the arrearage of grain crops is to be found in the condition of negro labor. "The negro will not raise corn," is a common remark. This indifference to corn growing and food crops generally, is an element of a large unit. The matter of inquiry here is the negro's relation to field crops, especially the grain crops.

By examining Table VI., showing the persons engaged in agriculture, we have the whole number so employed in 1880. After much inquiry of practical men, farmers and others, an analysis of the whole number of agricultural laborers, furnishes the following data : 25 per cent. of the whole are white men— it may be larger; the remainder are all blacks, 15 per cent. of the males are old slave negroes; 85 per cent. of the males, born since 1845, practically know nothing of slavery, and the others are females, assumed to be colored. These arranged in classes will give the following tabular statement with the per cent. each class is of the whole. The rate per cent. is approximately accurate.

TABLE VII.

PERSONS ENGAGED IN AGRICULTURE IN 1880, CLASSIFIED.

	NO.	PER CENT.
White males..........................	598,076	.25
Old slave negroes, males..............	269,135	
Younger negroes, males	1,525,100	.75
Colored females..............	550,166	
Total........................	2,942,473	

The concurrent testimony of farmers and others is that the value of the work of negroes on the farm, as compared with the same kind of work done in slave time under humane masters, and that work under no effective supervision to-day, may be thus expressed; the value of the work done by the old slave negroes is 50 per cent. of what it was in olden times ; that of the younger negro men, 30 per cent.; and that of the colored females, 20 per cent. We write of them as classes. The work done covers an entire year. The standard of measurement is reasonable work prior to the manumission of this people. The result of this investigation may be stated in the following :

TABLE VIII.

VALUE OF NEGRO WORK ON THE FARM IN 1880.

	NO.	PER CENT.
Old slave negroes, males..............	134,567	.50
Younger negroes, males...............	457,530	.30
Colored females.....................	110,033	.20
Total........................	702,130	

The substance of the estimate is that 2,344,401 negroes working on farms in 1880 do as much work as was done by 702,130 negroes prior to their emancipation. Is the estimate unreasonable? Accuracy is not claimed for the statement. It is not far from the truth.

The elements of deterioration in the quality and quantity of the work done by the colored people are known to all the Southern States. In their present condition this people as a class, undirected, waste much valuable time; their racial quality, laziness, here as in Hayti and the English West Indies, has few checks; they are proverbially poor managers of their own affairs; the future, with its interests, is one long day-dream. To them, more than any other people, the present hour is life. These are acknowledged facts. What reduction in work will these elements produce during twelve months?

The average value of this labor according to the estimate is 32 per cent. The average colored laborer that produced in 1860, 100 pounds cotton, 100 pounds corn, 100 pounds fodder, 100 pounds field peas, 100 pounds sweet potatoes, has reduced this average to-day in each of these productions to 32 pounds. Then he aided in raising the meat supply. Now the majority of colored people raise no hogs. He kept up the repairs of the farm; his work has been fully reduced to the same per cent. in this particular. As it takes three colored farm hands to produce as much to-day as one produced in a former period, the effect on food crops is evident.

Colored labor on an average produces more than 32 per cent. of cotton as compared with the quantity produced in the period before the civil war. As this is the crop bringing money, it receives special attention. The general opinion, however, is that the number of colored farm people producing two and three bales of cotton per hand is far in excess of those producing four and five bales per hand.

That the grain crops, essential to Southern prosperity, have not been in proportion to the increase in population, Tables I., II., and III. of this chapter fully exhibit, The facts showing this to the year 1880 are clear. The ten years following have been years of depression. The leading newspapers of the South have urged and warned the farming community to attend to the corncrib and the smokehouse —to live at home. These admonitory appeals have resounded through the land annually. A certain per cent. of farmers have heeded this important matter, especially small white proprietors, and some excellent colored landowners. But 75 per cent. of farm labor, according to the estimate in 1880, was colored people. In 1890, colored labor on the farm probably did not exceed 60 per cent. The majority of this people work under the metayer, or share system, or rent plan. This majority class neglect food crops of every sort. The fact that the overproduction of cotton has pressed the price down to seven cents is proof in itself of the evil here presented. This indifference or hostility of the colored people to the raising of corn is seriously affecting them and the country.

Seventy-five per cent. of the actual farm population producing less than one-third of the amount formerly raised is a fatal blow at prosperity. Detrimental as this is to the interest of both white and black, yet the situation wears a darker and gloomier hue when it is considered that horses and necessary farm appliances and food supplies furnished are based upon 100 laborers. This number, however, represents 32 hands, and these, without reference to the 68, raise an insufficient quantity of corn, potatoes, and peas for themselves, and the meat raised by them is a modicum of what they need. To our understanding of the facts, the conclusion is unavoidable, that the 2,344,401 colored farm laborers of the South, constituting three-fourths of the whole, have vastly reduced the *food crops*, their labor deteriorating to less than *one-third in value*, and have largely *diminished farm values*.

Corroborative testimony from other lands where the Hamites are in possession of freedom and civil rights, confirms the conclusion. The history of Hayti is a mournful record of misgovernment and retrogression. In 1789 the negroes massacred the French and achieved their independence. Their freedom extends over a century. At its beginning they numbered 56,666 freedmen, black and colored, and 509,642 slaves. It is reasonable to suppose that in a hundred years this population increased to a million and a half, even when full allowance is made for the loss of life incident to their numerous wars. The inspiration of freedom, the government in their own hands, sole masters of the western half of San

8

Domingo, every vocation in life and every avenue to advancement open, and the markets of the world ready to purchase the productions of their soil, should have increased productions threefold, and exports in the same ratio. The facts here recited are taken from the book on "Hayti, or the Black Republic," by Sir Spencer St. John. He was Minister Resident and Consul-General, representing the British Government in Port-au-Prince from 1863 to 1875.

PRODUCTIONS OF HAYTI IN 1789.

Coffee...........................	88,360,502 lbs.
Sugar, white and brown...............	161,000,000 "
Cotton............................	8,400,000 "

In subsequent years these productions never again reached the same quantity, nor were there any other productions that took their place. In 1821 the quantity of sugar was so small that it was struck from the custom-house lists. The figures now to be given will fairly represent the retrograde movement. They express the production of some of the best years during the period of freedom.

PRODUCTIONS OF HAYTI DURING THE ERA OF FREEDOM.

SUGAR.

Year 1821...........................	600,000 lbs.
" 1888...........................	1,900,000 "

COTTON.

Year 1835...........................	1,649,717 lbs.
" 1860...........................	688,735 "
" 1865...........................	4,000,000 "
" 1886...........................	2,037,000 "

COFFEE.

Year 1818...................... .... 20,280,589 lbs.
"   1863............................. .... 71,712,345 "
"   1886............... ... . 58,075,739 "

In 1875 the estimate was that population had increased to about a million and a half. The exports in 1789 were from $30,000,000 to $40,000,000. The following year they were $55,000,000. The highest exports since that period amount to $11,-500,000.*

An American poet has said, "The people make the country, but no country can make the people." † Energy and thrift and self-respect come not from the soil.

The evidence from the fifteen English West Indian colonies is similar to that of Hayti. In these colonies were, in 1834, 750,000 African slaves when they were emancipated. The government paid the owners $100,000,000, or £20,000,000, for the negroes. Let us examine the effect on agricultural production. Jamaica is one of the largest of these colonial islands.

PRODUCTION IN JAMAICA. ‡

	1834.	1860.	1867.
Sugar, cwts.............	1,500,000	599.737	515.902
Rum, gals.	2,697,324	1,694,606	1,769,716
Pimento, lbs............	3,605,400	6,850,548	4,866,239
Coffee, lbs.............	17,725,731	6,145,362	6,264,861

* Hayti, or Black Republic, p. 372.
† Alexander H. Stephens.
‡ Chambers' Encyclopædia, vol. v., p. 674.

Mr. James Anthony Froude visited these islands in
1887. A few of his utterances, or those quoted by
him, are here recited:

" The public debt had increased, and taxation was
heavy. Many gentlemen in Jamaica, as in the
Antilles, were selling or trying to sell their estates
and go out of it." *

" Col. J——, acting governor, confirmed the
complaint which I had heard so often, that the
blacks would not work for wages more than three
days in the week, or regularly upon those, preferring to cultivate their own yams and sweet potatoes." †

" Fine properties all about the island were in the
market for any price which purchasers could be
found to give. Too many even of the old English
families were tired of the struggle, and were longing
to be out of it at any cost." ‡

Of Grenada he says: "Such a scene of desolation
and desertion I never saw in my life save once, a
few weeks later at Jamaica." §

St. Lucia: " The chief complaint is the somewhat
weary one of the laziness of the blacks, who, they
say, will work only when they please, and are never
fully awake except at dinner-time." ‖

" The English of those islands are melting away ;
that is a fact to which it is idle to try to shut our
eyes. Families who have been for generations
on the soil are selling their estates everywhere, and

---

* The English in the West Indies, p. 200.
† Ibid., p. 211.   ‡ Ibid., p. 231.
§ Ibid., p. 54.   ‖ Ibid., p. 134.

are going off. Lands once under high cultivation are lapsing into jungle." *

Dominica: "The soil was as rich as the richest in the world. The cultivation was growing annually less." †

Barbadoes: "The great prosperity of the island ended with emancipation." ‡

The final outcome of this investigation is discouraging. Credible witnesses in large number, unbiased by passion or interest, from these lands, have placed themselves upon record. Free Hamitic labor deteriorates in value, year by year. The products of the soil diminish in like proportion. Debts and perplexities confront the people whose interests are endangered. The facts and figures of the Southern States cover a period extending over a quarter of a century; of the English West Indies, more than half a century; and of Hayti, a full century. The results of Hamitic labor, to which these American territories testify by authoritative record, is strikingly unit-like. It is not the report of a narrow district.

In Hayti, where the Hamites are in absolute control, the agricultural condition has steadily gone from bad to worse. In the English West Indies, where the negroes are proprietors, as in Grenada, or labor as tenants or on the share system, as in Barbadoes and in other islands, the outlook is gloomy. In the Southern States, a combination of causes have placed the people between the upper and

---

* "The English in the West Indies," p. 284.
† Ib., p. 143.   ‡ Ib., p. 105.

nether mill-stones. One of these is the failure to raise ample food crops. Unless the colored people can be induced to attend to food crops as essential to their material well-being, the day of agricultural prosperity is in the far-distant future. The history of the past twenty-five years, crowded with mistakes and delusions, furnishes not one ray of hope, without this essential basis upon which to build.

As proof of the tardy progress of the Southern people, traceable largely to the various causes related in these pages, note the value of farms in the two tables following:

TABLE IX.

VALUE OF FARMS.*

NOTE.—The valuation refers to lands, houses, and fences.

STATES.	1880.	1860.
Alabama	$78,954,648	$175,824,622
Arkansas.....................	74,249,655	91,649,773
Florida......................	20,291,835	16,435,721
Georgia	111,910,540	157,072,803
Louisiana	58,989,117	204,789,662
Mississippi	92,844,915	190,760,367
North Carolina	135,793,602	143,301,065
South Carolina..............	68,677,482	139,652,508
Tennessee...................	206,749,837	271,358,985
Texas.......................	170,468,886	88,101,320
Total	$1,018,930,517	$1,478,946,826

* Compendium, Tenth Census, Part I., p. 658.

TABLE X.

VALUE OF FARMS.

STATES.	1880.	1860.
Connecticut	$121,063,910	$90,830,005
Dakota	22,401,084	2,085,265
Illinois	1,009,594,580	408,944,033
Indiana	635,236,111	356,712,175
Iowa	567,430,227	392,662,441
Michigan	499,103,181	160,836,495
Minnesota	193,724,260	27,505,922
New Hampshire	75,834,389	69,689,761
Ohio	1,127,497,353	678,132,991
Vermont	109,346,010	94,289,045
Total	$4,361,231,105	$2,281,688,133

The increase of acreage referred to on a former page belongs wholly to the States of Arkansas, Florida, Tennessee, and Texas. They increased their acreage 13,606,469 acres in twenty years. Of this number, 9,999,633 belong to Texas alone.

Georgia, Louisiana, and Mississippi increased their acreage 331,008 ; on the other hand, Alabama, North Carolina, and South Carolina reduced the number of acres in cultivation 486,120. The six States considered as a whole show a deficit of 155,112 acres in cultivation. This reduction took place in spite of the fact that population increased 53 per cent. from 1860 to 1880.

Another determinate factor directly related to the question of food crops has been brought to our notice upon further investigation of the causes affecting Southern prosperity.

In 1870 the aggregate cotton crop was 3,011,996 bales; in 1879 the cotton crop was 5,755,359 bales.* The increase is 91 per cent. At the former period the price was 23½ cents per pound; at the latter period it was $9\frac{9}{10}$ cents per pound. This is a loss of $13\frac{6}{10}$ cents on each pound, or 1.37 per cent. That is, a bale weighing 450 pounds on an average brought, in 1870, $105.75; in 1879, $44.55. In other words, the smaller crop brought to the cotton farmer $62,117,333.55 more than the larger crop.

If there is any virtue in comparisons, such facts enforce attention. What effect did this large crop have on corn, oats, sweet potatoes, field peas, hay, fodder, and bacon? There is but one answer: less than was needed, and less money besides.

---

* Tenth Census, volume on Agriculture, page xxvii.

CHAPTER VIII.

THE FARM LEAKS.

THE history of the world is made up of a vast number of little things. Success and failure in life have their origin here. "Despise not the day of small things," is good counsel. The complaints against ill-fortune would rarely be heard, should attention to small matters become the rule. The road to poverty is a zigzag journey paved with neglect in little things. A little extravagance in domestic affairs, a little time lost this week, and a little lost every week, and a little inattention to this important matter, and then some other affair, will soon show their effects upon the prosperous condition of any man. These little things are efficient agents to reduce profits. A little leak will sink a ship; a little fire may do great damage; a little carelessness may wreck a railway train; and a little bad management may make prosperous farming impossible. Excellent management in all kinds of industry is a much rarer virtue than some people suppose.

Every man wishes to make headway in his business. This is right; it is praiseworthy. Without such reasonable ambition there is no progress. The man who is satisfied to live from hand to mouth deserves no commendation. It is a kind of contentment that is of no use. There is no glory in the resolve to be a beggar, and there is no manliness to fold one's hands in despair. It is brave to push forward. Improvement is the law of progress.

A thorough understanding of the particulars of any honorable industry is essential to success; what relation has each upon the other, and all of them upon the end to be attained? Then there must be a plan, faithfully carried out. This need not be of the cast-iron material, but some method must be adopted according to which the business shall be conducted. What is this but an orderly arrangement of time and labor to the objects demanding attention? The man who blunders and blusters about his work is not a model in any vocation of life, and is rarely prosperous. The calm, steady worker, cheerful and self-reliant, pursuing the course marked out, calculating gains and losses, is, as a general rule, the man that wins success, even from untoward circumstances. If one plan does not work, a better plan may.

Merchants may increase their gains by a number of methods. They may extend and enlarge their business; they may eliminate risky and unprofitable customers; they may decline to deal in certain commodities that experience has shown not to be remunerative; they may reduce expenses. In all this there is common sense.

Whenever there are leaks that reduce profits below the point of reasonable remuneration for labor and capital, there is always a first thing to do. To find the cause is the prime consideration. No remedy can be applied until this has been found.

It makes no difference where the leaks are, whether in the home, the mercantile house, the factory, or the farm, the same principles govern. It controls every business of whatever nature, however small or great. The leaks must be found before they can be stopped.

In great manufacturing establishments five factors are necessary to their prosperous management. There must be ample capital; sufficient labor, skilled and common; rapid production of goods; quick sales; and competent superintendence. A defect in any one of these elements may reduce dividends to zero, or bring disaster to the enterprise. Inefficient superintendence is a large and serious defect. The man who cannot grasp the parts of such a business is sure to bring swift misfortune to all concerned.

In former chapters various causes have been considered operating detrimentally to the farmer. Another is now to be examined. It is another leak, through which have trickled millions of dollars that should be in the pockets of the Southern farmers, or invested in permanent improvements. Let us call it the Southern Live Stock Leak.

The deficiency in animal products in the ten States is such that it is worthy the serious attention of all farmers. The year 1890 is compared with 1860. There can be no question as to the effect of this condition upon Southern prosperity. This lack of animals robs the farmer of a large percentage of profits. It is a factor that invariably adds to his poverty. It is a loss, especially the swine product, for which no cotton-lint, pound for pound, is a compensation.

The general condition in the number of the six classes of animals at two periods, thirty years apart, is indicated in the three tables following. If we omit Texas the loss in sheep was 23 per cent. in 1890; in all the ten States there were less hogs in 1890 than in 1860. In nine States, omitting Texas, the loss at the latter period exceeded a million head. It would take five hundred thousand bales of cotton to stop this leak. In milch cows there is a gain of 28 per cent. Omitting Texas, there is a gain of 12 per cent. in other cattle in the nine States. The gain in horses is 10 per cent., if Texas be omitted. The largest gain in the ten States is 72 per cent. in mules. Three-fourths of them were probably imported, and paid for in cotton.

As a digression from the topic under consideration, this increase in the number of mules, largely used on farms, furnishes strong grounds for the belief that agricultural laborers have increased nearly in the same ratio as population. It is believed that the increase of white labor is in excess of colored labor. Probably 30 per cent. of the colored population has been displaced from the farms and is now found in the towns and villages of the South. The displacement and depreciated labor of this people has in part been counterbalanced by the increase of white labor. The aggregate number of laborers is larger than in 1860; but the 29 per cent. increase in acreage is less than the gain in labor, and the gain in mules. Besides, nearly three-fourths of this increase in acreage belongs to Texas, as elsewhere shown, and in that State the white population has more than quadrupled since 1860.

The tables following furnish the material for any comparison between the two periods indicated, of the progress of any one of the ten States in reference to the increase or decrease of the six classes of animals named.

TABLE I.
LIVE STOCK, 1860.

STATES.	NO. SHEEP.	NO. SWINE.	NO. MILCH COWS.	NO. OTHER CATTLE.
Alabama..........	370,156	1,748,321	230,537	454,543
Arkansas..........	202,753	1,171,630	171,003	318,089
Florida...	30,158	271,742	92,974	287,725
Georgia...........	512,618	2,036,116	299,688	631,707
Louisiana	181,253	634,525	129,662	326,787
Mississippi	352,632	1,532,768	207,646	416,660
North Carolina.....	546,749	1,883,214	228,623	416,676
South Carolina......	233,509	965,779	163,938	320,209
Tennessee.	773,317	2,347,321	249,514	413,060
Texas	753,363	1,371,532	601,540	2,761,736
Total	3,956,508	13,962,948	2,475,025	6,346,192

TABLE II.
LIVE STOCK, 1890.

STATES.	NO. SHEEP.	NO. SWINE.	NO. MILCH COWS.	NO. OTHER CATTLE.
Alabama	286,238	1,530,001	311,805	454,042
Arkansas..........	269,484	1,663,275	329,121	587,212
Florida.....	110,351	358,021	54,951	565,201
Georgia.	411,846	1,627,008	354,618	580,816
Louisiana..........	115,082	706,947	177,613	295,731
Mississippi........ .	240,148	1,443,813	309,234	441,862
North Carolina.....	414,819	1,291,893	272,155	398,414
South Carolina.....	102,031	670,652	156,575	210,396
Tennessee..........	511,118	2,242,215	377,740	484,578
Texas..............	4,752,640	2,321,246	843,342	7,167,853
Total	7,213,757	13,855,071	3,187,154	11,186,105

TABLE III.

LIVE STOCK.

STATES.	1860.		1890.	
	HORSES.	MULES.	HORSES.	MULES.
Alabama	127,063	111,687	134,805	143,258
Arkansas.............	140,198	57,358	187,153	129,866
Florida..............	13,446	10,910	34,737	13,000
Georgia	130,771	101,069	115,629	155,700
Louisiana	78,703	91,762	124,650	94,785
Mississippi	117,571	110,723	139,468	196,436
North Carolina........	150,661	51,388	154,229	96,295
South Carolina........	81,125	56,456	70,303	79,269
Tennessee...........	290,882	126,345	303,206	229,246
Texas...........	325,698	63,334	1,350,344	213,146
Total	1,456,118	781,032	2,614,524	1,351,001

The large decrease in sheep and swine in 1890, as compared with 1860, is apparent. No compensating crop has been found to make up this loss. The loss pointed out is only partial. It does not express the full damage. Let us suppose that in 1860 one-half of the colored population were engaged in farm labor, and that one-twentieth of the white population were so occupied. A certain quantity of animal food was necessary to their sustenance. In 1890, the colored population had increased 77 per cent., and the white population 91 per cent., in the States under consideration. The increase of the two races was about 87 per cent., or, taking the above rates as a basis, 84 per cent. The white farming population in 1890 represented not less than one-tenth of this race. If, now, we make full allowance for the displacement of colored people from the farm, yet the increase of this race will justify the conclusion that the number on farms in 1890 is much greater than in 1860, whether the whole number is actively engaged in work or not. They are there, and must be provided with food. Whatever, therefore, may have been the changes in location and work of the colored people, supposed to be 30 per cent., their aggregate increase and the increase of white farm labor will warrant the conclusion that the total increase of farm labor, or those living on farms and so named, is equal to the aggregate increase of population. The people are on the soil, and the bulk are in the rural districts.

In order that the status of wealth of 1890 in these States may correspond with the increase of population, the increase of the six classes of animals should be 84 per cent. If eighteen thousand pounds of bacon were required to sustain one hundred persons in 1860, thirty-three thousand pounds will be required to sustain one hundred and eighty-four persons in 1890. ·The greatest diminution is in the supply of animals used for food.

The difference between that species of farm capital sustaining life in 1860 and the losses sustained up to the year 1890, on this capital, may be presented in tabular form. The figures represent, in round numbers, the 84 per cent. on the capital of 1860. It is an approximate estimate of annual losses.

BALANCE SHEET OF LOSSES.

Hogs, 12,000,000 @ $5...............	$60,000,000
Sheep, 175,000 @ $2..................	350,000
Corn and oats, 50,000,000 @ 50 cts......	25,000,000
Field peas, 15,000,000 @ 50 cts........	7,500,000
Sweet potatoes, 40,000,000 @ 50 cts....	20,000,000
Milch cows, 1,300,000 @ $15..........	19,000,000
Other cattle, 500,000 @ $6............	3,000,000
Total..................	$135,000,000

This is the annual leak. Put it at $100,000,000. It will take three million bales of cotton to pay this deficiency. By referring to the tables of this and the preceding chapter, it will be observed that the figures express an aggregate loss. The burden falls most heavily upon some of the States. Some of them raise considerable quantities of wheat—such as Tennessee, North Carolina, Georgia, and Texas. South Carolina raises rice, and Louisiana cane. The gain in sheep during thirty years in the ten States is a little over two and a half million, but as the increase in Texas is over three and a half million, nine of the States have a less number of sheep than in 1860. The increase in horses is a little over a million, but nine hundred thousand belong to Texas. The increase of mules is the most uniform in all these ten States.

In further illustration of this leak, the information was obtained from a merchant in a town of Mississippi, that, in fifteen years, the firm of which he was a partner had sold 4,500,000 pounds of bacon; average, 300,000 pounds a year. The firm bought annually from 2,500 to 3,000 bales of cotton. About one-third of the customers bought no meat. The price of meat is generally higher than the price of cotton. It is fair to suppose that one-third of the cotton delivered to this mercantile firm paid for bacon.

If for every 2,000 bales of cotton, being two-thirds of the whole bought, 300,000 pounds of bacon are sold, then a cotton crop of 6,000,000 bales represents a demand for 60,000,000 pounds of bacon. One-third of this crop goes for bacon. No man living in the South questions the fact that the quantity of Western meat sold in the South annually is enormous. Every furnishing merchant in the cotton belt is a witness to this truth.

The inference from these considerations is both just and practical, that, if the necessary quantity of meat is raised at home, the demand for credit is reduced one-third, with all its burdens and vexations. It is a long step toward independence and prosperity.

One commercial crop cannot secure this end in the Southern States. The experience of thirty years furnishes ample proof. The loss in quantity of corn, oats, sweet and Irish potatoes, rye, wheat, hay, sheep, and swine, in the State of Mississippi in 1880, as compared with 1860, at a moderate valuation, was $9,000,000. In 1890–1–2, her cotton crop of 900,000 bales brought between $35,000,000 and $40,000,000. The increase in mules, in 1890, was 77 per cent. An increase of nearly 86,000 mules over the number in 1860 would consume from 5,000,000

9

to 6,000,000 bushels of corn. There was also an increase of more than 130,000 horses. Her population had increased, in thirty years, 62 per cent. Notwithstanding this augmentation of more than 200,000 work animals, and nearly 500,000 human beings, the food products were less in 1870, less in 1880, less in 1890, and less in 1892, than in 1860.

With slight variations, this is the status in the States of the cotton belt. No argument can justify the policy of concentrating capital and labor upon the production of the one commercial crop, increasing it beyond the world's demand, steadily lowering the price, and then buying Western corn and hay and meat at an advance of 50 and 100 per cent. of that received for cotton,

If the fertilizers now used on cotton were reduced one-half, and this half, in addition to the quantity already used, was applied to corn land, the effect upon the financial condition of Southern farmers would show itself advantageously in twelve months. Hog and hominy are intimately related. The gain on the home-raised pork, it is estimated, is 50 per cent. on the nominal value of corn. When the smoke-house is five hundred miles from the farm, the railroad freight on bacon, the handling it by merchants, and buying it on long time, makes it a very costly article to the cotton farmer.

A table on the cost of fertilizers, and the cost of building and repairing fences, is here given. It will serve the purpose of information, and may lead to efforts to supplement the commercial fertilizers with the preparing of an invaluable home article. The figures refer to the year 1879. The fence question is a matter pressing more and more upon the attention of farmers every year. The old rail fence will soon be a thing of the past.

TABLE IV.

Cost of Fertilizers and Fences.

	* FERTILIZERS.	† FENCES.
Alabama........................	$1,200,956	$1,402,609
Arkansas	108,732	1,579,144
Florida.	72,642	366,180
Georgia	4,346,920	1,834,625
Louisiana......................	278,305	1,482,121
Mississippi	123,253	1,560,119
North Carolina.......	2,111,767	1,869,654
South Carolina.................	2,659,969	917,000
Tennessee	157,442	2,426,008
Texas.........................	74,796	3,676,603
Total	$11,134,784	$17,114,063

There is no doubt that active industry has been on the increase in the South during the past thirty years. The sum of workers is greater to-day than in 1860. Thousands of white men have gone to work. The number of colored men on farms is equal to, if not greater than, the number in slave times. Thousands, however, have gone to the towns and sought other employment. The colored women doing light work in the fields in slave times, do but a fraction of that work to-day. Yet when all the facts are fairly considered, the conviction is well

---

* Tenth Census, Vol. on Agriculture, p. 103.
† Ibid., p. 25.

grounded that the active labor force on Southern farms is larger to-day by 50 per cent. than in the past. The cotton crop has increased to nearly 8,000,000 bales.

Now, what is the compensation to the toilers? What is the financial status of the men who have produced twenty-seven commercial crops? Has all this money been consumed on food, clothing, and appliances? What is the increase in fixed capital? What in real estate? When the debts are subtracted, how does the valuation of property owned by 3,000,000 of farmers in the South compare in 1890 with 1860? No reference is here made to the slave property, valued at $1,250,000,000. It is not considered in the comparison. The prosperous farmers are few; those who have made a bare living are not many; those who have consumed their farm possessions and the crops made thereon are thousands; those who are poor to-day are legions.

There must be something wrong in the general management. Thirty years' experience ought to satisfy any man of the correctness of this proposition. It is high time to institute an earnest search for leaks, and, when found, close them forever. What a monotonous plaint we hear at the end and beginning of each year! The last eight are grumbling weeks about bills and prices; the first eight weeks are begging weeks for new advances. The leaks in management, the leaks in buying, and the leaks in waste have had much to do in bringing about this pitiable condition.

Suppose that the seven and a half million bales

of cotton are hereafter reduced to four and a half, and the capital, time, and labor heretofore devoted to the remaining three million bales be employed in raising food crops and live stock. In two years, when the surplus cotton shall be out of the way, the price of the staple would be remunerative. When the farmers can live at home, the dawn of a better day is at hand. The old plan has depressed the South and brought poverty and debts.

CHAPTER IX.

OUR BROAD ACRES.

HOW large is our landed estate! The States and Territories, including Alaska, cover an area of 3,605,000 square miles, or 2,307,200,000 acres. In the ten States which have been used as a basis of comparison are 697,383 square miles, or 446,324,320 acres. If Virginia, West Virginia, Delaware, Kentucky, Maryland, and Missouri be added, there will be an increase of 191,305 square miles, or 122,435,200 acres, making a total of 568,759,520 acres in these sixteen Southern States.

Even the ten States cover an area more than three times as large as the German Empire, even larger in area, by over 20,000 square miles, than France, England and Wales, Scotland, Ireland, Italy, Spain, Switzerland, the Netherlands and Denmark, all combined. But these ten European countries contain a population of 130,039,000, and support them on less territory than is contained in the ten States. Their population is more than twice as large as that contained in the United States in 1890, whereas the population of the ten Southern States was a little over 14,000,000 at this date.

LAND SURFACE IN TEN STATES.

STATES.	LAND SURFACE IN SQUARE MILES.	LAND SURFACE IN ACRES.	ACREAGE OF FOREST LANDS IN 1890.
Alabama.........	51,540	32,985,600	17,000,000
Arkansas	53,045	33,948,800	28,000,000
Florida..........	59,268	37,931,520	20,000,000
Georgia..........	58,980	37,747,200	18,000,000
Louisiana........	45,420	29,068,800	13,000,000
Mississippi.......	46,340	29,657,600	13,000,000
North Carolina...	48,580	31,091,200	18,000,000
South Carolina....	30,170	19,308,800	13,000,000
Tennessee........	41,750	26,720,000	16,000,000
Texas............	262,290	167,865,600	40,000,000
Total	697,383	446,324,320	196,000,000

The total number of acres in all the States and Territories is 1,856,108,800. About one-fourth of the entire area is occupied by these ten States. Forty-three per cent. of this Southern area consists in forest lands. The foregoing total number of acres does not include Alaska. It alone covers an area of 580,000 square miles. It should be stated here, that there are slight discrepancies between the figures given in the Tenth Census report and various geographical works. The figures are approximately correct, and will answer the purpose here in view.

These figures will interest the thoughtful reader, especially in their bearing on the question of ownership.

THE AMERICAN LANDED ESTATE.

Including Alaska, it is a splendid domain. This vast territory is the property of the Federal Union.

No single country in South America is equal to its area. Brazil has less territory by nearly 400,000 square miles. European Russia has less land by more than 1,500,000 square miles. The Chinese Empire has about 575,000 more square miles than the United States; but the empire has 341,000,000 more people than the United States. The American heritage is not only of colossal dimensions, but is diversified by every variety of soil and climate and production.

Unavailable Land.

This comprises 1,002,997,177 acres. It embraces 369,529,600 acres in Alaska; military and Indian reservations cover 157,000,000 acres; mountains, lakes, and rivers embrace 476,467,577 acres.

Available Land.

When these deductions are made, there remain for all uses, present and prospective, 1,304,202,823 acres.

Farm Land.

The land thus used comprises 687,906,375 acres. It is a little over half of all the serviceable land in the Union, north and south, east and west.

Ownership.

This important question of land ownership concerns all the American people. It is a matter of vast significance to know the drift of this inheritance, and what its effect will be in the near future upon every acre in value. The honor and the independence of being a freeholder may be an impossibility, fifty years hence, to millions of our people. The land movement during the last thirty years rings out alarm bells that should be heard by all the people. The situation, as nearly as it can be ascertained, may thus be indicated:

		ACRES.
I.	Farmers own	687,906,375
II.	Railroads own	209,344,233
III.	Foreigners own	61,900,000
IV.	American speculators own	20,500,000
V.	Doomed by mortgages, estimated	20,000,000

UNDISPOSED-OF LAND.

When the sum of these five classes is taken from the available land, there remain of the American estate 304,562,215 acres—not quite five acres to every man, woman and child living.

The wealthy men of Europe who own the vast territory as given in Class III., also have absolute control through mortgages of 90,000,000 acres of the railroad land given in Class II.

RAILROAD OWNERSHIP IN LAND.*

	ACRES.
Northern Pacific	47,000,000
Atlantic and Pacific	42,000,000
Southern Pacific	35,200,000
Texas Pacific	18,000,000
Union Pacific	12,000,000
Kansas Pacific	6,000,000
Central Pacific	11,000,000
St. Paul and Pacific	4,723,038

* Hist. Wheel and Alliance, p. 672.

	ACRES.
Oregon and California..........................	3,500,000
New Orleans, Baton Rouge, and Vicksburg...........	3,800,000
Cairo and Fulton................................	3,000,667
Atchison, Topeka and Santa Fé...................	3,000,000
Illinois Central and Mobile and Chicago.............	2,596,053
Missouri River, Fort Scott and Gulf.................	2,350,000
Burlington and Missouri River	2,441,600
Denver Pacific..................................	1,000,000
Oregon Central.................................	1,200,000
Wisconsin Central...............................	1,800,000
Pensacola and Georgia...........................	1,568,229
Mobile and Ohio River...........................	1,004,640
St. Paul and Sioux City..........................	1,100,000
Iowa Falls and Sioux City.........................	1,226,163
St. Joe and Denver City	1,700,000
Missouri, Kansas and Texas.......................	1,520,000
Pacific and Southwestern.........................	1,161,235
Jackson, Lansing and Saginaw.....................	1,052,169
Chicago, Rock Island and Pacific...................	1,261,181
Cedar Rapids and Missouri........................	1,298,739

ALIEN OWNERSHIP IN AMERICAN LAND.*

	ACRES.
English Syndicate in Texas........................	3,000,000
Holland Company in New Mexico...................	4,500,000
Sir Edward Reid in Florida........................	2,000,000
English Syndicate in Mississippi	1,800,000
Marquis of Tweedsdale...........................	1,750,000
Phillips, Marshall & Co...........................	1,300,000
German Syndicate...............................	1,000,000
Byron H. Evans	700,000
Anglo-American Syndicate........................	750,000
Duke of Sutherland..............................	425,000
British Land Company in Kansas...................	320,000
Wm. Whaley, M.P...............................	310,000
Missouri Land Company of Scotland................	465,000
Robert Penant of London	260,000

* Hist. Wheel and Alliance, pp. 673–677.

ACRES.

	ACRES.
Dundee Land Company of Scotland	247,000
Lord Dunmore.....................................	120,000
Benjamin Neugas	100,000
Lord Houghton	60,000
Lord Dunraven	60,000
English Land Company...........................	110,000
Albert Peele, M.P................................	10,000
Sir J. L. Kay	5,000
Alex. Grant.....................................	35,000
English Syndicate in Missouri.......................	110,000
M. Ellerhausen....................................	600,000
Scotch Syndicate in Florida.......................	500,000
A. Boysen of Denmark............................	50,000
Total	20,557,500

OWNERSHIP IN LAND BY AMERICANS, SYNDICATES, OR SPECULATORS.*

	ACRES.
Col. Murphy......	4,000,000
The Standard Oil Company.........................	1,000,000
Ex-Senator Dorsey in New Mexico	500,000
Diston of Pennsylvania, in Florida	2,000,000
The Vanderbilts †.......	20,000,000
Total	27,500,000

LOCALITY OF LAND BY ALIENS.‡

	ACRES.
In eleven Northern and Northwestern States..........	5,050,000
In thirteen Southern and Southwestern States........ ...	20,350,000
In eleven Pacific States...........................	39,500,000

LAND RESTORED TO THE PUBLIC DOMAIN.

From March 4, 1885, to June 30, 1888, the lands restored to the public domain for the benefit of the

* Hist. of Wheel and Alliance.
† Newspaper.
‡ Hand Books of Facts.

people amount to 83,158,990 acres. These broad acres were recovered through forfeitures of railroads, private land claims, entries under pre-emption given up, and invalid State selections. Over 60,000,000 acres of land are now recommended for recovery.

This was an eminently wise movement. It was begun during Mr. Cleveland's first administration, and while Mr. L. Q. C. Lamar was Secretary of the Department of the Interior.

COMPARISONS.

Comparisons are said to be odious. Why this should be so we are not informed. We do know that profligate sophistry is odious in essence and in practice. To contrast the abstract with the concrete is a method not to be despised in conveying information to the great body of the American people.

On September 20, 1850, Congress commenced passing Land Grant Bills to aid in the construction of railroads in different States.* The first bill granted to the State of Illinois, for the benefit and use of the Illinois Central Railroad Company, 2,505,-053 acres of land through the richest portion of the State. The company has realized about $30,000,000 from the sale of these lands. In the six years following 1850 some forty-seven Land Grant Bills were passed by Congress in furtherance of railroad building. But since the war colossal grants have been

---

* Hist. of Wheel and Alliance, pp. 671, 672.

made for the same purpose. The total number of acres thus granted for the building of railroads amounts to 209,344,233, or 311,475 square miles. This vast territory was granted to 1,482 companies, which up to June 30, 1880, had completed 87,891 miles of railroad ; 19,722 miles extension were projected, and 21,307 miles of new roads were projected.

COMPANIES AND MILES OF RAILROAD.*

COMPANIES.	MILES.	CONDITION.
1,146	87,891	Completed.
. . . . .	19,722	Extension projected.
336	21,307	New roads projected.
1,482	128,920	Complete and projected.

To encourage these 1,482 companies to build 128,-920 miles of railroad, the great-hearted and far-seeing Congress granted them a dominion greater than the German Empire, for this empire only covers an area of 211,000 square miles, and the railroad grants equal 311,475 square miles. These railroad grants cover an area of more land than is contained in the German Empire, England, and Wales and Scotland. In this land of vast mountain ranges and mighty rivers—this ocean-girdled republican empire—nothing is done on a niggardly scale, even if the Anglo-Saxon people are beggared by fabulous grants.

Maine, Vermont, Illinois, Tennessee, Indiana, Connecticut, Delaware, Massachusetts, South Caro-

---

* Compendium Tenth Census, Part II., p. 1257.

lina, Maryland, Louisiana, and Mississippi do not contain as many acres as those embraced in the railroad land grants, by 155 acres.

These land grants to 1,482 railroad companies are greater in area than all the land owned by 16,051,000 people in twelve independent States of the Federal Union.

Nor is this all. The situation portends nothing that is cheerful. Ninety million acres, or 140,625 square miles, of this railroad land are mortgaged to foreign capitalists who, in the elegant language of commerce, will hold "the corner" on this vast property and fix the prices handsomely to the native and industrious bread-producers in the years to come. In case of war, these hardy sons of the soil will even defend these broad acres, whose owners reside in gilded palaces beyond the blue Atlantic.

Titanic land-holdings require corresponding comparisons to express them. The land owned by an English syndicate in Texas equals 3,000,000 acres. It is an area of 4,687 square miles. Were this land in the form of a square, the distance would be covered by 272 miles. If a man rode twenty-seven miles a day, it would take ten days to ride around it and get back to the starting point. A dozen Englishmen own this splendid estate.

This syndicate owns more land in Texas than is contained in the following twelve counties selected at random: Bastrop, Baylor, Bee, Bell, Bexar, Austin, Burleson, Dallas, Galveston, Hardin, Houston, and Harrison.

In Florida, one Englishman owns 2,000,000 acres, and a Scotch syndicate owns 500,000 acres.

An English syndicate is in possession of 1,800,000 acres in the State of Mississippi. This means a strip of territory covering 2,812 square miles. A Mississippian, with a good horse, riding twenty-five miles a day, can ride around it in eight days. All the land improved and unimproved, in the counties of Adams, Alcorn, Amite, Attala, Benton, Hinds, and Marion is not quite equal to the body of land to which this syndicate holds the title.

This ownership of large bodies of land by wealthy foreigners is certainly a disquieting factor to the American bread-winners of the soil. Is landlordism to be the fate of this nation? Are the Anglo-Saxon people destined to become "the hewers of wood and the drawers of water"? Does African freedom mean the enslavement of the white people? Are the American people to be cheated out of their land, and denied the birthright privilege of becoming freeholders, paying for land at honest prices? Shall these colossal speculations go on until the great body of our people are at the absolute mercy of whatever price rapacity can demand? Alarm bells should ring out their earnest protest in every State of the Federal Union, against any further encroachment upon the public domain by either foreign or American speculators. Legislative assemblies in all the States, and the Congress of the United States, should be charged to protect the people from these greedy and pitiless vampires.

The land movement in the South presents another

phase. It is a twofold movement. The one is the American idea: toward many small farms, where each man is his own freeholder, independent, unconscious of grinding dependence—a freeholder, the " patent and passport of self-respect with the Anglo-Saxon race ever since Hengist and Horsa landed on the shores of England." The other is the European idea: it means landlordism, vast estates, a multitudinous tenantry, beggary, serfdom. Can this condition be imposed on the Anglo-Saxon race in the nineteenth century?

The following tables furnish a study.

TABLE I.

NUMBER AND SIZE OF FARMS IN 1860.

STATES.	UNDER 3 ACRES.	3 AND UNDER 10.	10 AND UNDER 20.	20 AND UNDER 50.	50 AND UNDER 100.	100 AND UNDER 500.	500 AND UNDER 1,000.	1,000 AND OVER.
Alabama ..	......	1,409	4,379	16,049	12,060	13,455	2,016	696
Arkansas ..	......	1,823	6,075	13,728	6,957	4,231	307	69
Florida	......	430	945	2,139	1,162	1,432	211	77
Georgia .. .	......	906	2,803	13,644	14,129	18,821	2,692	902
Louisiana..	......	626	2,222	4,882	3,064	4,955	1,161	371
Mississippi.	......	563	2,516	10,967	9,204	11,408	1,868	481
N. Carolina	......	2,050	4,879	20,882	18,496	19,220	1,184	311
S. Carolina	......	352	1,219	6,695	6,980	11,369	1,359	482
Tennessee .	......	1,687	7,245	22,998	22,829	21,903	921	158
Texas	......	1,832	6,156	14.132	7,857	6,831	468	87
Total ..	......	11,678	40,439	126,116	102,738	117,625	12,187	3,634

TABLE II.

NUMBER AND SIZE OF FARMS IN 1880.

STATES.	UNDER 3 ACRES.	3 AND UNDER 10.	10 AND UNDER 20.	20 AND UNDER 50.	50 AND UNDER 100.	100 AND UNDER 500.	500 AND UNDER 1,000.	1,000 AND OVER.
Alabama...	277	3,597	13,055	41,721	26,447	44,254	4,645	1,868
Arkansas ..	97	2,070	10,780	19,282	21,787	37,976	1,793	648
Florida	69	1,301	2,456	7,640	4,381	6,562	652	377
Georgia ...	101	3,110	8,694	36,524	26,054	53,635	7,017	3,491
Louisiana..	100	1,848	6,708	12,626	8,501	15,031	2,159	1,319
Mississippi.	84	2,336	11,936	26.836	19,318	35,493	3,936	1,833
N. Carolina	277	7,273	13,314	34,148	34,007	61,806	5,063	1,721
S. Carolina	118	7,035	12,519	27,517	13,612	27,735	3,693	1,635
Tennessee .	220	5,821	17,335	34,783	39,541	63,315	3,549	1,086
Texas	34	3,554	16,780	43,675	29,539	70,821	5,988	3,793
Total ..	1,377	37,945	113,577	284,752	223,187	416,628	40,495	17,771

TABLE III.

1880.

NUMBER AND SIZE OF FARMS CULTIVATED BY OWNERS.

STATES.	UNDER 3 ACRES.	3 AND UNDER 10.	10 AND UNDER 20.	20 AND UNDER 50.	50 AND UNDER 100.	100 AND UNDER 500.	500 AND UNDER 1,000.	1,000 AND OVER.
Alabama...	92	956	1,652	8,501	16,282	38,814	4,194	1,724
Arkansas ..	33	585	1,417	8,981	18,135	33,962	1,561	571
Florida	53	815	1,238	3,532	3,461	6,132	607	360
Georgia ...	35	906	1,353	6,605	14,401	43,505	6,392	3,254
Louisiana..	59	811	1,942	5,425	6,780	13,243	1,884	1,142
Mississippi.	36	732	1,499	5,708	13,032	30,931	3,564	1,712
N. Carolina	128	2,141	3,851	13,973	25,929	52,810	4,447	1,608
S. Carolina	34	1,168	2,609	5,914	8,750	23,358	3,276	1,536
Tennessee .	102	2,447	3,996	15,028	29,257	53,515	3,121	988
Texas	21	1,463	3,015	10,312	21,374	63,440	5,508	3,583
Total ..	593	12,024	22,572	83,979	157,401	359,710	34,554	16,478

10

TABLE IV.

1880.

NUMBER AND SIZE OF FARMS RENTED FOR FIXED MONEY RENTAL.

STATES.	UNDER 3 ACRES.	3 AND UNDER 10.	10 AND UNDER 20.	20 AND UNDER 50.	50 AND UNDER 100.	100 AND UNDER 500.	500 AND UNDER 1,000.	1,000 AND OVER.
Alabama...	51	1,058	3,251	11,858	3,995	2,343	248	84
Arkansas ..	8	414	2,563	3,464	1,417	1,848	145	57
Florida ...	6	262	582	1,980	452	236	24	6
Georgia....	27	978	1,631	8,205	3,616	3,680	280	140
Louisiana..	26	464	1,831	2,524	634	887	179	124
Mississippi.	23	605	3,341	7,931	2,859	2,381	217	83
N. Carolina	23	921	1,553	3,023	1,305	1,639	145	35
S. Carolina.	46	4,418	5,096	8,443	1,866	1,811	225	69
Tennessee .	44	984	3,732	6,369	4,019	3,846	217	55
Texas	5	547	2,222	5,678	1,503	1,877	168	89
Total ..	259	10,651	25,802	59,475	21,666	20,548	1,848	742

TABLE V.

NUMBER AND SIZE OF FARMS RENTED FOR SHARES OF PRODUCT, 1880.

STATES.	UNDER 3 ACRES.	3 AND UNDER 10.	10 AND UNDER 20.	20 AND UNDER 50.	50 AND UNDER 100.	100 AND UNDER 500.	500 AND UNDER 1,000.	1,000 AND OVER.
Alabama. ..	134	1,583	8,152	21,362	6,170	3,097	203	60
Arkansas...	56	1,071	6,800	6,837	2,235	2,166	87	20
Florida.....	10	224	636	2,128	468	194	21	11
Georgia. .	39	1,226	5,710	21,714	8,037	6,450	345	97
Louisiana ..	15	573	2,935	4,677	1,087	901	96	53
Mississippi .	25	999	7,096	13,197	3,427	2,181	155	38
N. Carolina.	126	4,211	7,910	17,152	6,773	7,357	471	78
S. Carolina.	38	1,449	4,814	13,160	2,996	2,566	192	30
Tennessee..	74	2,390	9,607	13,386	6,265	5,954	211	43
Texas.......	8	1,544	11,543	27,685	6,662	5,504	312	121
Total...	525	15,270	65,203	141,298	44,120	36,370	2,093	551

TABLE VI.

NUMBER AND SIZE OF FARMS BY TOTALS IN EACH CLASS.

SIZE OF FARMS.	CLASS AS TO SIZE.	OWNERS.	RENTERS.	SHARE WORKERS.	TOTALS.
Under 3 acres............	I.	593	259	525	1,377
3 and under 10............	II.	12,024	10,651	15,270	37,945
10 and under 20.........	III.	22,572	25,802	65,203	113,577
20 and under 50	IV.	83,979	59,475	141,298	284,752
50 and under 100..	V.	157,401	21,666	44,120	223,187
100 and under 500........ ...	VI.	359,710	20,548	36,370	416,628
500 and under 1,000.......	VII.	34,554	1,848	2,093	38,495
1,000 and over....	VIII.	16,478	742	551	17,771
Total.................		687,311	140,971	305,430	1,133,712

TABLE VII.

THE TENURE OF FARMS IN THE TEN STATES, 1880.

STATES.	NUMBER OF FARMS CULTIVATED BY OWNERS.	NUMBER OF FARMS RENTED FOR FIXED MONEY RENTAL.	NUMBER OF FARMS RENTED FOR SHARE OF PRODUCT.
Alabama........	72,215	22,888	40,761
Arkansas.......	65,245	9,916	19,272
Florida........	16,198	3,548	3,692
Georgia........	76,451	18,557	43,618
Louisiana...... ...	31,286	6,669	10,337
Mississippi	57,214	17,440	27,118
N. Carolina	104,887	8,644	44,078
S. Carolina.....	46,645	21,974	25,245
Tennessee......	108,454	19,266	37,930
Texas....	108,716	12,089	53,379
Total......	687,311	140,791	305,430

TABLE VIII.

DIFFERENCE IN THE NUMBER OF FARMS BETWEEN 1860 AND 1880 IN
THE TEN STATES.

SIZE BY ACRES.	1860.	1880.	INCREASE IN 20 YEARS.
Under 3........	None	1,377	1,377
3 to 10.........	11,678	37,945	26,267
10 to 20........	40,439	113,577	73,138
20 to 50........	126,116	284,752	158,636
50 to 100.......	102,738	223,187	120,449
100 to 500......	117,625	416,628	299,003
500 to 1,000....	12,187	40,495	28,308
1,000 and over..	3,634	17,771	14,137

It is now proposed to arrange these eight classes
of farmers into three great groups according to the
quantity of land cultivated. Those cultivating less
than 3 acres; 3 and less than 10; and 10 and less
than 20; will constitute Group I. They are the
single farmers whether proprietary, renters or share
workers, employing no hired help. Group II. will
embrace all those cultivating 20 acres of land and
less than 500 acres. They are the middle class of
farmers. The last class will be Group III., consisting of plantations cultivating from 500 acres upward. These three groups will be presented for
1860 and 1880. They are indexes to the economic
movement in the South, as well as the strong tendency to multiply large plantations.

TABLE IX.

NUMBER AND SIZE OF FARMS IN THREE GROUPS.

	SIZE IN ACRES.	1860.	1880.	GAIN PER CENT.
Group I............	3 and less than 20.	52,117	152,899	1.93
Group II..............	20 and less than 500.	346,479	924,567	1.66
Group III.............	500, 1,000 and more.	15,821	58,266	2.68

No thoughtful man can study the land movement toward large plantations without fear for the future. When the uncertainty of labor is considered, and that cotton is the main crop of the South, as soon as the owners find that these plantations do not remunerate them, many plantations will fall into the hands of wealthy syndicates. The English West Indian history will repeat itself in the South. If 800 acres is the average size of these plantations of Group III. in the ten States, they embrace all combined 46,612,800 acres. It is less than the land owned by aliens in the United States.

We take it for granted that in 1860 there were very few farmers in the South who cultivated land as renters, and land cultivated on the share system was unknown. If there were any in either class, the per cent. was so small that it attracted no attention. Following the plan of Table IX., we will group all places according to ownership.

TABLE X.

Number and Size of Farms as to Ownership.

	SIZE IN ACRES.	1860.	1880.	LOSS AND GAIN PER CENT.
Group I..............	3 and less than 20.	52,117	35,189	Loss .32
Group II..............	20 and less than 500.	346,479	601,090	Gain .79
Group III............	500, 1,000 and more.	15,821	51,032	Gain 2.22

Comparing Tables IX. and X., we find that according to Group I., in 1880, 117,710 farms were cultivated by renters or shareworkers. In Group II. there were 323,477 farms cultivated by renters or shareworkers, and in Group III. 7,234 large plantations were thus cultivated. These renters and shareworkers, were chiefly negroes. Nearly a half million of farms were in the sole charge of the negroes. This fact will explain in part the decrease in the grain crop of the South, referred to in a former chapter.

The ownership of these farms reveals a far more important consideration in its bearing on the land question in the future. By the overwhelming testimony from ten States and the South generally, farmers have made no money at farming. Mortgages and debts form the burden of their complaint.

In Group I., while there has been a decrease in ownership of 32 per cent. since 1860, our inference is, that between two-thirds and three-fourths of the land cultivated by 117,710 renters and shareworkers belongs to white farmers.

But in Group II. there has been an increase of ownership in twenty years of 79 per cent., in Group III. an increase of ownership of 222 per cent. Who owns this land?—the speculator in part, the town and country merchant in part, the commission merchant in part, and the farmer in part.

To say that the ownership is all vested in farmers can not be reconciled with the uncontradicted and well-known report of "blue ruin" coming from the great farming community in every State of the South.

Making allowances for the breaking up of old farms since 1860 in Group II., parceling their farms out to children, in other cases selling portions of old farms, our opinion is, that of the increase in ownership of farms in twenty years, 50 per cent. in Group II. and 75 per cent. in Group III. are vested in other persons than farmers.

A large portion of this land is destined in the near future to be the property of some syndicate unless some remedy by law can be found to prevent it. The movement to monopoly of land is sure and steady.

We can not impress with sufficient emphasis the danger that threatens our people in the strong movement toward land monopoly. Land now sold for two dollars an acre will, long before the year 1925 is reached, cost our children twenty-five dollars an acre, if that land is held by a syndicate.

" The condition of the English and Irish peasantry to-day truth-fully mirrors the near future of the American farmer, if land consolidation and landlordism is not checked." *

" For various reasons the farms of the South have not been mortgaged to the extent of those in the more fertile regions of the North and West. But Shylock has already turned his greedy eyes upon this beautiful Southland, and is now establishing his loan agencies. We can not too strongly urge upon the Southern farmer to beware of the net that is being spread for him. Shun it as you would a deadly plague, if you would save your homes from his relentless grasp." †

" The syndicates that loan money at from one to three per cent. are mainly made up of Scotch, English, and New England capitalists, who have their agents throughout the South and West. These mortgages are falling due, and soon an immense number of Southern and Western farms will be in the hands of foreign mortgagees." ‡

The credit system and the high prices under that system are stealthily conveying a large percentage of Southern farms into the possession of some syndicate. For private and generous reasons, merchants who have come into possession of land ranging from 10,000 acres to 500,000 acres, will sell this land to resident farmers and planters. This is patriotic. But money is scarce in the South, and particularly so among farmers. When the merchant is pressed for money, patriotism will lose its aroma, and the land will go into the market; the highest cash bidder will get it. If this cash bidder is a company of capitalists, it will be held until a " corner " can be produced, or it will be cultivated by tenants. "Colonel Church, of New York, owns and collects

---

* Wheel and Alliance.
† *Ibid.*
‡ American Farms, p. 50.

rents from 180 farms in that State; some of them contain more than 500 acres each." * How many Colonel Churches are there already in the South? Silently and almost imperceptibly, here and there a farm is slipping out of the possession of some small owner.

An editorial in the St. Louis *Republican* is quoted in "The Tramp at Home," by Mr. Lee Meriwether, p. 160:

" There is not a single one of the twenty-nine agricultural States that is not, to a greater or less extent, under mortgage to the money-lending creditor States. . . . It is stated that the insurance companies of Hartford, Connecticut, hold $70,000,coo in Western farm mortgages; that the loan companies hold 1,000 mortgages, representing $76,000,000; and in the little State of New Hampshire, Western farm mortgages to the amount of $35,000,000 are held. . . . These agricultural States pay annually to the money-lenders $180,000,000 in interest alone.

" According to the Michigan Labor Commissioner, February, 1888, the mortgages on farms in the single State of Michigan amount to $64,000,000, paying an annual interest of $5,000,000." †

Could accurate data be obtained, what would not the South reveal in regard to farm mortgages? In a former chapter the testimony has been given from ten States. These mortgages are fatal to the future native ownership of the soil.

Let us turn our attention to the Old World—to England, standing high in the scale of Christian civilization. This is a land of churches and schools, of renowned seats of learning, of famous statesmen, orators, historians, poets, and preachers. Great as

---

* Wheel and Alliance, p. 674.
† The Tramp at Home, p. 161.

England is, what about the barriers to the progress
of her millions?

Has England any pity for her oppressed farm
tenantry? To become a landowner is to millions of
her people an impossibility. The door to land
ownership by the poor is closed by wealth. The
cruel dilemma presented to every poor man is:
"Work on our terms, or starve." Yet wealthy
Englishmen wish more land.

The condition of the dependent English farm
tenantry has a lesson for the American farmer—a
lesson for all the Southern people engaged in agriculture. To learn that lesson, at whatever cost of
self-denial and rigid economy, is an act eminently
wise.

Senator D. W. Voorhees, in the *North American
Review* of November, 1891, thus states the condition
of England's farm tenantry: "According to reliable
official statements the population of the United
Kingdom, embracing England, Wales, Scotland,
and Ireland, may be put down at 28,000,000,
and her land at 72,119,962 acres. Of these lands,
51,885,148 acres, more than two-thirds of the
whole landed property of the kingdom, are owned
by less than 11,000 persons. These vast landowners draw a rental from an oppressed tenantry
of over $562,000,000 per annum, and as the
amount of money circulating in the kingdom is
contracted, and its volume diminished, so is the
purchasing and governing power of these enormous
millions increased, and the privileged few aggran-
dized by grinding the faces of the poor. The for-

eign policy of England is often denounced for its brutal rapacity, but her home policy, whereby an idle, sensual, income-devouring aristocracy enjoys full and free license to prey upon her toiling masses, wears a darker hue than even the perfidious and crimson stains she has left on distant shores, and with which she has incarnadined the seas."

This means an average of 4,717 acres to each one of the 11,000 persons, and not quite three-fourths of an acre to each of the 27,989,000 poor people. If civilization is the condition of a people's progress in physical comforts and conveniences, in intellectual enlightenment and expansion, and in those virtues that lie at the foundation of individual happiness, social order and well being, then England's civilization is not for the masses. Eleven thousand Englishmen have the power to prevent twenty-eight million other English people from ever becoming freeholders; and to be a freeholder, Mr. Blaine said in his eulogy on President Garfield, "had been the patent and passport of self-respect with the Anglo-Saxon race ever since Hengist and Horsa landed on the shores of England." That self-respect is denied to this people by inexorable conditions. The moneyed power has encrusted her civilization with a deadly blight.

Notwithstanding these remorseless conditions—those cruel laws that confront the poor man in his efforts to improve his surroundings—the scale upon which England pays by law the clergy of her State church bears no proportion to the poverty, oppression, and burden of her millions.

	Per annum.
The Archbishop of Canterbury's salary is..............	$76,000
Bishop of London....................................	50,000
Archbishop of York.................................	56,000
Bishop of Durham..................................	40,000
Bishop of Winchester	35,000
Bishop of Ely........	27,000
Six Bishops, each $25,000...........................	150,000
Eight Bishops, each $22,500.........................	180,000
Eight Bishops, each $21,000	168,000
Twenty-nine Deans, each $7,400.....................	217,500
One hundred and twenty Canons, each $5,000..........	600,000

177 Clergymen are paid annually...............$1,599,500

In the United States this large sum would support several thousand ministers who claim no higher title than the sublime purpose to serve their divine Lord and the high interests of humanity. It is a melancholy portrait to contemplate in these closing years of the nineteenth century; a wealth-enthroned clergy representing Him who was lowly of heart, and millions of worshipers ground down into the dust. This is the boasted civilization of the age. This is grim progress. This is Christianity emasculated, its efficacy and healing power lost in gorgeous ceremonials, fit only to captivate and enthrall for an hour the sensuous intellect. The poor, the lowly, the despised, the disconsolate, are forgotten and neglected, and everywhere encircled by crushing laws. Wealth is everywhere intrenched in strong and protecting statutes, not merely as wealth should be protected, but to the detriment and serious disadvantage of the poor.

It is stated that less than 200,000 men in England

have an annual income of $700,000,000, and eight persons in the United Kingdom own more than 220,000 acres of land.

ENGLAND'S LANDLORDS.

Duke of Sutherland	1,358,425	acres.
Duke of Buccleugh	459,260	"
Sir James Matheson	406,070	"
Earl of Breadalbaugh	372,609	"
Earl of Seafield	305,891	"
Duke of Richmond	286,407	"
Earl of Fife	257,629	"
Alexander Matheson	220,433	"
Duke of Athol	194,640	"
Duke of Devonshire	193,121	"
Duke of Northumberland	185,515	"
Duke of Argyle	175,114	"

If we take 50,000 acres as the average number of acres cultivated in many a county of the Southern States, then these twelve rich Englishmen own as much land as is cultivated in eighty such counties. In England, the land question is settled. It is owned by the moneyed power, and that power will hold it.

"Though England is deafened with spinning wheels, her people have no clothes; though she is black with digging coal, her people have not fuel, and people die of cold; and though she sold her soul for gain, they die of hunger." * Such is the condition of England, reputed one of the wealthiest nations of the earth. Wealthy she is, but wealthy in the midst of overwhelming and appalling poverty and distress.

---

* Ruskin.

The causes that have brought about this condition in England are not unlike the causes that operate now in these United States, and that are at work in these Southern States to bring about similar disastrous results.   One phase of these results is the land question.   If the agencies now in existence go on unchecked, men now living may see the day when land ownership will be out of the reach of the poor man.   These agencies are:

1. Titanic land grants to build railroads ;
2. Land bought by foreign syndicates ;
3. Land bought by American syndicates ;
4. Land that will fall into the hands of syndicates through loan associations ;
5. Land that will ultimately fall into the hands of syndicates through the credit system and its accompaniment, deeds of trust.

THE PERIL THREATENING THE AMERICAN ESTATE.

That the danger of land being wrested from the people of these United States, North and South, East and West, is real, is supported by unequivocal testimony.   The methods to accomplish this land spoliation are often insidious and unscrupulous, and no less bold and arrogant.   Bribes and perjury have been invoked when necessary to the fell achievement.

"There are no morals in politics and governmental affairs," said a State official to a farmer, whose sound, rugged common sense remonstrated against certain vicious proceedings.   That a falsehood, charged with the very essence of the doctrine of Machiavelli, should be formulated into words,

and should be given publicity, is sufficiently start-
ling. Such profligate sophisms are used as the
clumsy weapons to silence common sense. Bribery
and arson, perjury and felony, according to this
hideous falsehood, wear no moral complexion. But
why argue against so monstrous a perversion of
the fundamental idea of all government? Yet it
should surprise no one, when an artist so corrupt
should bring forth his masterpiece of villany by
lending his official influence to any scheme however
nefarious. That there are such men, no one can
doubt. That the influence and the official station
of such men are a menace to the interests of the
people, there can be no question.

The danger of land spoliation is thus portrayed
by the *World:*

" There are many reasons why aliens living in their own countries,
yet desiring to benefit by the prosperity of this, while not sharing
the responsibility of citizenship, are anxious to own land and houses,
and reap the benefit of our countrymen's toils and industry. Chief
among those reasons is the desire for a permanent and safe investment, especially for the future. There is no longer either honor or
profit in being a landlord in Ireland, and those who could sell their
properties have done so. The Land Restoration Leagues of England and Scotland have reached such proportions that the future holding of real estate is of doubtful value ; while the Social Democrats,
who seek the establishment of a social republic, are enlisting the
workingmen and poor of both countries, and a general uprising is
only a question of time. . . . There is nothing under the sun
so sensitive as capital. Those who hold it foresee coming disaster
afar off, and desert the sinking ship before others have an idea of
the proximity of danger. Thus the capitalists of the Old World
have sought new and sure fields in which to invest, and the United
States furnish all the requirements desired by the most careful
money-lenders of the world. . . . Their willingness to own

land, to invest in business enterprises, to possess the patent rights of machinery, to run breweries, to tunnel or bridge rivers, to build houses, to work mines, or to operate railroads, is not from any love of this country. It is altogether that they may lay every man, woman, and child, under tribute—not only the present, but all future generations ; that every one here who toils may pile up for them riches to be spent in their own countries : that they may perpetuate here the conditions against which their own countrymen are about revolting. They would fasten on the people of the United States the curse of ' absentee landlordism.'

" In order to obtain these holdings, the most corrupt practices have been resorted to. Congressmen have been bribed, government officials silenced, witnesses suborned, and perjury resorted to. Millions of acres of the best farming land in the nation have been stolen, and hundreds of thousands of acres of magnificent forests have fallen into their hands. Let those who believe in America for Americans study the figures given, and act accordingly." *

The *Galveston News* as reported in the " Economist Scrap Book," Part II., for May, 1891, page 124, says : " The fathers of Texas saw further than their sons. They forbade the holding of Texas lands by aliens. Otherwise, nearly all the lands in the country might have passed into the hands of foreigners. In less than fifty years, citizens of Texas will curse the day that an empire in extent of her territory passed into the hands of men living abroad, and spending money there drawn from Texas renters."

Similar causes are operating in all the Southern States, and in the same direction.

A few years ago, the attorney-general of Texas entered suit against a railroad company to restore to the State lands granted that corporation. A

---

* Handbook of Facts for January, 1891, p. 65.

delegation from the Panhandle of Texas visited the State Capitol, and formally requested the attorney-general to withdraw the suit, as the suit was throwing a cloud upon the titles of lands in that section, and injuring the Panhandle and its people. The attorney-general declined to comply with the request of the delegation. He is reported as saying, speaking of the greed of the corporation in grabbing Texas lands, that to-day they controlled one-fourth of all the lands in Texas, they would control it in perpetuity, and he predicted that in less than twenty years, the people of the Panhandle, instead of owning and controlling their own homes, would be vassals of rich English landlords.*

This is the dreary condition of servitude awaiting the Panhandle people of prosperous Texas. But Texas is waking up. The alarm is sounded. The recent message of her Governor has an earnest ring on this all-important land question.

We quote that part of the message relating to land corporations. It has direct practical value to all the Southern States.

LAND CORPORATIONS.†

" The constitution declares that ' perpetuities and monopolies are contrary to the genius of a free government, and shall never be allowed, nor shall the law of primogeniture or entailments ever be in force in this State.'—Article I., section 26. The laws of this State regulating the estates of deceased persons, are amply sufficient to give full force and effect to the spirit of the constitution against primogeniture and entailments. But there is no law to check or

---

* The Economist's Scrap-Book, Part II., for May, 1891, p. 124.
† Message by Gov. A. S. Hogg of Texas, Jan., 1893.

limit title to lands owned by corporations nor to prevent monopolies of real estate by them. While land corporations can not, as such, be chartered under the laws of this State, yet under the law authorizing the Secretary of State to grant permits to foreign corporations to do business within the State, they are chartered in other States and foreign countries, and are operating here in the purchase and ownership of lands. Titles to many million acres are now vested in them, the lands withheld from settlement except at exorbitant prices, without any law regulating or controlling or limiting the corporate rights in any respect whatsoever. There is danger in this condition, which seems to have aroused the people; for, in their convention last August, they adopted the following platform on that subject :

"'16. We demand the enactment of a law that will define perpetuities and prohibit the operation of land corporations in this State, requiring those now holding title or possession of lands for agricultural, horticultural, grazing and speculating purposes, excepting overflowed and irrigation lands, to dispose of the same within such reasonable time as may not impair vested rights.'

"The purpose of this demand is wise and just. Land corporations, having in view the ownership of large bodies of soil, portend land monopoly with titles in perpetuity. There is no institution more inimical to the genius of a free government; none that should be more strenuously prohibited. Permit corporations of this class to operate much longer in this State, grouping together large bodies of agricultural and grazing lands, and the time is not far off when, if the people are permitted to buy homes at all, they can only do so at prices and on such terms that bondage of themselves and their posterity must be the result; for an excessive mortgage debt on a home, bearing annual interest high enough to demand the surplus products of labor to meet it, means no more nor less than bondage of an aggravated form. The condition of other States in this respect can not fail to be a valuable lesson to Texas.

"A corporation has been defined to be an artificial being, invisible, intangible, existing only in contemplation of law, with life perpetual. No power can check its franchises nor limit or destroy its life, except the government that grants its charter. Operating in Texas lands now are Scotch and British corporations and those of other States. While the State has no power to destroy them nor to revoke their charters, she has the right to tax them and to limit their right to acquire property, to prescribe the time and method of its alienation, and to exclude them from the State on conditions and terms consistent with vested rights, at will. Many of them are chartered abroad with the provision in the grant that they shall not own lands within the grant or government, but may go elsewhere for that purpose. If they were good, this condition would not be in them. It is not well for a great people, in the exciting race for wealth, to overlook this germ now being sowed among them, which, if neglected long, will spring into an overshadowing growth that can neither be checked nor destroyed. There is a *land famine* in most of the Old World and in many sections of the New. In the natural drift of affairs it may reach Texas within the next generation. Nothing can so readily precipitate it as the land corporation. When known that there are in nine of the old States only seven acres per capita ; that in nine of the others there are only twenty acres per capita ; that in twelve others, comparatively new States, there are only twenty-two acres per capita ; that in nine strictly Southern States there are only thirty-five acres per capita; and that in the whole United States, including the Territories, there are only thirty-seven acres per capita of the whole population, and that about one-tenth of these lands are possessed by land corporations, there is at least some excuse for a thoughtful people to be agitated at this time over the land problem.

"While the whole area of Texas amounts to about seventy-four acres per capita of her population, she is confronted with the most serious condition of corporate ownership of about one-fourth of it all. Statistics show that in the United States from 1870 to 1880 the cultivable lands in stable crops increased sixty-six per cent ; while from 1880 to 1890 the increase thereof was only twenty-six per cent. The evident cause of this is the growing scarcity of agricultural lands throughout the government. The bread-producing land of the world is fast being exhausted, while the bread-consuming people are increasing. As the ratio of production decreases, the ratio of bread consumption from year to year steadily increases. The land problem, after all, underlies the bread problem. It is the duty of the government to understand this and to act wisely for the good of posterity. This can best be done by restrictive laws, making corporate land monopoly impossible for the future. While the American people have escaped the evil of land monopoly under the laws of primogeniture of the Old World, they may yet find themselves involved in a more serious condition—that of land monopoly from titles in perpetuity caused by corporate ownership.

"To comply with this demand of the people of Texas, therefore, who had the right to make it, a law now becomes necessary by your honorable bodies, and the following suggestions therein are respectfully made :

" 1. Declare that land corporations are contrary to the genius of a free government, and shall hereafter exercise no rights in Texas except such as may be expressly authorized by law.

" 2. That no such corporations shall hereafter be chartered or be permitted to do business in the State after a limited period named.

" 3. That further acquisition of title or interest in land for speculative, agricultural, or grazing purposes shall be prohibited.

" 4. That those now holding title to or interest in lands for agricultural or grazing purposes, or that may, under the provisions of the law authorizing them to purchase real estate in collection of debt, hereafter acquire interest in or title to such land, shall within a specified time, consistent with vested rights, alienate them to natural persons, wind up their corporate affairs, and leave the State on prescribed penalties and forfeitures."

CHAPTER X.

BUSINESS is an honorable term. It does invaluable service in commerce and exchanges. Freighted with blessings, it is the servant of the rich and the poor. Its purview embodies method, exactness, and punctuality. In a moral sense, it stands for equitable transactions.

From these functions, in numerous individual instances, it has been deflected. It has often done degrading service. Its fair visage is besmirched. To discriminate legitimate business from disreputable transactions is not always an easy task. Extortion is business; fraud is business; peculation and speculation have appropriated the title; the taking advantage of ignorance and necessity has employed the term; corners in trade, dealing in "futures," and gambling in "stocks" have been so styled. Confiscation prices are fair in business. The cheat's transactions come under the term. According to this perverted usage, legitimate and illegitimate, reputable and disreputable dealings are styled business. Crime is not the violation of law, but business. Oppression is business. Thus it happens, that moral distinctions between right and wrong are defaced in trade.

The science of exchange occupies a prominent place in political economy. The appliances necessary to effect the end, require vast capital. Steamship lines and railways have not only destroyed the isolation of distant communities, removed the barriers to progress, but have made the exchange of productions possible, and have brought them to the doors of the rich and the poor alike.

The merchants constitute a large class of those concerned in exchange. Their position in society and the service rendered are quite as important as that of the producer. Without them the factory would be of no use, and the cotton and grain fields might as well be abandoned. They are a highly useful and intelligent class in society, honored for their integrity and business sagacity. Their service is indispensable to progress.

The tillers of the soil, or the farming class, in these United States differ widely from a similar class in the Old World. We have no peasantry here in the European sense. Caste has taken no root on American soil. Of twenty-one Presidents of the United States, fifteen came from farms; they were either farmers, or the sons of farmers, and four of the number spent their young manhood tilling the soil on small farms. Thousands of merchants, senators and members of Congress, eminent lawyers and preachers, and men in the various professions and vocations in life had early acquaintance with plough handles. Farm life is simple. Industry is regular. Temptations to evil are few. The circumstances furnish strong supports to virtue. Morality is robust. The unanimous verdict is, the best men and women, not by nature, but environments, are found in the rural districts—on American farms. They are hospitable, unsuspecting, honest, true and faithful to their obligations.

We shall not be suspected of any intention to do injustice to either one of the great classes portrayed. As classes their record is unsullied. Bad and faithless men are found in all the conditions of life. Among the twelve apostles, there was a Judas. Among gentlemen, there are those who belie the title. In every club, lodge, association and convention, are faithless men—false to avowed principles. Farmers and merchants are no exception to the weakness or the wrong that pertains to humanity.

With this understanding we may study the perversions in business relations. There is wrong done. No doubt about it. We do not believe that the guilt belongs altogether to the individuals of one class. Business has not all been fair. Crookedness has cut a large swath. There is guilty splendor on the one hand, and honest poverty on the other. What causes brought about these conditions? Were they normal?

Without discussing these questions, attention is directed to the fact that the Southern situation since 1865 was an invitation and a temptation to a great deal of crooked business. The situation deserves consideration. The people were poor. The credit system was the mode of doing business. Tens of thousands of white farmers were incapable of doing business in this way, without ruin. They did not understand what they were doing, even when the merchants were thoroughly honest dealers. They could not afford to pay long-time credit prices. If this is not true, how shall we explain the impoverished condition of Southern farmers in general? If the dealer was dishonest, swift ruin was inevitable. The negroes were all ignorant. Their custom was sought. They bought without rhyme or reason, as long as the prospect to pay was good. The lien law, intended as a blessing to them, proved a curse, as it practically alienated them, by their own choice, from their old masters. Those who fell into the hands of unscrupulous dealers, became bondsmen a second time. These peculiar circumstances were favorable to rascality. The successful cheat, if a dealer, soon became rich; if a farmer, white or black, he made a little which the high prices paid by the honest farmer covered.

Some of the underlying principles that gave rise to rascality are well worth consideration. Disowned they may be, but their existence is real, and, as active governing motives, the results show them potential. Men love power. It is inherent in the constitution of man. There is no real " Wamba " or " Gurth " in all the Southland to-day. A condition exists but little removed from that of an age gone forever. Many an Anglo-Saxon has a collar around his neck quite as galling as the iron ring worn by Wamba. Upon its gorget may be read the significant inscription: " Harry Yellowly, the son of Hardfate, is the lienserf of Isaac Shellwell," or, " Dick Fitzurse, the son of Riskall, is the thrall of Wagter Brothers."

Merchants that succeeded under existing business methods, became rich in a few years—some very rich. Failures were inevitable. Bad debts were rarely paid. Debts secured, in many instances, the land paid the claim. When every circumstance is considered, the farmers fared the worst. None are rich. Thousands are miserably poor — even men that started with no debts encumbering their property. These hard and unreasonable conditions upon which the necessities of life, the bread and meat supply, were made dependent, were fruitful in conduct that can not be reconciled by any principles of common justice. " Thou shalt not muzzle the ox when he treadeth out the corn," is a merciful command for the interest of the ox. But to impose a percentage which can not be extorted from the soil shows less consideration for the man than the beast. Frankness demands, and justice, " You can not buy on these terms and avoid beggary and bondage."

" Might is right " is expressive of oppression as old as humanity. It fills a dark and dreary chapter in history. The clumsy and brutal weapons employed to enforce it in ages past, are no longer in use, but the doctrine is still in the world. Power still confronts weakness. Its false and vicious intent is not blazoned to the world. It uses delicate machinery for the enforcement of its end. All power unjustly used is of this nature. " I have him in my power," is too often the expression not of right, but of might; and to use that might

unjustly is atrocious.   The tools used in the practical application of the maxim to business are,
money employed to produce monopoly values in
food supplies; advantages of every sort that the
creditor may have over the debtor, or the debtor
over the creditor; and circumstances as varied as
human wants.   The tricks of trade, the jugglery of
laws, the art of deception, perjury itself, a wanton
disregard for truth and honor, have all been called
into requisition to support this species of tyranny.
An adept in this sort of crookedness is vulgarly
styled "a smart business man."   Rehoboam's yoke
is heavy.

Mr. Hacker is reputed an honest man—he pays
his debts promptly.   This is well, but is this one
virtue to be used as a substitute for meanness and
avarice?   Is it not Mr. Hacker's rule to use every
advantage over those with whom he has dealings,
that money and circumstances give him?   Did he
not buy Mr. ——'s school warrant, face value $40,
for $18, when he knew that it would be paid at
farthest in two years?   That teacher had a large
family.   Hacker asked an old neighbor 40 per cent.
for the use of $100 on twelve months' time.   He
took a yoke of oxen from a man who was owing
him for $30, and sold them next week for $65, and
this was "cheap as dirt."   He bought at the highest
market price.   In trade, he was exorbitant, unmer-
ciful.   One hundred per cent. profit was fair.
"Stubbs!   This is the way to do business."   It was
a favorite saying of his.

A gentleman thus philosophized concerning hon-

est Mr. Hacker and his one vicarious virtue:
" Were the leading men in the various counties of
the Southern States all honest Mr. Hackers, in a
few years there would neither be a school nor a
church in the land. Professional men would take
their talents elsewhere; public enterprise would
die a still death; the people would, in a few years,
be reduced to a state of serfdom. He never attended a meeting of his fellow-citizens, save from
compulsion; from choice and interest in the public
good, never. His epitaph will read: ' Here lies
the body of Nabal Hacker. His life was selfish;
his ruling passion asserted itself in death—Save the
property.' His one vicarious virtue, honesty, is on
record; his dominant selfishness and his other qualities must be read in the poverty and the desolation
of the homes and the people over whom he had
the advantage."

Another bad doctrine that has gained favor in
practice, is that right and wrong are contingent on
knowledge. The obsequious Uriah Heep could not
look more humble than some men in expressing
their entire confidence in its soundness. "There
is big money in nigger trade." Certainly, there is
no telling what a benumbed and tattered conscience
will permit a man to do when money-making is the
life-blood of such a soul. " To do justice to all men,
black and white, ignorant and informed, is the law
of God. The negro has rights—to deal fairly with
him is one of the simplest. Justice demands it.
The lowest consideration that it is bad public policy
forbids injustice in every form, especially to the

ignorant and the weak. 'It is business.' This is
a diabolical defence. 'Niggers cannot tell twelve
ounces from a pound; twenty-four inches from a
yard; and they don't know the cost or the qualities
of goods.' The very best reasons why they should
be protected. How have ignorant white men fared
under such a guardianship? How many liens have
been recorded in the county clerk's office whose
fatal cross mark was never made by a black hand?
'Guilty wealth!' Chuckle over it, who will. It
is an infamous load to carry down to the grave.
Vicarious virtues will be published in the 'In
Memoriam,' and then go down to dust and forget-
fulness. But such acts will be embalmed in the
memory of living sufferers, and read on the historic
page of 'splendid guilt.'"

The retaliatory idea has also played a part in the
conduct of men. Wrong means wrung, twisted,
bent, perverse. All wrong is a twisted affair. It
soils heart and hands. It has stings for the ap-
pointed hour. It is a horrible companion in the
midnight watches. One wrong is not an adjustment of another wrong, but a shoot from the same
perverse stock. The fact that A —— cheated the
people out of $50,000 can never be pleaded in justi-
fication of B's conduct to cheat A. One robbery
does not adjust another robbery. Such measures
knock the bottom out of character, and no wreck in
life is attended with such far-reaching consequences
as character scarred by injustice or passion. The
inheritance is transmitted to children's children.
No amount of wealth can compensate for the loss

of incorruptible integrity. On this subject, the counsels of an old book have stood every test—tried in the furnace. Every misfortune has declared the lessons of wisdom pure and true. Some of these lessons are : " A good name is rather to be chosen than great riches;" " He that walketh uprightly, walketh surely ; " " He that getteth riches, and not by right, shall lose them in the midst of his days, and at his end shall be a fool." Whatever else may be depreciated, these truths in their wide application have never been discounted. To retaliate wrong with wrong is a vengeful cheat.

Wrong-doing has many phases. All failures in business are not honest. The true man compelled to yield to inevitable circumstances may become poor, but he comes through the fiery trial with a spotless name. His word is still his bond, and the synonym of truth and honor. The circumstantial evidence in many a failure points to a different result. What an amount of artful work must be necessary to prepare for such a fraudulent scheme! The books must be doctored ; merchandise must be spirited away, if it be part of the plan ; notes given for fictitious money and passed to the credit of bills payable to make one of the preferred creditors look like a decent, honorable gentleman. Preparation for the solemn act of perjury is essential, as well as for the hard and disturbing questions of the lawyers. Assets and liabilities must be arranged. Accounts of good debtors must be closed in the main ledger, and transcribed to a separate book, and payments by these debtors agreed upon by private arrangement.

These methods and others that have not been brought to our attention are more or less necessary in fraudulent failures to make these scurvy transactions look fair and honest. The liabilities are greater than the assets, yet the poor man in a short while appears to have more money than he had before his credit went to zero. These dark occurrences in business are sledge-hammer blows to confidence.

We would not add a feather's weight to the misfortunes of a true man. Legitimate business amid disaster deserves that generous consideration which misfortunes always evoke from noble spirits. Such business when prosperous will always obtain the award due to the high qualities of character and management which make success possible. Wealth legitimately and honorably made can not be the object of envy or reproach. It is the fruit of merit and business capacity.

There is a terrible evil in the country, striking herculean blows at truth. The solemn appeal to God in our courts, with the implied belief in retributive justice, is often a heartless mockery. Perjury riots with demoniacal glee in the temples of justice. Forsworn witnesses suborned in desperate cases defy the law. Legal talent of the highest order too often racks ingenuity to exalt a technicality into a fundamental principle, beclouds the plain intent of the law, and minimizes the value of conclusive testimony. "A sharp legal practitioner" is a common term. "Elaborate tissues of circumstantial falsehood, chicanery, forgery, and perjury" are the common weapons used to destroy the plain import of

the law. Life, liberty and property are in danger.
The too frequent use of this villanous enginery has
brought the courts of the country into disrepute.
The veneration for law and the confidence in courts
are jostled by the miscarriage of their intent. Is
there no legislative wisdom in the land to provide a
remedy against these evils, so damaging to the
interests of society?

In the marts of trade, in the administration of
government, in all those relations of life, in which
money, property or interest is the main consideration, truth is mangled. We have confidence in the
statements of thousands. Were it not so, business
would come to a dead halt. Into this goodly fel-
lowship of truth-loving men, have crept the liars.
"The Cretians are always liars, evil beasts," and the
Cretians are found where a penny is to be made or
a personal interest is at stake.

A lie is a confession of weakness. It resorts
naturally to secresy and darkness, to whispers, and
to reticence when nearing the confines of truth. A
lie can be a mute, and thus affects prudence, wisdom
and dignity in the drapery of falsehood. What can
not be accomplished by a straightforward course, is
attempted by circumvention. Many an unworthy
enterprise would fail, if truth directed the issue.
The hope of attainment depends upon truth carved
and clipped. A lie dares not reveal itself. The
Bengalee on the Lower Ganges typifies the tribe.
"Courage, independence, veracity, are qualities to
which his constitution and his situation are equally
unfavorable. What the horns are to the buffalo,

what the paw is to the tiger, what the sting is to
the bee, . . . deceit is to the Bengalee."

An American writer has given quite a variety of
lies prepared in the manufactory for the demand of
the market to impose on the weak and the unfortunate. They are not the literal tools of burglars and
highway robbers, but the equally dangerous instruments of the children of the Bengalees and the
Cretians. Here are the samples furnished: "Large
lies and small lies; lies private and lies public, and
lies prurient; lies cut bias and lies cut diagonal;
long limb lies and lies with double back action; lies
complimentary and lies defamatory; lies that some
people believe, and lies that all the people believe,
and lies that nobody believes; lies with humps like
camels and scales like crocodiles, and necks as long
as storks and feet as swift as an antelope's, and stings
like adders; crawling lies and jumping lies and soar-
ing lies." Honor is prostituted; shame is without
a blush; evils national, municipal, civic and private,
have too often their substratum in a compact of
lies.

There is another evil not coördinate with any of
those named, but intimately related to them, and to
wrongs of every sort. It is the doctrine that a man
in a public position must not express his convictions concerning any wrong that affects the interests
of society. It is a doctrine firmly rooted in the
general belief. It is entertained by many excellent
men, whose motives are pure. Others there are who
see through the thin gauze, the naked falsehood.
Men of convictions are many, but men who dare

express these convictions for the public good are not so numerous.

Men in public positions are merchants, ministers, teachers, lawyers, physicians, politicians, and all persons who in any way are dependent upon the people for support, patronage, or votes. Society is the sum of the individuals composing it. Moral evils exist in this society—they must not be assailed; there are pernicious laws, promotive of the interest of a few, hurtful to the many—their ill effects must not be analyzed; an unwise and unhealthy mode of business takes root in the thought and habits of the people, its pecuniary benefits accrue to a class and its damaging effects touch every other member of the community—no reformatory influence must be put in motion; the surreptitious selling of liquor is quite common, it is designated by the term Blind Tiger, the law is cheated, and the community is injured—no one must speak out. Individual responsibility is nowhere to be found; it is a worm-eaten commodity, and as thin and small and " scentless as a cake of soap in a public bathing room." The guilty vendors of the article, and their patrons, and all those who wish to prove that prohibition does not entirely prohibit, no more than the laws against fraud, theft, robbery, or murder entirely and absolutely prohibit these crimes, nevertheless they are wise laws—are silent, even if they have guilty knowledge. Those in public positions are mute for prudential reasons. To speak out, may hurt the trade, the business, or may cost some votes. He who antagonizes any evil is sure to excite the ill-will of

12

somebody. In short, this fallacious doctrine flatly asserts that men, whatever may be their position, are not responsible for the influence they are competent to exert. This negative character thus taught is a deadly poison. The moral dry-rot must go on. The contagious, inflammatory distemper must be allowed to send out its putrid effluvia into every household.

Another view. Public opinion is the prevailing opinion of the community. You and I help to make it. If it is virtuous, it is a blessing. But it can only be a blessing when it is a dominant force in society. It can never be a controlling force if the men who make this opinion are " all dumb dogs that can not bark."

There is not an evil in society to-day that could not be largely checked or exterminated, were it not for this vicious doctrine of irresponsibility. But " what is everybody's business is nobody's business." The fallacious adage conveys less than a half truth. If A, B and C are charged to do a certain work, it is their duty solely to perform it. Nobody else has anything to do with it. This feature finds large application in practical life. But human responsibility and moral influences have no such narrow limits. It is everybody's business to do right, to promote sound morals, to obey and uphold the laws of the country, to be loyal and true, and to stand up in a manly way for principles.

What about prudence? It is a good quality in its place. To be cautious—to consider what is to be done and how the end is to be attained, are

valuable in every undertaking. Do this and act.
It is a mere preliminary step to the more important
thing, action. If it is all prudence—all selfish considerations—balancing of gains and losses when
moral questions demand attention, it is as valuable
as a cracked bell when the town is on fire. The
house will burn to ashes before prudence can resolve
to extend a helping hand. The man who makes
prudence his sole guide in moral questions is selfish.
This is the law of ethics. The man who is governed
by duty is virtuous. Selfish considerations enter
not into the equation. Prudence consults ease,
pleasure, money, gains, losses and votes. Duty is
governed by no such earthenware considerations.
What is the right, and the obligations that it imposes? Duty has nothing to do with consequences.
Prudence queries: "Am I my brother's keeper?"
Selfishness in all its deep loathsomeness is in the
skulking interrogatory. The reply of duty is calm
and majestic: "Thou shalt love thy neighbor as
thyself." And this means, render him service, and
the highest service that can be rendered to humanity
is to emphasize the right by every available means.

Away with the delusion of the wretched doctrine!
Away with the accursed peace it would purchase by
selfish considerations! Away with all the deadly
evils lurking in many noxious recesses, which mere
selfish prudence would rather endure and tolerate
than by manly efforts exterminate!

The gist of the whole matter is: there are times and
occasions when it is the duty of all men to speak
and to act. Convictions must find a voice. When

laws are surreptitiously and shamelessly violated;
when grievous wrongs artfully enslave the unwary;
when crimes go unwhipped of justice, and the evasion of the laws by means subtile or desperate is
the order of the day, then this duty to speak out
is imperative.   To be silent under such circumstances is not manly—it is immoral.

Dr. J. G. Holland pertinently remarks on this
subject:

"It is for this peace that numbers have failed to set themselves
against great evils that threaten their neighbors, themselves and their
children.

"A man who only asserts so much of that which is in him as will
find favor with those among whom he has his daily life, and who
withholds all that will wound their vanity and condemn their selfishness and clash with their principles and prejudices, has no more
manhood in him than there is in a spaniel, and is certainly one of the
most contemptible men the world contains."

The whole truth is, the selfish man, with sordid
aims, "seeks to make the world useful to himself,"
even if the attempt bankrupts the people in life and
in property.   He risks nothing, and does nothing
that will affect his interest.   Such a man may die
amid affluence and be buried with fashionable éclat,
but he did not "live well."   The true man, with
higher instincts and nobler aims, "seeks to make
himself useful to the world."

The character of Sir William Temple, as described
by Macaulay, illustrates this bad doctrine to decline
a public service when that service might endanger
personal interest.

"Yet Temple is not a man to our taste.   A temper not naturally
good, but under strict command,—a constant regard to decorum,—

a rare caution in playing that mixed game of skill and hazard, human life,—a disposition to be content with small and certain winnings rather than go on doubling the stake,—these seem to us to be the most remarkable features of his character. This sort of moderation when united, as in him it was, with very considerable abilities, is, under ordinary circumstances, scarcely to be distinguished from the highest and purest integrity ; and yet may be perfectly compatible with laxity of principle, with coldness of heart, and with the most intense selfishness. Temple, we fear, had not sufficient warmth and elevation of sentiment to deserve the name of a virtuous man. He did not betray or oppress his country ; nay, he rendered considerable service to her ; but he risked nothing for her. . . . If the circumstances of the country became such that it was impossible to take any part in politics without some danger, he retired to his library and his orchard ; and while the nation groaned under oppression, or resounded with tumult and with the din of civil arms, amused himself by writing memoirs and tying up apricots."

This complacent attitude which ignores responsibility and manly expressions upon questions of the highest moment, is found in all the gradations of society. Men wink at crime, connive at vice, and sometimes shut eyes and ears to wrongs of every hue and type. It is not meant that they approve these things, but they shirk the responsibility to express condemnation, and to bring guilt before the proper tribunal. And this want of individual responsibility has enfeebled the administration of justice, lowered the tone of public morals, and affected the material interests of the people. The man who expresses his convictions on any important matter, however sound, however true, however pure the motive, if he antagonizes personal or class interests —interests hurtful to the community, may expect maledictions. The Ephesian coppersmith is more concerned with gains than sound morals and the public welfare. The successful fraud is more likely to receive fulsome congratulations. Public opinion must be toned up to a higher standard, and individual obligations and individual responsibility must be vitalized with truth and principles.

The moral forces of society are not only entitled to high and earnest consideration, but the intense obligation upon all classes of men to make them dominant is the demand of the age. Great principles must be reinforced and grounded in the belief. Their supreme importance must be established in the thought and the affections of men. Every agency by which this is done is a boon to society. All hostile influence to such agency is also hostile to the best interests of the community. Wealth is of far less value to society than robust morals. It may not be fashionable to say this, but it is the truth nevertheless. "Breeding, brains, or bullion," it is said, determine the laws for the " best society," and bullion is generally the controlling spirit. But when did wealth make any attempt to regenerate society, reform an abuse, or seek the elevation of humanity? An eminent writer thus expresses himself : "There is hardly a fact in all history more patent than this, that in the undertaking and prosecuting any humane or Christian reform, the fashionable classes are never to be relied upon for aid, while their opposition in one form or another is certain." Wealth and fashion, in varying degrees, go hand in hand. We point to the general rules, and not to the noble exceptions. Is wealth, then, to be despised? No! The meaning is: its place is subordinate to the far higher consideration of the moral forces in all the interests that affect man.

This view of the value of great underlying principles of morality is forcibly presented by a Southern statesman. He says:

"Our public men reflect the conscience of the nation, and are our representatives in politics and morals. By them are the people judged and influenced. . . . False notions of moral responsibility undermine all solid ground for virtue ; destroy courageous self-reliance and independence ; elevate expediency and availability above worth and principle ; beget vacillation and time-serving, encourage a habit of appealing from eternal verity to the force of numbers ; and generate a brood of slimy sycophants, who fawn and flatter in order to fatten on popular credulity.' The common distinction betwixt political and personal honesty is a delusion and a fraud. The politician who is disingenuous, tricky, untruthful, dishonest, is unfit to be trusted in public or in private life. Virtue is permanent, and circumstances cannot efface the distinction between right and wrong. The capriciousness of human nature does not ally duplicity and honesty ; nor do vicarious virtues compensate for crime. Marlborough was an invincible warrior of consummate courage and ability, loved his ambitious wife devotedly, but these should not win forgiveness for his cruelty, hardness of heart, falsehood, avarice, and treason. Colonel Turner, a gallant cavalier, was hung after the Restoration for a flagitious burglary. At the gallows, he told the crowd that his mind received great consolation from one reflection—he had always taken off his hat when he went into church. To be the wisest of mankind is no excuse for being the meanest. . . .

"Commerce, mechanic arts, agriculture, literature, heroes, battle-fields, internal improvements, free institutions, will not regenerate a nation nor insure its permanent welfare. Christianity, breathing mercy, justice, truth, fraternity, must be its basis, and give sanction to its laws. The vices which degrade men will destroy a republic. Meanness, avarice, drunkenness, extortion, insolence, cruelty, sycophancy, falsehood, bribery, will dishonor and ruin any people. A low standard of integrity will demoralize, corrupt, overthrow. The right and true must find embodiment in statutes. God's law and civil laws must run in parallel lines. Mischievous and meaningless

else are representation, trial by jury, ballot-box, common schools, habeas corpus, constitutions, and 'checking and balancing of greedy knaveries.' When contracts and vows are treated as idle things; when oaths from frequency or levity in administering become idle jests; when vices are licensed by statute, and revenue is coined from crime; and when in the shameless facility for divorce 'the statute of heaven intended for the purity of home and lying at the foundation of all society,' is trodden under foot, a people may well study the history of dead nations, that Tekel, Tekel, be not written over the doors and on the walls of their capitols, seats of learning, and sanctuaries." *

It has been fashionable to boast of the wealth of this nation. Here are sixty million people, and sixty thousand million dollars represent their aggregate wealth. Who are the owners?

200 people are worth	$4,000,000,000
400 people are worth	4,000,000,000
1,000 people are worth	5,000,000,000
2,500 people are worth	6,250,000,000
7,000 people are worth	7,000,000,000
20,000 people are worth	10,000,000,000

This was the schedule in 1890. By this time, three years later, it may be that forty thousand people own two-thirds of the national wealth.

We would not be misunderstood. There should neither be prejudice nor hostility against wealth in any form. Righteously obtained and used, it is a blessing. This is the inflexible condition. Governments, railroads, steamship lines, inventions and wealth are all to be construed as favorable to the interests of mankind when equitably used. They are curses to the people when they are transmuted

---

* Hon. J. L. M. Curry.

into engines of oppression. Money is not an oppro-
brious term. " Money-borrower " and " money-
lender " are not humiliating epithets.

" The laborer is worthy of his hire." This is good
doctrine. All the agents employed in production
are entitled to their full pro rata of reward according to their effective capacity. These agents are
the common laborer, skill and talent in all their
diversified phases and wide application, responsibility and honor attached to positions of trust and
importance, and capital. The classification is general and will serve to convey the thought intended.
We have no metric system by which to determine
with exactness the distributive share of any production due to the agents employed in its creation.
Equity will have little trouble in approximating the
just portion to each. Fairness will solve the problem on just principles. Unreasonable labor is just
as hurtful to justice as unreasonable capital. When
one acts the Nero and the other the Caligula, then
both are tyrants.

In 1860 there were few millionaires in these
United States. In thirty years from this period
less than forty thousand people own nearly two-
thirds of the national wealth. The statement is
amazing. What is to prevent this forty thousand,
with their vantage ground, from securing in the
next thirty years, full ownership of the remaining
one-third of the wealth? It may be announced to
the world: America is the wealthiest nation on the
earth—she is so to-day. Fifty thousand people own
the aggregate property of the great Republic. And

then in 1920, this announcement may be made: The American Republic is the greatest pauperized nation on the face of the globe. We hope it will not be so. There is certainly something wrong to make this millionaire condition possible. There is injustice somewhere.

What part the National Government has contributed to this condition; what part capital itself has done; what is due to speculation; what is due to inventions—the great labor-saving machinery, and the inability of labor to adjust itself to these new conditions—all these furnish vast material for inquiry. This one thing is certain, the gains of capital are enormous.

In the South, capital in trade, when successfully managed, has been by far the most remunerative investment. A return to normal methods may avert untold calamities.

CHAPTER XI.

TOWNS—THEIR INFLUENCE.

A TOWN means more than a square mile of territory. We use the term in a general sense, whether its inhabitants number 1,500 or 15,000. The community of such a place will have in view an object, more or less clearly defined. The essential idea is *occupation*. Other considerations, such as convenience to schools and churches, and various privileges and facilities, may govern individuals; but the main thing for the majority is the work of such a place that can secure to them a living. Without employment the breadwinners are a burden to themselves, and something worse in numerous instances to the community.

The principal industry of the Southern people is agriculture. To this chief employment, the business of the majority of towns in the South is directly related. Towns where railroad shops are located, or where manufacturing interests and the lumber business furnish employment, are few. Probably ninety-five per cent. of all Southern communities gathered in towns depend for their support and existence upon the busy workers in distant cotton, cane, and rice fields. If this industry is depressed, the town suffers. The industries of these towns are expressed with sufficient exactness by the terms, "trade and transportation, professional and personal service, mechanics and laborers." There is work for all of the four classes in every town. There is no danger that the three first named will overcrowd their vocations long. The fourth class is equal in number to all the other classes in many communities, and in some places double and treble the three classes. The complexion of our population accounts for this fact. The suburbs of Southern towns and villages are alive with colored people. No observant person can fail to note the fact that the supply of laborers, so styled, in these communities, is greater than the demand. The town is the reservoir into which the stream of this class from the adjacent country flows.

Every town is ambitious of its business prosperity, its schools and its churches, and an important evidence of its growth is the increase of its population. It is human nature so to boast. No one doubts that Southern towns generally have a large surplus population. The truth about this matter can hurt no one. A larger laboring population in any place than the work there requires is not a sign of health, but of disease. The outside world and reflecting men may construe the parade about population as a satire on this unfortunate status and the burdens it imposes on the municipal government. Five hundred people, less or more, in a town, without money, work or bread, are not convincing proofs of a prosperous condition. "Nudity and rags," says Horace Mann, "are only human idleness or ignorance out on exhibition." It is a cheap exhibition, save the effect it has on the tax schedule to provide for the expense of the criminal docket. There is no question about the statement that there are large numbers of colored people in our towns whose condition would be greatly improved were they on farms where their labor is in demand. As it is, they eke out a precarious existence. According to the tenth and the eleventh census, in the ten Southern States used as a basis of comparison, out of 6,937 townships, 2,061 lost population. This is nearly thirty per cent. in ten years. These figures do not indicate the entire movement to the towns. There is not a township probably in any Southern State, notwithstanding the general increase of population, from which there has not been a colored exodus.

"Let us reason together." A depletion of this labor in the country can not benefit the town. The Southern farm is the town's remunerative workshop. The prosperity of the town hinges on the success of the farm. This is quite evident. But is even this gainful idea a matter of thought—a matter of sympathetic interest? Good roads to a town are necessary, but labor on the farm is more so. Indifference on the part of those most concerned will not help matters. A dealer that will sell a farmer $500 merchandise on time, and buy him a mule besides, may not regard himself under any moral obligation to turn the idle labor at his door into a useful channel. "It is not my business." Certainly not. But a man can be humane—can be helpful to those who make business prosperous, especially when a little right influence costs not a nickel. A man need not crowd his life with all sorts of excuses, yellow, green, and speckled, when a little service is to be done, that would be helpful to the poor colored man, helpful to the merchant himself, and helpful to everybody. A little helpful influence exerted by all good and earnest men would do good. Generally speaking, there is altogether too much dependence upon law and law officers, and too little effort in life and practice to make virtuous opinions dominant. The best laws are evolved from virtuous public opinion, and this same opinion must aid to enforce these laws, stand by the officers when they execute the laws, and frown down upon unfaithful public servants when they wink or connive at infractions, or fail in any wise to do their duty. It is too often the case, that the man who is loud in condemnation of unfaithfulness in public men, is the last man to put in motion one right influence to check the evil he condemns, or root up the causes that produce the evil. Idleness is one of them. It is not a virtuous commodity. It makes no man rich. It is a rotten thing within and without. It is a cruel thing. Hope is not in it—nor right. It produces no bread. It cheers no living man. It breeds crime.

What can be done? Much every way. In union there is strength. Concert of action can do a vast deal in town and country. Let the best men, the most influential men, come to the front. Let right motives and right actions dominate. Let an earnest inquiry go forth from such a source: "Why stand ye here all the day idle?" A committee on "Industrial Morals" is in order everywhere. Let the inquiry be made when the sun is high in the heavens. Moral suasion, wholesome counsel, and sympathetic interest will not be fruitless. The let-alone, do-nothing, irresponsible, negative policy has been weighed in the balance, and found wanting.

"Upon an area of six square miles," said a friend, "live eight hundred men and grown boys, who practically live from hand to mouth. They are colored people. They could make 2,400 bales of cotton, 80,000 bushels corn, 80,000 bushels sweet potatoes, and other produce." Yet not a friendly hand is stretched out to help them. It is manly to say to them : "There is no work for all of you here. It is not to your interest to remain."

If it be true that the country is the town's work-shop, much may be done to add to the efficiency of that workshop. Friendliness must show itself to be so. There is a reciprocal relation between them. If one is injured, so is the other. Absolute independence is nowhere to be found. The utmost good will and friendliness should exist between the merchant and the farmer. Fair dealing and hearty kindliness will cement this relationship. They apply to both alike.

There is another matter of no small interest to the people. We refer to education ; especially to the public schools of Southern towns. It is one thing heartily to approve the education of the children of the State at the public expense, and it is another thing to indorse all the particulars of the plan to accomplish the desired end. There is no question as to the duty of the State to give a common-school education to all her children.

Our observations relate to the policy. In other words, to the quantity of the work that is attempted in the public schools of our agricultural towns ranging from 1,000 to 3,000 inhabitants. Wealthy cities can afford to do what these can not.

In the first place, a common-school course of studies should be definitely confined to its proper work, as the term implies. It is the school for the masses in town and country. Spelling, reading, geography, arithmetic, English grammar, and United States history make an ample common-school course. This elementary course should be well taught. Thoroughness is the crying need in these schools.

Why not add other studies to this list? The reasons are plain : our people are poor ; the pay of superior teachers is small ; inefficient teachers are numerous. From ninety to ninety-five pupils out of every hundred pursue the studies named. From a half-dozen to a dozen girls and boys in such a town are ready to take up advanced studies. This number is divided into three or four classes. They are generally the sons and daughters of well-to-do and influential parents. Of course, there is more or less forcing done ; not so much by the instructor as the parents. Another dozen of ill-prepared material may swell these higher classes, much to their injury, and to the hurt of those that are ready for the advanced work.

Let us see how it works. The town builds a new

schoolhouse, costing from $5,000 to $10,000.   Now for a name.   In a city of a hundred thousand or more inhabitants, a school of such material is styled " public ; " in a small city, a graded school—quite appropriate ; in the country, the village, or the town, such an institution takes a more ambitious title : it is a normal school, or a high school, or a college.   The town is on a boom, the college is on a boom, and a new broom sweeps clean.   Everybody favors the school. Tuition costs nothing, except in the music department.

In ten years the children of the few wealthy and influential patrons are educated ; they have finished the higher studies, taught under disadvantages, by teachers burdened with elementary work.   But the taxes go on.   These may amount for State, county, and town, to two and a half to three per cent.

Who pay these taxes?   In towns such as described, the bulk is paid by two or three dozen men ; and of that number, a dozen merchants pay by far the larger portion.   Leave them out, and the bottom drops out of the school.

If meagre salaries are paid the one or two teachers of the high school, or if the whole number of teachers in the common and high school course is not sufficient for even the common free-school course, to do first-class work, since the number of pupils generally attending the public school of a town is large, inefficiency follows, however competent the teachers may be.   If a requisite number of teachers are employed, and living salaries are paid, the expenses are increased, and this burden falls heavily

13

on the large business class of these towns—the merchants.   It will not be borne many years.   A limited
course well taught, is far better than a long course
ill taught.

The country public school of four months' session
imitates the town school with sessions from eight
to ten months.   Higher studies are added for two
or three favorite pupils, and the attention these
receive from the teacher is equal to the attention
given to the second, third, and fourth reader classes.
Three pupils in physical geography, general history,
elementary algebra, and rhetoric, will take up more
time in their recitations than twenty-four pupils in
the lower studies.   These studies are added when
the demand is made, or when the circumstances are
favorable for their introduction.

A very common opinion is, " the four months'
free school" in the country is a failure.   It has been
the complaint for years.   We have assigned a cause.
Instead of doing well in this short time a small
amount of work, a great deal is attempted, and that,
as is the case in seventy-five schools out of a hundred, by inexperienced teachers.   In a number of
schools of this sort, personal inquiry revealed the
fact, that a young lady teacher having from twenty-
five to thirty-five pupils, attempted to teach the
six common-school studies mentioned on a former
page, and eight advanced studies besides, pursued
by three pupils.   She worried through the four
months, attended one or two teachers' institutes,
closed with a general examination and a concert,
and she was paid for her work from $120 to $140.

The best pupil in the school could not tell whether there were eight or fifteen parts of speech in English grammar, and was perplexed to know to what the product of a half of a half referred.

Better work in elementary studies is the need in these schools. To it every effort should be directed. The great evil of too much work, too many studies, is apparent. The towns set the example. They imitate the city; the village and the country school, the town.

The tendency of the town schools, especially if high-school studies form a part of the course, and instruction in the latter is free, is to invite country patronage. Several dozen children board with their relations or friends to enjoy the benefits of the town institution which furnishes free tuition to all that can come. The poor man's children can not come. The enrolment of the town school is thus increased a few dozen pupils. Here and there a few farmers move to town to secure these benefits, and generally leave the town with more experience than money.

The town is not benefited, and those that come are not compensated for the loss sustained. People in pinched circumstances, perhaps involved in debt, leave their farms, upon which they are dependent to support their families, and come to town to educate their children. The inducement is, education in town is free. Others move their families to town, governed by the same motive. This is all well, if a man is out of debt, and can see how to make ends meet, and support a part of the family on the farm and a part in town. The motive to educate is laudable, but experience has shown that these methods adopted by anxious and ambitious parents to accomplish the object are in the end unwise. Not a few farmers have thus crippled themselves financially for years, and that without educating their children in a free school.

We need high schools, intermediate between the common schools and the colleges. They should be genuine, not makeshifts. Burdened as the Southern States are with debts, crippled and uncertain as are the great farming interests of the country, the people are in no condition to maintain them at the public expense. Very few are the communities able to do this. The well-to-do people will patronize these schools, and they are able to pay for such education.

The condition pointed out in educational matters can not last. There is confusion. It is difficult to tell where the common free school ends its work, and where the high school begins. Nothing is defined, nothing limited. Schools with all sorts of pompous names are springing up in the country. At every cross-road, village, and town there is a high school or a college. They flourish a few years, then die the death. Like Jonah's gourd, they spring up in a night, and perish in a night.

The counterfeit always damages the genuine, for in many things they may be alike. The discerning alone can tell the difference between the true and the false, that which is permanent and that which is temporary. The tendency of the movement is hostile to gradation in school work, and discouraging

to every man who desires to make educational work
a profession. No man with liberal preparation cares
to enter this field at from $40 to $75 per month,
with no hope of permanency or improvement in the
remuneration. The counting-room, medicine, law,
and mercantile business offer more inviting fields
under these circumstances, and require no such
intellectual equipment.

The influence of towns, morally, is worthy of
attention. There are good people in every town.
But wherever population is massed, whether the
number is 1,000, 5,000, or 100,000, there are moral
dangers. Here the assaults on virtue are fierce.
The term "virtue" is used in a generic sense as
standing for the entire circle of moral principles.
The town is a life centre, a trade centre, an enterprise centre, a crime centre, a vice centre, a centre
of various influences put in motion by all sorts of
people, differing widely in their motives and objects in life.

We note the influence of a class highly honorable
on many accounts. The reference is to the business
portion of the community; not the merchants alone,
but all men engaged in honorable, honest, legitimate
vocations in life. They constitute the respectable
class in the town. Diligent, attentive, and punctual
in their professions, callings, and business, they
contribute their share to material prosperity. It is
the industrious class. Take them out, and the
bottom drops out of the place.

The central object with the major portion of this
class in society is business, and the dominant motive

is material prosperity. To accumulate property is the end in life, worthy of every effort. If honor and distinction are added, they grace the fruit of their exertions. We are sure that we do no injustice to any one in the affirmation, that the majority of our law-abiding, industrious, and influential citizens in every community propose to themselves, as the supreme object in life, material prosperity. With not a few, every other consideration is secondary; and, we are confident, with many, every other consideration is zero. It is not meant that they are indifferent to their families, the ordinary social relations, or the amenities of life. No! The very appeals of charity are made to them, and will obtain a hearing with most of them. Much that is pleasant and amiable is found here. Earnest efforts to secure material well-being are indorsed by principles human and divine. It is a means to an end. It is not half of that for which life was given.

Moral influences are needed everywhere, and especially in those places where temptations to evil are numerous, and the strain upon morals is the greatest. Habits, customs, certain social influences, idleness, a low public opinion, fashionable acquiescence in wrongs of various types—these make a tremendous strain on the right. The pernicious example of a man of influence is incalculable. He may poison the minds of whole platoons of men whose conduct he despises. That example may consist in nothing more than placing a discount on morals, in depreciating their value. Wealth is necessary to individual comfort; morals are essential

to hold society together. The latter is entitled to
the first place in the affections, esteem, and practices of men. This gives power and beauty to character, and lies at the foundation of all well-ordered
society.

It is a great truth that no man lives to himself.
No life is isolated. Every man is in a community,
and of a community. He can not separate himself
from it. The vicious influence which he shuns, and
about which he is indifferent because it does not
concern him, is in the community of which he is a
part. Its miasma reaches his home and his place of
business. He may wish to have nothing to do with
it, but it will have something to do with him. This
is certain. Vice and wrong of every kind are threats
against everybody. For these reasons, the depreciation by word or act, of great moral principles, is
an incalculable injury.

The town is also a political centre. The opportunity is here furnished to impart lessons of patriotism. Governmental affairs so directly concern all
the people, rich and poor, that it would seem any
matter of a political nature relating to the munici-
pality, county, or State, would enlist the interest of
the most responsible and influential citizens. If
good government is so important to the welfare of
the people, it seems that they would emphasize its
value by interest in its affairs. The interest should
be commensurate with the exalted end in view. It
is the solemn duty of all good citizens to show by
their acts, and by sacrifices if need be, that " this is
a government of the people, by the people, and

for the people." Individual responsibility to the government is the essential condition to make this possible.

We hear much in our day of "thug-rule, ring-rule, and class-rule." A government of a dozen, by a dozen, and for a dozen, is a sign of decay both as to interest and responsibility. But who is to blame? Not the dozen. Blame those who plead indifference, who plead excuses and dissatisfaction, who plead, perhaps, despair of improvement. Blame those who will not help to remove bad men from office, and aid in the enactment of wise and beneficent laws. Dispassionate discussion defines the boundary of truth. Individual interest and responsibility of all the people are signal marks of healthy progress. It is a lamentable sign when a large number of the poorest conditioned men, morally and intellectually, are the guardians of political interests.

CHAPTER XII.

THE PROGRESS OF THE NEGROES.

THEY were brought to America by compulsion; they were sold to Southern planters when interest dictated the bargain; others were brought from Africa and sold to the Southern people by reason of the same selfish motive; and they were liberated by no act of their own. Whether enslaved or made freedmen, the effort was not their act. They have ever been the football of superior races. Degraded in slavery, or elevated by philanthropy, the moving force, whether a curse or a blessing, is from without. No Joshua has appeared among them. White captains dared the dangers incident to their enslavement. Adventurous cunning and cupidity placed upon the neck of the negroes the yoke of bondage. In submission they yielded to the curse. White statesmen, white philanthropists, and white organized efforts have exerted themselves untiringly, and in large and noble measures, to elevate them during the last five and twenty years. What has been done for the negroes, in bane or in blessing, has neither been proposed nor done by the negroes. White men write and speak in their behalf; white men give their money in the interests of the negroes, and white men do the effective thinking for their good. The negroes are passive. All the predominant influence for their elevation is extraneous. This is a luminous fact in the history of this people. They have been a fruitful cause of contention to the American people. They are a bone of contention to-day. The negro problem does not concern them as a class, but the white people are anxious about its solution. The negroes are an amazingly helpless people.

Amid the strife and progress of the ages, what book, what invention, what trophy in the arts or letters, what achievement in the field of industry, what brave and wise leadership on some ensanguined battle-ground, and what persistent and triumphant victory in any great moral contest of humanity, signalize the part which the sons of Ham have taken in civilization? On the North American Continent they have been in close touch with the stirring activities of the Anglo-Saxon people. What have they absorbed and utilized? The encouragement of friends, the leverage of government, the presence of inspiring Anglo-Saxon examples, have given birth to no high purpose and to no generous spirit of self-dependence among this people. The very incentives of personal and political freedom have impaired their energy. The story of their wrongs, and the results of all the intellectual and moral agencies instituted for their advancement, are written by Anglo-Saxon pens. The world is still waiting for some pen-mark, some epic, that shall chronicle the deeds of a pure Hamite, some granite monument that shall commemorate the heroic or civic services

of a son of Ham. The past is a dreary waste, bar-
ren of results. The hope and the inspiration of the
future are palled by the past.

" The great primordial nations of Ham were first four—those of
Mezer, Cush, Phut, and Canaan. Of these, the nation of Canaan
was much the largest, consisting of twelve nations ; that of Mezer
was composed of seven nations ; Cush, of six ; while Phut made
only a single nation. Five of the nations descended from Canaan
were destroyed, enslaved, or expelled from Judea by Joshua, and
six have left no written history. . . . Turning to Africa, we
find,' according to ethnologists, four great types, the Moorish, the
Egyptian, the Berber, or Abyssinian, and the Negro. Of these the
Mauric type seems descended from Phut, the Egyptian from Mezer,
the Abyssinian from Cush, and the Negro from Canaan."

" The negro type is found aboriginal in Africa, in the Fejee
Islands, New Guinea, New Caledonia, and Madagascar. Its nations
are all black or brownish-black. The hair of the negro is woolly
and wiry ; his features generally broad and flattened, though there
are several tribes of them who have, in connection with woolly hair
and dusky skin, the most elegant forms and features, as among the
Caffres and Iolofs. . . . There seem to be six or seven kinds
of negroes, which we enumerate as follows : (1) The Hottentots, (2)
the Caffres, (3) the Guinea negro, and (4) the Iolofs, all of Africa ;
(5) the Papuan of Oceanica, (6) Negrillo of New Guinea, and (7)
the Australian negro. The *Guinea negro, common with us*, has
woolly hair and *black skin, thick lips*, a *broad, flat nose, prognathous
jaws, narrow* and *receding forehead*, a *slender waist, high hips,
slender limbs*, and *massive feet, rounded on the bottom*. . . . The
Iolofs, in addition to *woolly hair* and *jet-black skin*, possess a *fine
form* and strictly *European features*. The Caffres are of *woolly
hair, blackish-brown complexion*, and have *fine form* and *features*." *

If this description of the descendants of Canaan,
the son of Ham and the grandson of Noah, be

* Dominion ; or, The Unity and Trinity of the Human Race.

accurate, we have in these United States the
Guinea negro, the Iolofs, and the Caffres. To
these must be added those in whose veins flow one-
half, three-fourths, or seven-eighths white blood, or
the mulattoes, the quadroons, and the octoroons.
(The last three will hereafter be designated by the
common title, mulatto.) These four classes are
found on American soil. The Guinea negroes constitute an overwhelming majority. The close ob-
server may have seen a few Iolofs and Caffres.
What per cent. these are of the whole negro population can not be determined. The mulattoes constitute a little more than one-seventh of the entire
population. The Guinea negroes, the Iolofs, and
the Caffres will be classed as black. According
to the eleventh census, Bulletin No. 199, these
Canaanites, or persons of African descent, may be
arranged as to numbers thus:

```
Blacks.................................. 6,337,980
Mulattoes......................... 956,989
Quadroons...................... 105,135
Octoroons...................... 69,936—1,132,060

     Total............................7,470,040
```

According to their residence they are found, as
per Census Bulletin No. 199, as follows:

RESIDENCE.	BLACKS.	MULATTOES.
North Atlantic States............	207,175	62,731
Western Division..............	16,477	10,604
North Central States............	297,331	133,781
South Atlantic States...........	2,823,905	438,785
South Central States...........	2,993,092	486,159

Of the whole African population in the North Atlantic States, 23 per cent. are mulattoes; of those in the Western Division, 62 per cent. are mulattoes; of those in the North Central States, 31 per cent. are mulattoes; of those in the South Atlantic States, 10 per cent. are mulattoes; and of those in the South Central States, 13 per cent. are mulattoes. In the three Northern Divisions were, in 1890, 728,099 persons of African descent; of this number, 28 per cent were mulattoes. The Southern Divisions had at this time, 6,741,941 persons of African descent. Thirteen per cent. of this number were mulattoes.

MOVEMENT.

Of the entire mixed population—mulattoes, quadroons, and octoroons—17 per cent. are in the North. Of the black population, 8 per cent. are in the North. The ambitious, aspiring portion of this people are either mulattoes, quadroons, and octoroons, or the Iolofs and Caffres. The mulattoes inherited the superior intellectual qualities of their fathers, and often their bad moral qualities. Ambition, pride, cunning, and resentment show themselves much more clearly in varying degrees in the mixed race than in the pure negro. The Guinea negro is submissive, humble, always jolly, cares little for the future, and is wanting both in resentment and gratitude. The jet-black and the blackish-brown negroes, styled by the author of *Dominion*, Iolofs and Caffres, show far more intelligence than the Guinea type. They may constitute from 5 to 10 per cent. of the pure African race.

LEADERS.

The majority of those esteemed leaders of this race are mulattoes, with a small per cent. of higher type pure negroes. Generally it is the white blood of the mulattoes that pushes forward, that seeks the professions, looks with resentment upon the past, and boasts of its relationship to a white father. The Iolofs and the Caffres are less ambitious, but more conservative. The lower strata, the great bulk of this population, have given no sign of an upward movement. The worthy specimens indicating progress belong to these higher types. Rev. Henry M. Turner, Bishop of the African M. E. Church; Rev. J. A. Beebe, Bishop of the Colored M. E. Church; Rev. Isaac Lane, Bishop of the Colored M. E. Church; Rev. Lewis H. Holsey, Bishop of the Colored M. E. Church, are fine examples. Their photographs are found in a work entitled *The Gospel among the Slaves*, published by the Publishing House of the M. E. Church South. In a book published by G. P. Putnam's Sons, entitled *Prisoners and Paupers*, by Henry M. Boies, M.A., are four photographs of pure negroes, whose features are not those of the Guinea type. They are Rev. Joseph C. Price, D.D., President of Livingston College, Salisbury, N. C.; Rev. C. N. Grandison, D.D., President of Bennett College, Greensboro', N. C.; Hon. John H. Smyth, ex-United States Minister, etc., Washington, D. C.; also a group of five well-developed pure negroes in private life is given. There is no doubt that three or more types of pure negroes are found in this country. That progress and leadership belong to these pure higher types, and that the mulattoes outnumber these in leadership, is, I believe, a common opinion. Hon. Frederick Douglass, Hon. Blanche K. Bruce, and Hon. John R. Lynch, stand in the front rank. The chief characters portrayed in " Uncle Tom's Cabin " are mulattoes, quadroons, and an octoroon. Madame de Thoux, George Harris, and Susan are mulattoes; Cassy and Emmeline are quadroons; and Eliza is an octoroon. Uncle Tom is an exceptionally good negro, whose living reality it will be difficult to find. Sambo and Quimbo belong to the genuine Guinea type. At a recent public school institute in the county of Lincoln, Mississippi, we counted fifteen teachers in attendance. Of this number, six male and seven female teachers were mulattoes.

Progress.—What have education and freedom done for this people in twenty-seven years? What progress have they made? If by progress is meant political, civil, and religious privileges, improvement in knowledge, in morals, and in all those elements that pertain to the well-being of the race, the question is difficult to answer in the affirmative or negative without committing a grave error. If it were a question relating to individuals, truth demands an affirmative answer. The inquiry refers to the race—to 7,470,040. The answer to the inquiry may be stated thus: Let the figure 5 represent the general condition of this people in 1865, and the figure 10 the reasonable progress of the race in twenty-seven years. The aggregate condition of

100 persons would be represented by 500 in 1865.
Ten persons have gained five points each ; their total
is 100 points, measuring reasonable progress. Ninety
persons have retrograded two points each; 270
points measure their general condition to-day.
Three hundred and seventy points express the
general condition of the race in each group of 100
persons in 1892, as compared with 500 points expressive of the condition of this race in 1865. The
race has sustained loss in the general condition of
well-being; choice individuals have made commend-
able improvement. They have had the privilege to
vote, to sit on the jury, and many other privileges
accorded the white race. They have schools and
churches. They are masters of their own time and
work. Some hold property. The number is small
—it may be five per cent. There has been progress in knowledge. It may be that 3,000,000 can
read, and many can write. They had, in 1880, in
the Southern States, 1,140,405 children in the public schools, and over 1,000,000 did not use these
privileges. There were 18,219 teachers. In 69
schools of science, theology, law, and medicine were
15,639 students. In industrial schools there were
perhaps 500 * students. There are not less than
5,000 † ministers of the gospel. Here are some of
the elements of progress.

---

* This number is too small. The Tuskeegee Institute of Alabama
has from 900 to 1,000 students of this class, according to the *Review
of Reviews* for April, 1894.

† Too small. There are in the Southern States, 7,991 ordained Baptist colored ministers alone. See *American Baptist Year-Book* for 1894.

The things in which some of the best negroes have made advancement do not counterbalance the elements of retrogression of the legions. In other words, the uplifting forces have carried on an unequal contest with the down-grade forces. The latter have done more injury to this people in their new relation as freedmen and citizens than the former have aided them to a better life. Moral or physical forces must govern every life. Moral considerations play an insignificant part in the life of the majority. Physical restraints are the most effective. Note *the idleness of a large and increasing class.* It is their great curse. Reason can not induce them to work, and compulsion is out of the question. Wise laws might do much. This one trait is the parent of a whole brood of evils. The progress in this direction is fearful. The truth may be distasteful, yet 15,000,000 people are witnesses to the fact. Should the public schools introduce *lessons in industry* and *morality*, and place them on an equality with *reading, writing*, and *arithmetic,* they would be of matchless importance to this race.

This one racial quality visible everywhere, in town and country, can be easily verified by those who have direct dealings with this people. The mere theorist who judges them at a distance, or judges the whole people by a few choice specimens that have come under his observation, is sure to paint the prospects of the race in rose-colored terms. Thousands of men would gladly have dealings with such characters as Uncle Tom, but the Uncle Toms are few. The numerous family of Sambo, Quimbo,

14

and Topsy makes " the negro problem " so serious.
The African people as a class—there are noble exceptions—have made no advance to a better life
in *industry*. By the concurrent testimony of all
those whose business forced them to note the character of their work, and of those who worked with
them side by side, and compared results, negro
industry has decreased 66 per cent. Besides, *licentiousness, lying, thieving, drunkenness, gambling*, and
perjury have made alarming gains in twenty-seven
years. *Promises* are idle things, utterly valueless
in their estimation. Consequences do not affect
them. Confidence in their promises is reduced to
the minimum. They will not testify against each
other in court unless envy, jealousy, or hatred in-
spires them. These things exist ; they are reality ;
and are not the product of prejudice or of exaggera-
tion. James Anthony Froude relates a similar condition existing in the West Indies. He says : " The
*negro morals are as emancipated in Dominica as in
the rest of the West Indies*." * Of a former period,
the same author thus writes : " Dominica had then
been regarded as the choicest jewel in the necklace
of the Antilles." † Again, speaking of the negroes
near Mandeville, on the Island of Jamaica : " They
stole cattle, and would not give evidence against
each other. If brought into court they held a
pebble in their mouths, being under the impression
that, when they were so provided, perjury did not
count." ‡

---

* The English in the West Indies, p. 152.
† *Ib.*, p. 153.   ‡ *Ib.*, p. 249.

The progress of this people, as a class, in knowledge, in accumulating wealth, and in orderly life, are outweighed by the retrogression of the great body of negroes in morals. The various forms of immorality that mark their downward course are not done in a corner; they are on record. A great body of white people, especially the farming people, are weary of the struggle. Every farmer of the South knows that the odds to successful farming are tremendous when he is dependent upon this labor.

As early as 1874 Rev. Dr. E. J. Winkler, an eminent minister of Georgia, said in an article on "The Negroes in the Gulf States," published in the *International Review*, vol. i., No. 5:

"Labor they esteem as a humiliation. They will not engage in any service unless compelled by urgent necessity; and, when employed, are neglectful and resentful to a degree. Although they afford the only material for the future supply of menial service to the home and the field, the growing desire of good citizens is, that most of them remove to other regions. The more industrious must be retained, for they can be used to their own profit and for the advantage of the community. *The others will only consume and destroy what more industrious hands may produce.*"

The Southern people will testify to the accuracy and severe truthfulness of this statement. The only difference that eighteen years have made, is, that the condition now is far worse; it is more embarrassing. No argument can explain away the facts. More than this, the matter of the last statement of Dr. Winkler furnishes one of the causes of much of the lawlessness of the country. Men are crazed with the struggle and their desperate surroundings. The lawless deeds are paraded in the newspapers, but no inquiry is made into the condition that gave them birth. Peaceable Anglo-Saxon farmers of meagre intelligence, maddened by their hard surroundings, not knowing which way to look for relief, growing poorer every year, and more despondent, in an evil hour startle the community. The situation is dreary and menacing. Lawlessness is not the route out of the difficulties. There can be no sympathy with anarchy, but to relieve it by lawful means is the dictate of virtue.

In further illustration of this retrograde movement, we quote from Mr. Froude's book, *The English in the West Indies,* as a realistic companion portrait of the condition in the South.

" Mr. ——, however, *did most really* convey to me the *convictions of a large and influential body* of West Indians—*convictions* on which they are *already acting,* and *will act more and more.* With Hayti so close, and with opinion in England indifferent of what becomes of them, *they will clear out while they have something left to lose, and will not wait till ruin is upon them, or till they are ordered off the land by a black legislature.* There is a saying in Hayti, *that the white man has no rights which the blacks are bound to recognize."* (p. 192). . . . Col. J——, acting governor of Jamaica, " *confirmed the complaint which I had so often heard, that the blacks would not work for wages more than three days in the week,* or *regularly upon those, preferring to cultivate their own* yams and sweet potatoes " (p. 211). . . . " The negroes in Mandeville were, perhaps, as happy in their old condition as they have been since their glorious emancipation, and some of them to this day speak regretfully of a time when children did not die of neglect ; when the sick and the aged were taken care of, and the strong and healthy were, at least, as well looked after as their owner's cattle. Slavery could not last ; but neither can the condition last which has followed it " (p. 246).

Men who live in the South, familiar with what has been going on for twenty-five years, seeing the strong racial qualities of this people, involving black and white in ruin, and who dare speak out without gloss or varnish, and with no selfish motive governing them, are bound to say the situation is full of alarm.

Those that decry the endeavors of the South to educate her children, have not examined her condition and her trying environments. Some comparisons may emphasize the truth of what the South is doing.

TABLE A.

1880.

SCHOOL POPULATION, ENROLMENT, AND ATTENDANCE.*

STATES.	SCHOOL POPULATION.	SCHOOL ENROLMENT.	SCHOOL ATTENDANCE.
Alabama	388,003	179,490	117,978
Mississippi	426,689	236,704	156,761
Georgia	433,444	236,533	145,190
New York	1,641,173	1,031,593	573,089
Massachusetts.....	307,321	306,777	233,127
Iowa.............	586,556	426,057	259,836

* Report of the Commissioner of Education, 1880, pp. 406, 407.

TABLE B.

1880.

EXPENDITURE PER CAPITA ON SCHOOL POPULATION, ENROLMENT, AND ATTENDANCE.*

STATES.	EXPENDITURE PER CAPITA ON SCHOOL POPULATION.	EXPENDITURE PER CAPITA ON SCHOOL ENROLMENT.	EXPENDITURE PER CAPITA ON SCHOOL ATTENDANCE.
Alabama	$0.96	$2.09	$3.17
Mississippi	1.56	2.70	4.01
Georgia	1.08	1.99	3.31
New York	6.34	10.09	18.16
Massachusetts.....	14.91	14 93	19.66
Iowa.............	8.17	11.25	18.45

TABLE C.

1880.

PER CENT. PER CAPITA OF SCHOOL EXPENDITURE ON VALUATION OF PROPERTY.

STATES.	ASSESSED VALUATION OF PROPERTY, REAL AND PERSONAL.†	TOTAL PUBLIC SCHOOL EXPENDITURE.‡	PER CENT. OF PUBLIC SCHOOL EXPENDITURE ON ASSESSED VALUATION OF PROPERTY, REAL AND PERSONAL.
Alabama..........	$122,867,228	$375,465	.003 +
Mississippi........	110,628,129	830,704	.007½ +
Georgia	239,472,592	471,029	.002 —
New York	2,651,940,006	10,412,378	.004 —
Massachusetts.....	1,584,756,802	5,156,731	.003 +
Iowa	398,671,251	4,921,248	.012 +

* Report of the Commissioner of Education, 1880, pp. 412, 413.

† Compendium Tenth Census, 1880, Part II., p. 1508.

‡ Report of the Commissioner of Education, 1880, p. 412.

The valuation of property of the State of New York, in 1880, was $2,651,940,006; the expenditure for public education during the year was $10,412,-378; and the school population of the State was 1,641,173.

According to the sources of information referred to—the Compendium of the Tenth Census, and the Report of the Commissioner of Education for 1880 —the valuation of all property, real and personal, in thirteen Southern States, namely, Virginia, West Virginia, North Carolina, South Carolina, Georgia, Florida, Alabama, Mississippi, Louisiana, Texas, Arkansas, Kentucky, and Tennessee, was $2,370,923,269. The difference in valuation between these thirteen States and the State of New York is $281,016,737. That difference alone more than equals the value of all the property in Florida, Alabama, and Mississippi. The expenditure of these thirteen States for public education in 1880 was $7,132,651. The school population in these thirteen States that year was 2,943,180 white children, and 1,680,273 negro children, making a total of 4,623,453 children of school age. These thirteen impoverished States had 2,982,280 more children for which to provide education than New York.

According to wealth, in 1880 Alabama expended 3 mills for educational purposes; Mississippi, 7½ mills; Georgia, 2 mills; New York, 4 mills; Massachusetts, 3 mills; and Iowa, 12 mills. Iowa leads in this comparison, giving three times as much money as New York; yet New York has six times as much wealth.

The per capita comparison , accoding to Table B, places the Southern States at a disadvantage. By this rule Alabama expends $3.17 per capita on school attendance; Massachusetts spends $19.66. Measured by property, each of these States spends 3 mills.

There are two men whose school expenditure may be thus stated : Mr. Hogan is worth $150,000. He sends a boy to college, costing him $500 per annum. Mr. Samuel is worth $250. He sends two children to school at a total expense of $25 per year. According to the per capita illustration, the figures of Hogan stand at $500; Samuel at $12.50. By the rule of wealth, Hogan expends of his wealth on the education of his son, 3⅓ mills ; Samuel expends of his wealth, 100 mills, or ten cents. In other words, Samuel does thirty times as much for the education of his children as Hogan, and Samuel is by far less able to afford it. Hogan can pay $5,000 per annum with far greater ease to himself and family than Samuel can pay $25. The same reasoning holds good as States.

The whole force of these remarks is to show that the Southern States in their poverty, embarrassed by hard surroundings, have bravely met their responsibilities in this matter. They have done what they could. Our " Brother in Black " has been a full sharer in the educational blessing.

Organized benevolence coming from Northern citizens has made splendid contributions to the education of the negroes. The resources from which revenues are derived, as far as they are known, may be thus stated :

American Missionary Association	$6,000,000
Freedman's Aid Society (Methodist)	2,225,000
Baptist Home Missino	2,000,000
Presbyterian Home Mission	1,542,746
John F. Slater	1,000,000
Daniel Hand	1,000,000
Other individual gifts	1,000,000
The different Woman's Societies	500,000
Quakers and others	500,000
Total	$15,767,746

The following contributions have been made by Southern States in aid of common and normal schools for this race. The statistics were prepared by the Rev. Dr. A. G. Haygood (General Agent of the Slater Fund, now Bishop of the M. E. Church, South). As the article in *Harper's Magazine* for July, 1889, from which these statistics are taken, was written in the early part of 1889, the expenditures by States do not extend beyond the year 1888.

Alabama	$3,404,293.24
Arkansas	3,409,110.00
Florida	849,000.00
Georgia	2,702,276.00
Kentucky	1,362,873.00
Louisiana	2,150,000.00
Mississippi	7,136,800.00
North Carolina	2,441,062.00
South Carolina	3,000,000.00
Tennessee	2,358,000.00
Texas	4,064,259.00
Virginia	4,500,000.00
Total to the close of 1888	$37,377,673.24

To this sum must be added the contributions for the same purpose, made to the close of the year 1888, by West Virginia, Delaware, Maryland, Missouri, and the District of Columbia. These, with the appropriations of all for the five years following 1888 will swell the aggregate of the Southern States for the education of the blacks to $55,000,000. The money given by the North, and the appropriations of the Southern States, with the District of Columbia, will make from $70,000,000 to $80,000,000.

When, in the ages of the past, have seven million people on the Dark Continent, during a quarter of a century, received such generous aid from organized benevolence and State governments for their elevation? The woe-begone condition of the children of Ham in their native land pleads in vain for help; but their cousins and their kindred on American soil, though 260 years held them in bondage, have in recent years been the objects of unwearied and benevolent attention. What is the fruitage?

Crime.—We must face the painful facts, and write the melancholy truth that, in spite of the ennobling agencies and of the social and civil incentives, crime among the sons of Ham is on the increase. Passion and license are stronger than reason.

There is no disposition to make a worse showing for this population than the facts warrant. These are sufficiently alarming. Neither is there any purpose on the part of the Southern people to treat them more severely because their color is black. It is frankly admitted by those who understand their character, that they need greater restraints than the

Anglo-Saxon race. Fear with them is a far more potential factor in the maintenance of good order than reason.

If the charge that the Southern people and Southern courts are unjust and harsh to them be true, how is the disparity between the excessive number of African convicts in Northern prisons as compared with white convicts to be explained? We would not charge our Northern citizens of Anglo-Saxon lineage with cruelty toward this people. Compare Tables D, E, and H, with Tables F, G, and I.

TABLE D.

POPULATION IN 1880, IN SIX STATES, NORTH.*

STATES.	WHITE.	AFRICAN.
Connecticut	610,769	11.547
Illinois.........................	3,031,151	46,368
Iowa	1,614,600	9,516
New York	5,016,022	65,104
Ohio...........	3,117,920	79,900
Massachusetts	1,763,782	18,697
Total	15,154,244	231,132

* Compendium, Tenth Census, Part I., page 3.

TABLE E.

PRISONERS IN PENITENTIARIES IN 1880.*

STATES.	WHITE.	AFRICAN.	IF CRIME AMONG THE WHITES HAD BEEN EQUAL TO THAT OF THE AFRICANS, WHAT THE NUMBER OF WHITE CONVICTS WOULD HAVE BEEN.	NUMBER OF AFRICAN CONVICTS TO WHITE CONVICTS PER POPULATION.
Connecticut..	224	28	1,465	6 A. to 1 W.
Illinois......	1,690	148	3,396	5 A. to 1 W.
Iowa........	522	24	4.068	7 A. to 1 W.
New York....	5,848	444	34,159	6 A. to 1 W.
Ohio...... ..	1,130	148	5.768	5 A. to 1 W.
Massachusetts	1,046	39	3,668	3¼ A. to 1 W.
Total	10,460	831	52,254	5⅝ A. to 1 W. Av'ge.

TABLE F.

POPULATION IN 1880 IN SIX SOUTHERN STATES.†

STATES.	WHITE.	AFRICAN.
Alabama......................	662,185	600,103
Arkansas.....................	591,531	210,666
Louisiana.....................	454.954	483,655
Mississippi..........	479,398	650,291
North Carolina.................	867,242	531,277
South Carolina.	391,105	604,332
Total	3,446,415	3,080,324

* Compendium, Tenth Census, Part II., pp. 1694, 1695.

† Compendium, Tenth Census, Part I., pp. 2, 3.

TABLE G.

PRISONERS IN PENITENTIARIES IN 1880.*

STATES.	WHITE.	AFRICAN.	IF CRIME AMONG THE WHITES HAD BEEN EQUAL TO THAT OF THE AFRICANS, WHAT THE NUMBER OF WHITE CONVICTS WOULD HAVE BEEN.	NUMBER OF AFRICAN CONVICTS TO WHITE CONVICTS PER POPULATION.
Alabama........	75	312	344	4⅔ A. to 1 W.
Arkansas.......	200	364	1,017	5 A. to 1 W.
Louisiana.......	81	466	436	5¾ A. to 1 W.
Missi~~-~~ippi......	82	653	479	5⅘ A. to 1 W.
North Carolina..	428	383	624	1⅔ A. to 1 W.
South Carolina..	22	237	152	7 A. to 1 W.
Total	888	2,415	3,052	5 A. to 1 W.

TABLE H.

1880.

NUMBER OF CONVICTS IN PENITENTIARY TO 100,000 OF THE POPULATION.

STATES.	WHITE.	AFRICAN.
Connecticut.............	36	240
Illinois............	55	310
Iowa...........................	32	252
New York.....................	116	681
Ohio.........................	36	185
Massachusetts.................. ..	59	208

* Compendium, Tenth Census, Part II., pp. 1649, 1695.

TABLE I.

1880.

NUMBER OF CONVICTS IN PENITENTIARY TO 100,000 OF THE
POPULATION.

STATES.	WHITE.	AFRICAN.
Alabama..................	11	52
Arkansas....	33	172
Louisiana............................	17	96
Mississippi.........................	17	100
North Carolina......................	49	72
South Carolina.................... ..	5	39

There is a difference between the Anglo-Saxon
people and the negro race. Color is the least
difference. Character, exhibiting itself in honor, in
high incentives to action, in rational obedience to
law and constituted legal authority, characterizes
the white race in a far higher degree than the black
race. The black man is far more disposed to construe liberty into license than the white man. Self-
restraint is a hard lesson for him to learn. To this
quality of his character is to be traced the increase
of crime. It matters not whether his residence is
in Connecticut or Massachusetts, Alabama or Mississippi. Wherever restraints are the least felt by
the blacks, there crime is on the increase.

Making allowances for differences in the laws and
the enforcement of laws in various States of the
Union, the facts brought out in Table H can not be
disguised. Table E shows the crime record in still

darker colors. Had crime been as prolific among the white inhabitants of Connecticut, Illinois, Iowa, New York, Ohio, and Massachusetts as among the 231,132 Africans of these States, in 1880, there would have been in their penitentiaries 52,524 white convicts, instead of 10,460. In this statement no invidious comparison is intended between the North and the South. It is the criminal record of the blacks in six Northern States, where the influence for their elevation and progress is favorable. The charge of prejudice to this people that has been preferred against the Southern people would be resented there. The remorseless criminal record of this race in these States stares us in the face, and the people, North and South, dare not shut their eyes to its significance.

Had the Africans in these States numbered 15,-154,244, and the white people 231,132, it is probable crimes would have increased in geometrical ratio.

Another fact: In the Northern States are quite a number of educated Africans, and all the people of African descent have, in common with the Anglo-Saxon people, enjoyed in unstinted measure the superior advantages of the common-school system, as well as the advantages of the well-equipped higher institutions of learning; and all this superior intellectual leverage has been applied in its full strength to the sons and daughters of this people, for a period of nearly one hundred years. There they have had the sympathy of the white people in a large degree. In view of this may we not say, in all candor and kindness, and in no spirit of bitter-

ness, it is time to look for fruit? What are the
results of this magnificent outlay of money and
endeavor to elevate the children of Africa in these
Northern States? Connecticut spent in 1880,
$1,408,375 on her public schools, and had propor-
tionally six African convicts in her penitentiary to
one white man; Illinois expended that year $7,531,-
942 on the public schools, and had proportionally,
during the same year, five African convicts in her
penitentiary to one white man; Iowa's expenditure
for common-school education in 1880 was $4,921,-
248, yet Iowa had proportionally seven negro convicts in her penitentiary to one white; New York
expended during that year on her public schools
$10,412,378, and had proportionally six African con-
victs in her penitentiaries to one white man; Ohio's
expenditure in 1880 for public education was $7,166,-
963, and she had proportionally five negro convicts
in her penitentiary to one white man; Massachusetts gave that year to the support of her common
schools $5,156,731, and had, in proportion to popu-
lation, three and a fourth black convicts in her
penitentiary to one white man. The average num-
bor of convicts in the penitentiaries of these six
States, in proportion to population, was five and a
third negroes to one white man. The long-hoped-for
fruitage is not indicated by this record.

In these six Northern States were, in 1880, 47,007
persons of African descent, from ten years and
upward, who could not write, and 517,850 white
persons from ten years and upward who could not
write. If we compare the crime record with the

illiteracy of the two races, then seventeen negro convicts and twenty white convicts for one thousand persons would be the ratios for each race. This can be true only upon the condition that all the convicts were illiterates. One fact, everywhere prominent, account for it as we may, that however favorable or unfavorable may be the environments of this race, there is a wide disparity between the crime record of the blacks and the whites.

In the South we note the same increase of crime among the negroes. A Mississippi judge says that eighty per cent. of the crimes in the State are either caused by the blacks, or can be traced to them. The number of negro convicts in the penitentiary of Mississippi in 1869 was 259; in 1880, there were 653.* In Louisiana the negro convicts in 1880 were 466; in 1890, 751.† In Florida, the negro convicts in 1869 were 102, in 1892 there were 407.‡ In Texas the negro convicts numbered, in 1882, 1,183; in 1890, 1,523; and in 1892, 1,681.§ In Alabama, the negro convicts in 1868 were 199; in 1880, 312. The number of State convicts in Alabama, September 30, 1890, was, white, 167; negro, 956; and the number of county convicts in the State was 63 whites, and 573 negroes. This gives a total for

---

* Letter from T. B. Stone, Secretary Board of Control, Penitentiary.

† Letter from J. W. Bates, State Clerk, Louisiana State Penitentiary.

‡ Letter from Hon. L. B. Wombwell, Commissioner of Agriculture.

§ Letter from Hon. L. A. Whatley, Superintendent of Penitentiary.

county and State of 230 white convicts, and 1,529
negro convicts. The ratio of convicts in the State
is $6\frac{6}{10}$ negroes to 1 white. There were 27 white
convicts to 100,000 white people, and 225 negro
convicts to 100,000 negroes.*

In 1880 the negro population of the United
States was 6,580,793.† The negroes—those of
African descent, whether pure or mixed—in the
penitentiaries were 7,347; negroes in reformatories,
workhouses, and houses of correction, were 1,935,
making a total of 9,282.‡ The negro population
in 1890 consisted of 6,337,980 pure Africans, and
1,132,060 mulattoes, making a total of 7,470,040.
The pure negroes in the penitentiaries were 10,-
889, mulattoes 3,378; total, 14,267 negro convicts.§
Negroes in reformatories, 1,730. Total in penitentiaries and reformatories, 15,997.‖ Increase in ten
years 6,715. The gain of the negro population
in ten years is a little over 13 per cent. The increase in crime among the negroes from 1880 to
1890 is a little over 72 per cent. Crime increased $5\frac{1}{2}$
times as fast as population. Two hundred and four-
teen negroes in every group of 100,000 are criminals.
Had the aggregate population of the United States
in 1890 been Africans, there would have been 134,011
black criminals in the penitentiaries and reformatories. "What of the night?" The future is dark.

---

* Report of Inspectors of the Alabama Penitentiary.
† Compendium, Tenth Census, Part II.
‡ Census Bulletin, Eleventh Census, No. 199.
§ Census Bulletin, Eleventh Census, No. 31.
‖ Census Bulletin, Eleventh Census, No. 72.

But the 15,997 do not represent in full the black criminal class. The convictions due to numerous minor offences, tried in the lower courts during every month of the year, in every county of the Southern States, must be considered. This will add 20,000 offenders in the Southern States to the dark catalogue. The majority of all the trials in the courts of every justice of the peace are negro cases. Ninety per cent. of these trials consist in offences among themselves.

Southern society is burdened with this crime. Let no reader in a distant State where negroes are few, imagine that the more heinous offences such as felony are committed by negroes altogether against white men. Many are so perpetrated. There are now in —— County six negroes in the county jail charged with murder. Four of the six took the life of four negroes. Two of them each killed his man at a negro dance. One of the six killed another negro over the gambling-table. A dispute about ten cents led to the crime. All the blacks that can do so, and few can not, carry pistols, and that in spite of the law against carrying concealed weapons. Many have shotguns. The factors of ruin among the black people are making steady progress.

This exhibit of crimes among this people is not born of ill will to this race. Wherever they enjoy freedom and mingle with the Anglo-Saxon race, their crimes are far in excess of the white race. In 1833, Mr. Everett, in a speech before the Colonization Society, said : " The free blacks form in

Massachusetts about one seventy-fifth part of the population.   One-sixth of the convicts in our prisons are of this class." *

In 1834 a memorial presented to the Legislature of Connecticut, draws a portrait of the negroes in that State nearly sixty years ago, very similar in many phases to what any man can see in every Southern State in 1893, who can write the facts as they exist.   The memorial reads : " Not a week, hardly a day, passes, that they [the negroes] are not implicated in the violation of some law." †   This is true all over the South to-day.

" Assaults and batteries, insolence to the whites, compelling a breach of the peace, riots in the streets, petty thefts, and continual trespasses on property are such common occurrences, resulting from the license they enjoy, that they have ceased to become subjects of remark.   It is but recently that a band of negroes paraded the streets of New Haven, armed with clubs and pistols and dirks, with the avowed purpose of preventing the law of the land from being enforced against one of their species.   Upon being accosted by an officer of justice and commanded to retire peaceably to their homes, their only reply consisted of abuse and threats of personal violence. The law was overshadowed, and the officer consulted his own safety in a timely retreat."

The memorial then proceeds to show that the evil complained of has so rapidly progressed, that the whites have become the subjects of insult and abuse whenever they have refused to descend to familiarity with them ; that themselves, their wives and children, have been driven from the pavements where they have not submitted to personal conflict ;

---

* The Gospel among the Slaves, p. 108.
† Ibid., pp. 108, 109.

that from the *licentiousness* of *their general habits* they *have invariably depreciated the value of property* by their location in its neighborhood, and that from their *notorious uncleanliness* and *filth* they have become *common nuisances to the community.*

This was the complaint and charge of Connecticut in 1834. In 1880 there were 240 negro convicts in Connecticut to 36 white convicts for 100,000 citizens of each race.*

"In Ohio the black population (1835) is 1 to 115 whites; convicts, 7 whites to 100 blacks. Vermont, by the census of 1830, contained 277,000 souls; 918 were negroes. In 1831 there were 74 convicts in the prison, and of these 24 were negroes. [This means 1 white convict to 145 negro convicts.] When compared with what is reported of the proportion of negroes in the prisons of the slave-holding States, it is shown that the proportion of negroes in the penitentiaries of the free States is in the ratio of more than 10 to 1 in favor of the slave-holding States. The free negroes in Ohio in the aggregate are in no better condition, therefore, than the slaves in Kentucky. They are excluded from social intercourse with the whites, and whatever of education you may give them will not tend to elevate their standing to any considerable extent."—From the Report of the Committee on the Judiciary, relative to the repeal of laws replacing restrictions and disabilities on blacks and mulattoes, by Mr. Cushing, February 21, 1835. Agreed to unanimously. Legislature of Ohio.

In 1880 there were 185 negro convicts to 36 white convicts for 100,000 citizens of each race in Ohio.

A Southern State in which there is a large black population, as is the case in all the Southern States, has dangerous and pernicious evils with which to contend, unknown to the older States. Many good

---

* The Gospel among the Slaves, p. 109.

citizens North and South, in strong sympathy with
the negro's condition, intellectually and morally,
and genuinely desirous for his elevation, have studied
the poor, wronged negro only as they see him in
the past, and believe that he will yield to the leverage that has been so efficacious in the general
elevation of the Anglo-Saxon race. They see him
in his Sunday dress, but neglect to examine him in
his every-day garb. We think it more than probable that a slave-owner raised with the negroes, who
saw them at their work day by day up to the year
1860, and then left the South, would be amazed
should he return to the South in 1890, at the transformation in the every-day life of this people.

We are informed by reliable men, police officers,
that negro boys and negro men, some old men, are
readily employed as agents of vice. For a nickel,
it is said, they will aid in the prostitution of their
own race. Girls with a little common-school education do not seek service with good families, notwithstanding that their parents are poor and can not
support them, yet they are well dressed—far better
dressed than the girls who make their living by
honest toil. Every village and town in the South
is thus embarrassed. The significance of this condition can not be too soon considered by Anglo-
Saxon parents. The thoughtful blacks, having the
interest of their race at heart, have cause for deep
concern.

The enormous licentiousness existing among this
people is well known. It is a moral contagion. It
deadens the perception of the right. Here are

negro women by scores in every county, with houses full of children, but no fathers to own them.   Here is a mother with four girls; she has no husband, and never had.   Her oldest daughter has two children, and that daughter has no husband.   It is a common state of things, and no one talks about it.   Can this condition go on without terrible consequences?   Can virtue bloom in Sodom?   Can the degradation of our "Brother in Black" go steadily forward in its progress of ruin, and the white race escape the contagion?   In a high moral sense, the civilization of the Huguenot, the Cavalier, and, the Puritan is in danger.

"One crime" may not be attempted by negroes in the South without swift retribution.   The fiery temper of the Southern people will brook no delay in meting out punishment to the guilty.   We plead in vain to let the law have its course in this as in other heinous offences.   In spite of this well-known Southern sentiment, attempts at this "one crime" by negroes are alarmingly on the increase. A person can not pick up a newspaper without an account of this "one crime" with all its revolting details.   There is a timidity and dread among the white women of the South, unknown in the days of slavery.   Rev. Dr. MacVicar of the American Baptist Home Mission Society, is represented in the *National Baptist* as saying: "The young negroes in the South live lives of unending debauchery and gambling." *

---

* From *Religious Herald*, July 20, 1893.

According to the Third Biennial Report of the Inspectors of Convicts for the State of Alabama, 1890, of 31 State convicts sentenced for forgery, 21 were negroes; 28 convicts sentenced for rape, 23 were negroes; 34 convicts sentenced for arson, 28 were negroes; 235 State convicts sentenced for murder, 183 were negroes. What is true in Alabama, is true in the Southern States.

The Biennial Report of the Board of Control of the Mississippi State Penitentiary for the years 1890 and 1891, shows that of the convicts received for the year ending December 4, 1891, 20 were sentenced for forgery, 17 of whom were negroes; 28 were sentenced for rape, 26 of whom were negroes; 21 were sentenced for arson, and 21 were negroes; 115 were sentenced for murder, and 112 were negroes.

The criminal docket, Circuit Court of the County of Pike, State of Mississippi, September Term, 1893, presents the following record:

OFFENCES.	WHITE.	NEGRO.
Murder..........................	2	5
Arson...................		1
Rape		2
Retailing liquor............................	1	7
Burglary................................		4
Total...........................	3	19

In this county there were, in 1890, whites, 10,581; blacks, 10,620.* The negroes have in this county

* Compendium, Eleventh Census, Part I., p. 494.

from 30 to 35 public schools, and from 40 to 50 churches, all with pastors of their race. In 1880 the whites raised 4,018 bales of cotton in this county; the negroes, 2,489 bales.*

The lumber business and the railroad shops may employ 500 negro men. The relations between the two races is cordial. The most influential white citizens are the best friends of the colored people. The demand for agricultural laborers is ample. Some most excellent colored men live in this county. They are regarded by their white neighbors as trustworthy. A few own property. The number of trustworthy negroes is very small—from one to two per cent. Here, as elsewhere, the colored people all belong to the laboring class, with the exception of the preachers, the teachers, here and there a physician, a few small shopkeepers, a few shoemakers, blacksmiths, carpenters, and barbers.

Crimes are frequent. The obtuse moral faculty leads to all sorts of violations of the laws. Personal property is in danger whenever there is an opportunity. Homicides are common. Illicit selling of liquor is conducted by negro women quite as extensively as by negro men. This is the settled belief. In every town are scores of negro boys and girls, from twelve to twenty years, who do not attend school. This is a matter of sheer unconcern with them and their parents. They do no work the year round that deserves the name. The boys are street loafers. They run on errands for small storekeepers,

---

* Map of Mississippi.

when needed, and are rewarded with a nickel or with a piece of cheese and a few crackers. The girls do less than this. They wish no honorable employment. Where there is one colored house-girl making an honorable living, there are twenty such girls who can not be employed to do work, though there is not a pound of meal in the house, nor money. Infanticide is a common charge against colored mothers without husbands. Ignorance and carelessness are, no doubt, chargeable with many a death. Still, the crushed skull of an infant demands a sounder explanation. The law in some States against the selling of laudanum without a physician's prescription is good. One intent of this law is to discourage the opium habit ; the other, no doubt, is to prevent crime. We mince matters. Checks and preventives are good, but why not go to the root of this moral condition? "The fire of London was upon the whole a blessing. It burnt down the city and burnt out the plague." The "torpid content" of reposing communities needs to be vastly disturbed. And laws, wise and humane, need to be enacted, that shall go down to the noisome recesses where lurk the germs of these enormous moral maladies.

The court expenses for 1893 in the County of Pike, State of Mississippi, were more than $10,000; from six to seven tenths of this sum was chargeable to crime by negroes. The amount expended on the public schools for this race in the county is $7,790 per annum. What is the fruit of this noble agency? What of the forty or fifty churches? We would not put a straw in the way of these approved instrumentalities, but rather strengthen their efficiency. Our motive, therefore, will not be misconstrued, and the truth of what we are about to say will not be gainsaid, that the meagre acquirements of a common-school education have had the general effect thus far of disqualifying the colored boys and girls as servants and as laborers. It is the voice of the South. We see the effect at home—it is the common judgment of the Southern people.

In Mississippi there are from 150,000 to 200,000 colored church members, connected in the main with two denominations, Methodists and Baptists. During the scholastic year 1892–93, there were in this State 2,569 colored public and 79 private schools. The amount expended for the colored public schools was $340,914; that is, for salaries of teachers. When other expenses are added, with the appropriations to the colored normal schools and Alcorn University, the total annual educational expense bill for this race will not fall far short of $400,000. What is the fruitage of these intellectual, moral, and religious instrumentalities for the elevation of this race?

It is our profound conviction, that the white people here and in the South mean well to the negroes. Kindness and forbearance have characterized their relation to them, in large measure. This truth will stand every adverse criticism, and still it is the truth.

CHAPTER XIII

THE NEGROES AS FARM LABORERS

THE negroes have enjoyed freedom nearly thirty years. It is natural to suppose that the incentives of this new condition would prompt them to industrious habits. There is no ill grace in telling the truth concerning the racial qualities of this people. The evidence of personally seeing this people at their work by living witnesses all over the South, during the entire period since their emancipation, is entitled to credence. It is not necessary to judge the black man harshly to tell the truth about him. The truth without any ingredient of hate or prejudice is sufficiently disheartening. What is this truth? As independent laborers, i.e., laborers not supervised by intelligent white men in planning and directing, they are a failure. Planters and farmers, whether they employ five or five hundred, concur without dissent in this opinion. We submit that the concurrent judgment of these farmers living in various States is good proof. During a period of years, to our personal inquiry of hundreds of our best farmers, "What is the value of the work on farms by the old slave negroes to-day as compared with their work in slave times under humane masters?" but one answer has been given: "Half, and less than half." The old slave negroes are everywhere regarded in the South as the best farm hands. The habits of industry taught them abide in a degree. They are bad managers when left to themselves, waste a great deal of time, and are self-indulgent ; still, they are the most reliable and industrious workers.

" What about the younger generation of colored people—those who practically know nothing of the life prior to the emancipation of the negroes, or who were born since then ? "

" The men do much less work than the older class, and the women do next to nothing." This is the judgment of white men, and this is the opinion of every old negro consulted by us. The agricultural condition of the South corroborates these statements.

In using the work done in slave times as a standard, the unjust inference is not to be drawn that Southern people, as a rule, were severe, cruel, and unreasonable. Where there was one Simon Legree there were a thousand just and kind-hearted masters. We dare affirm that the great body of this people were better fed, better clothed, and better housed then than to-day. Slavery is dead, and may it remain so forever.

Their work to-day is very inferior. It has depreciated in quantity and quality. When supervised, their work is not now what it once was ; when their work is entirely under their own control, it is very poor. It takes on an average to-day two negroes of the old class to do as much as one did formerly, three of the class of young men to do the work that one did in a former period, and five women of this latter class to do the work of one in past time. There are worthy exceptions in these groups, but they are few. The equation resulting from the character of this labor may be thus expressed: the work of three negroes in 1860 equals the work of ten negroes in 1890. The result is equivalent to this: that if three do their full quota of reasonable work, seven are idle.

From these facts certain deductions follow. As a race, they are not self-sustaining. They produce less than they consume. A man doing half work, his wife rendering no help, can not make sufficient to support himself and his wife. When there are small children the situation is worse.

With this condition of Hamitic labor in the South, the people are confronted with a serious state of things. The colored producers are few, the non-producers are many. The Tables A, B, and C will exhibit the non-producing classes.

TABLE A.
NON-PRODUCTIVE NEGRO CLASS.

1.	Children under 5 years	1,114,365
2.	Public school children enrolled	1,140,405
3.	Teachers in public schools	18,219
4.	Students in 30 normal schools	5,439
5.	Students in 15 secondary schools	3,705
6.	Students in 16 colleges	5,066
7.	Students in 2 schools of science	434
8.	Students in 13 schools of theology	725
9.	Students in 1 law school	160
10.	Students in 2 schools of medicine	110
11.	Students in industrial schools, estimated	500
12.	Ministers of the Gospel, estimated	5,000
	Total	2,294,128

TABLE B.

NON-PRODUCTIVE NEGRO CLASS.

1. Convicts in State penitentiaries........................ 15,997
2. County convicts, estimated—small..................... 5,000
3. Insane in 1880....................................... 5,995
4. Idiots in 1880....................................... 9,490
5. Blind in 1880.. 7,384
6. Deaf-mutes in 1880.................................. 3,177

    Total.. 47,043

TABLE C.

NON-PRODUCTIVE NEGRO CLASS.

1. Aged negroes from 70 to 100 years old 111,434
2. Men from 35 to 69 years old, half of the class........ 347,048
3. Women from 35 to 69 years old, half of the class..... 338,674
4. Men from 15 to 34 years old, two-thirds of the class .. 1,039,714
5. Women from 15 to 34 years old, four-fifths of the class. 1,086,010

    Total.. 2,922,880

These data furnish us with 5,264,051 people belonging to one race who practically produce nothing. Make an exception for 1 and 2 of Table B.
They constitute expensive groups. The others of
this table are the unfortunate groups. There will
be little difference of opinion concerning Table A.
Group 1 of Table C consists of persons deserving
the commiseration of the communities in which
they live. The remaining groups of this table
make up the hard problem. What to do with
them is the question. They perplex wise men.
Can it be true that nearly three-sevenths of this
people, able to work, practically do nothing to sustain life? It is not difficult to obtain evidence.
The villages and towns of the country can furnish

the facts. What a moral dynamite this is in the land! What a hot-bed of vice! What convulsions sleep within this tremendous force! What material for hospitals, asylums, and criminal courts! What is the prospect in the future—twenty-five years hence? When this population shall number twenty million, the race friction will be intense, unless history is reversed.

But let us notice the working classes of this people—the bread-winners.

TABLE D.

WORKING NEGROES.

1. Men from 35 to 69 years old, half of the class........	347,048
2. Women from 35 to 69 years old, half of the class.....	338,674
3. Men and boys from 15 to 34 years old, one-third of the class......................................	302,734
4. Women and girls from 15 to 34 years old, one-fifth of the class..	271,502
Total	1,259,958

They do their full quota of work. This number represents the total of the three out of ten. It is supposed that their productive work now is equal to the work done in 1860.

The classification of this people in these four tables presents 1,259,958 producers against 5,264,051 non-producers. Only the Africans in the Southern States are here considered. The defective groups in Table B are based upon the Tenth Census Report for 1880.

Not quite nineteen per cent. toil to make a living. Eighty-one per cent. are dependent. Add to this dreary picture the fact that a kind of Chinese wall encircles this people. It is referred to here, to show that the labors of the most cultured Hamite in any one of the professional groups in Table A are confined to his own people, and the masses of this people are ignorant. Life among them is very depressed. His sympathies, hopes, and aspirations are hemmed in by race conditions. Beyond, the atmosphere is cold and repellent. The labors of the one hundred and sixty colored lawyers will in the main be confined to their own race. Will these barriers give way? The subject will be referred to again.

The defective industrial quality of the negroes is the greatest hindrance to their progress. It not only breeds vice, but, poor as they are, this sluggish disposition makes them poorer every day, and widens the breach between them and the white people. Here are a million negroes who can not claim the roofs that shelter them as their own, and yet they are more independent than the richest man in the country. A vast number of them would rather work by the day than by the week, and so on through the other time periods. Penniless, they would rather postpone work for a week or a month than begin to-day. They believe in the blessings of procrastination. It is a matter of sheer unconcern whether they please their employer or not. Do the work as they please, quit when they please, begin when they please—this is the Hamitic idea of labor. This state of things can not continue. The notion is gaining ground that the Hamites are a vast

16

pauper race. The struggle to secure labor is becoming more difficult every year, and the labor itself
when obtained is uncertain and unsatisfactory. The
farmer who has ten families on his place in February, may not have half that number in March.
Under these circumstances farming is a risky business. The sons of farmers that can do so are seeking more inviting fields of labor.

Something must be done. It is certain, notwithstanding the fact just stated, that the white labor
on farms is increasing, and black labor on farms is
constantly decreasing. All the hill country of the
South will be occupied by white labor first. The
negroes, as the years go on, will gather in vast numbers in the swamps and alluvial bottoms of the
South. This is the movement. There the last bat-
tle will be fought.

Let us note this labor movement. In thirty
years, population increased 87 per cent. in the
Southern States. The whites alone increased 91
per cent. During this period a large number of
native white people have, by necessity, been forced
to cultivate the soil. This number has annually aug-
mented. They have brought to their work a degree
of intelligence and management that could not be
expected from the blacks. The persistence, energy,
and enterprise of the white people is so far superior
to the blacks, that the work and the results show in
everything marked contrasts. We write of them as
classes. The gentle rain that drives the negro from
the field is a stimulus to the white man. The trifle
that discourages the black is a matter of contempt

with the white. Besides, the white men introduce improved farm tools and machinery wherever they can be used to advantage. Take the cotton-planter —one man with one mule does as much work and does it better than was formerly done by three men and two mules. In 1865 it took eight mules and two boys to run a gin. The ginning of three bales of cotton was a day's work. Now a small engine does twice the work at less expense. The white man is quick to see what is to be done, and does it. The black man is slow to see, and slower to act. What he does, is done awkwardly. Tell him to do two things, and neither is performed. He delights to dally at his work. It takes him twice as long as it does a white man to fasten a hame's string or adjust a backband. His house, corn-crib, hennery, and garden fence, if they are of his own construction, are models of their kind. Blind men could do better. One picket of the fence is seven feet long; the next, four; then, five; next, seven again, and so on to the end. Some overlap each other; between others there are gaps of three and four inches. Some touch the ground, and some fail to reach it by six inches, and the fence is as straight as a crooked line can be. All this is characteristic of his work in general. He prefers to be his own manager—live to himself, and plan for himself—away from white influence. His progress is of the sort that makes himself poor, and his friends too.

White labor, it was said, is steadily increasing. The superiority of this labor in the general management of farm work, the native energy of the white

race, and their disposition to seize upon improved
implements and new methods, make the advantage
over the colored man immense. This superiority
adds a large per cent. to the increase on production.
The negro labor is steadily leaving the farm; yet
upon the whole, for the masses of this race, with a
few exceptions, this work is best suited to them.
They can make it profitable to themselves and to
others, upon the condition that their labor is subject to direction in detail. Without such superintendence, the experience of years shows that their
work is an egregious failure. A farm under their
management means bedlam let loose. There are exceptions to this general statement; but, like all
exceptions, they are numerable.

This fact, that the colored people are leaving the
country for the towns, suggests another subject:
" Can the white people raise the cotton demanded
by the world ? "

We find the following statement and table in the
Report of the Commissioner of Agriculture for
1876, p. 136:

(1) " Some writers have assumed, prior to the change of the labor
system, one-sixth as the proportion of white laborers in the cotton
fields. The proportion has been increasing for the last ten years,
until now there are *two States*, according to the reports of our correspondents, in which *the larger part of the product is grown by
whites.* Returns from *more than half* the cotton area of Texas make
the proportion of cotton grown by white labor *five-eighths*, and data
representing three-eighths of the Arkansas area establish the proportion of six-tenths. *In every State there is a large increase of white
labor production.* While the percentage for each State might be
nearer to perfect accuracy if the information covered every acre of
the cotton area, the *actual canvassing of about half the field*, ranging

in each State from three-eighths to five-eighths of its area, furnishes the best attainable means of estimating the proportion of the cotton crop grown by whites. On this basis the proportions are, 60 per cent. by black labor, 40 per cent. by white. The proportions, by States, are as follows:

STATES.	BLACK.	WHITE.
North Carolina	65	35
South Carolina	68	32
Georgia	66	34
Florida	72	28
Alabama	59	41
Mississippi	68	32
Louisiana	77	23
Texas	38	62
Arkansas	40	60
Tennessee	59	41

" The proportion of white cultivators will not decrease. As population increases, the white element will be stronger in numbers, and a larger proportion of the cotton will be grown by small proprietors ; while the African element will drift into menial service in towns, and in manufacturing and mining enterprises, and many who aspire to occupancy of land will earn only a precarious existence."

This was in 1876, seventeen years ago.

(2) " King Cotton's days of prosperity, it was gravely predicted, would end forever with the emancipation of the slaves. But the South raises thirty per cent. more cotton to-day than it ever did before the war, and raises it on a smaller number of acres. And note the increase of white labor in the production of the cotton crop. Before the war, white labor produced only ten per cent. of this staple ; in 1883, forty-four per cent.; in 1884, forty-eight per cent ; in 1885, over fifty per cent. . . . The white man of the New South has gone to work in the cotton fields as well as everywhere else."*

* The Century Illustrated Monthly Magazine for March, 1887, p. 771.

If the gain in cotton production by white labor is two and one-half per cent. annually since 1883, then the cotton produced by white labor in 1893 is about seventy per cent. of the entire crop.

(3) " Mr. Edward Atkinson has shown that the crop produced in twenty-one years by free labor was 35,000,000 bales in excess of the crop produced in the preceding period of twenty-one years by slave labor. The claim has been often iterated in the South that this difference is due to the white labor that has entered the cotton fields since the war ended."

" This old nonsense about our climate and the inability of the white man to toil under a blazing Southern sun, is so transparent that it is scarcely necessary to show its falsity. White immigration has poured into Florida of late, passed over the negro districts, and, settling in the extreme southern portion, the hottest section of the State, has built up there, amid its waste swamp lands, an agricultural prosperity that Florida never knew under slavery and negro labor. The white men who have poured into Texas since the war, from all sections of the Union, have shown that the climate did not affect their labor in the slightest degree ; but they have worked to such good purpose, that they have placed Texas at the head of the cotton States, the producer of nearly one-quarter of the entire crop."

"Cotton has long since ceased to be the product of the negro. . . . The white States and white districts have become the cotton centres of the South. The negro parishes of Carroll, Tensas, and Madison, the finest cotton country in the world, where the yield is greater and the staple the finest, produce far smaller crops than they bore thirty years ago, while the white counties of Texas have increased their production four and five fold. This fact attracted the particular attention of Professor Hilgard, who prepared the census report on cotton, and he notes the singular coincidence that the bulk of the crop of Mississippi is raised in the hills, where the yield per acre is small, instead of in the bottoms where every condition is favorable. The fact did not seem to strike him that the true reason lay in the fact, that in the hills the cotton was raised by the whites, in the bottoms by the negroes."

With this condition of Hamitic labor, and all the resultant racial influence of this people upon pros-

CHAPTER XIV.

NEGRO COLONIZATION.

HISTORY has no record of two races as unlike as the Anglo-Saxon and the African, living together in harmony under like conditions. The superior race is energetic and ambitious. Every door of enterprise, of industry, of knowledge, of preferment in civil and political life, is wide open to them. It is a masterful, dominant race.

The other race is sluggish and unenterprising. Its past history is a vast Sahara. Every door of advancement, or nearly so, open to the Anglo-Saxon, is closed to the African. Hayti, with a hundred years' experience and opportunities, and the British Colonies in the West India Islands, with nearly sixty years of freedom, and educational, civil, and political advantages, furnish no ground of hope for the Hamites of the Southern States.

The Indian has long ago been forced to move toward the setting sun. The number of Indians is insignificant. When interest puts forth its claim, the imperious superior race will demand the removal of the sons of Ham. Interests moral, social, industrial, and political are already demanding a hearing. "What shall we do with the negroes?" is impressing itself more and more upon the South-

perity, upon morals, upon the civilization of the South, the time is at hand when the future of this race should be dispassionately considered. Southern agriculture can not always remain in its present paralyzed condition. It is mercy to consider the race question now. It may be far otherwise twenty-five years hence.

ern people. To impose political disabilities upon the black man removes one difficulty, but leaves the grave moral and industrial perplexities untouched. With these the people have to do every day.

The consensus of thoughtful observers is, that two races, not homogeneous, can not live on the same soil.

Mr. Froude thus expresses himself concerning this subject, after his visit to the English West Indian Colonies in 1887:

" The races are not equal and will not blend. If the white people do not depart of themselves, black legislation will make it impossible for any of them to stay who would not be better out of the way." " The whites are leaving the islands. Negro labor can not be controlled, and negro labor is the only kind of labor on the islands that can be employed by the English planters. Dominica has 29,900 negroes and 100 English."

Of this island, he says:

" The soil was as rich as the richest in the world. The cultivation was growing annually less. The inspector of roads was likely to have an easy task, for, except close to the town, there were no roads at all on which anything with wheels could travel, the old roads made by the French having dropped into horse-tracks, and the horse-tracks into the beds of torrents. . . . The island goes on in a state of *torpid content.*"

Of St. Vincent:

"The prosperity has for the last forty years waned and waned. There are now two thousand white people there, and forty thousand colored people."

Concerning Barbadoes:

"The great prosperity of the island ended with emancipation. Barbadoes suffered less than Jamaica or the Antilles, because the population was large and the land limited, and the blacks were obliged to work to keep themselves alive."

Speaking of the English West Indies in general, Mr. Froude remarks : " The whites whom we planted as our representatives, are drifting into ruin." The whites are leaving the islands, since they can not employ the negroes as laborers for a common benefit. This is the chief industrial obstacle. The blacks can not leave, but in the West India Islands, as in the Southern States, they enjoy a "torpid content." This cause alone is hastening the day of negro deportation.

As early as 1845, United States Senator J. H. Hammond of South Carolina said :

" It is the most fatal of all fallacies to suppose that these two races can exist together, after any length of time, or any process of preparation, on terms at all approaching to equality. Of this, both of them are finally and fixedly convinced. . . . Every scheme founded upon the idea that they can remain together on the same soil beyond the briefest period, in any other relation than precisely that which now subsists between them, is not only preposterous, but fraught with deepest danger."

Elsewhere in the same paper, Senator Hammond draws a pen picture of a state of things following emancipation, which will be recognized as a condition largely true in 1893 :

" Very few of them could be prevailed on to do a stroke of work, none to labor continuously while a head of cattle, sheep, or swine could be found in our ranges, or an ear of corn nodded in our abandoned fields. These exhausted, our folds and poultry yards, barns and storehouses, would become their prey. Finally, our scattered dwellings would be plundered, perhaps fired, and the inmates murdered."

The negro convicts in our penitentiaries are in part the fulfillment of the dreary prophecy. The labor question and the moral condition of the Africans are making more and more conclusive every month why the two races can not dwell on the same soil in peace.

In 1782 Thomas Jefferson wrote concerning the negroes:

" Nothing is more certainly written in the book of fate than that these people are to be free ; nor is it less certain that the two races, equally free, can not live in the same country." *

Senator J. J. Ingalls is thus reported in the *Atlanta Constitution,* December 3, 1888:

" Unless history is a false teacher, it is not possible for two distinct races, not homogeneous—that is, which can not assimilate by intermarriage and the mingling of blood—to exist upon terms of political equality under the same government. *One or the other must go to the wall.*"

Mr. Lincoln said, in his joint debate with Stephen A. Douglas on September 18, 1858, concerning the negroes:

" I am not, nor ever have been, in favor of bringing about in any way the social and political equality of the white and black races. I am not, nor ever have been, in favor of making voters or jurors of negroes, nor of qualifying them to hold office, nor to intermarry with white people ; and I will say, in addition to this, that there is a physical difference between the white and black races which I believe will forever forbid the two races living together on terms of social and political equality."

When opinions are the outgrowth of a large observation of facts, and the operation of causes and their effects upon the industrial, social, and

* Plea for Progress.

political relations of society, then such opinions are entitled to high consideration.

If the negro is here to stay, justice demands that he shall have an even chance in all political privileges, and that all the avenues of industry shall be thrown wide open for his advancement. To educate the negroes—fit them for high service—and then close all the doors of progress, is trifling with their destiny. In all the Northern States, there is no record of a negro judge, negro governor, negro State senator, negro mayor of a town or city, negro sheriff, negro officer of any sort, negro president or negro professor of a college. No negro minister of the gospel, however learned and however devout he may be, has up to this time, in all the years of the past, been called to serve a white church of any Christian denomination in the North. As far as we can learn, all these doors are closed there. Yet Northern sympathy, Northern philanthropy, Northern pleas, social, educational, and political, in behalf of the negroes, have been most emphatic. If this is the state of affairs in the North, what can be expected of the South, where the traditions of master and slave, to say nothing of other vital considerations, shut the door?

But history vetoes these privileges to the negroes on the soil of the Anglo-Saxon race. Hayti sends out its warning. The British Colonies in the West India Islands bring the intelligence of the whites leaving the islands, weary of the struggle with the negroes, and of " drifting into ruin ; " and this intelligence, so crushing to the hopes of Christian men, comes sixty years, nearly, after the manumission of the blacks. The reconstruction period of the South is replete in its lessons to the whole country, that the Anglo-Saxon people must and will rule this land. The North and the South are agreed upon this subject practically; their history runs in parallel lines, with this difference, that in the South are some sheriffs, State senators, and other civil officers of African descent, generally mulattoes.

These privileges denied, all these doors closed, the negroes " must go to the wall." Their progress is hemmed in by conditions rooted in the natural antagonism and superiority of the Anglo-Saxon people, and this is stronger than the Chinese Wall. Add to this the moral causes characterizing the twenty-seven years of the negro's freedom, filling the land with violence and convulsions. Seventy-five per cent. of the criminal expense bill in the South is due to the negroes ; 26,046 negroes crowd the asylums.

This status claims attention. Separation is the path of safety for both races. Wisdom, humanity, and Christian duty demand it. The best interests of the children of the white race and the black race require that the separation of the races receive speedy and earnest consideration.

If there is any other feasible plan to remove existing evils, and impending dangers increasing five times as fast as population, it has not been revealed. It is madness to trifle with the situation. Separation is better and cheaper than armed battalions.

The leading men of this race are waking up and

are looking to Africa as the future home for their
people. During the session of the Colored Institute, held in the city of Birmingham, Alabama, in
the month of August, 1893, Bishop Abram Grant,
D.D., is reported as having expressed himself thus:
In his opinion "the condition of things is such, that
*the colored people need to consider the subject of eventu-
ally making Africa their future home.*"

In the special to the New Orleans *Times-Democrat*, from which the statement is taken, this is
added:

"The Institute is made up of some of the ablest colored men of
the South. Graduates of colleges will take part in the discussion
touching on the future of the sons of Ham. Rev. W. H. Sheppard,
the colored missionary to Africa, is here, and in attendance upon
the Institute. *He believes Africa to be the proper place for the negro
race.*"

Following this, appeared an article in the Phila-
delphia *Press*, from Bishop Turner, in which he
takes strong grounds in favor of negro emigration
to Liberia. This is a negro republic in Africa,*
"extending 500 miles along the grain coast of
Upper Guinea, and reaching about 50 miles into
the interior. It was originally established by an
association of which Henry Clay was president,
for the purpose of furnishing a home for emancipated negroes, and giving them opportunities of
self-improvement and self-government, in 1821."

Bishop Turner's position is thus stated:

"The Anglo-Saxon race that controls this country is a peculiar one.
It is a masterful and dominating race. *Wherever it has settled among*

* The People's Family Atlas of the World.

other races by colonization, it has always either subjected the native races or exterminated them. It has subjected the native races in India, and at the Cape of Good Hope in Africa. It has practically extermi- nated the Indians in the United States, and it has, to all intents and purposes, wiped out the natives in Australia and New Zealand. . . . We do not believe that the Caucasian will accept the African as an equal in every respect. We are in favor of a judicious emigra- tion to Liberia. We should like to see a large number of young men with ambition and energy, of middle-aged or old men with experience and capital, of old and young men and women with edu- cation and culture to train the young, of mechanics and agicultur- ists, to go ,there to settle that country, the only one in addition to Hayti where the problem of negro government is being solved. We have visited Africa more than once, and have inspected the territorial domain of the Liberian republic, modeled after the United States in its legislative, executive, and judicial departments, and we speak of what we know and have seen."

Colonization is the hope of the African race. It is best for them and their children. It is best for the white people. All the facts of the case lead to this conclusion. It ends the strife, the turmoil. It is the one foundation for hope to prevent untold suffering to both races, and final extinction to the Hamites. Even now the land is full of violence. The discontent and the dissatisfaction of the Anglo- Saxon people, due to the thriftless habits, the wide- spread idleness and crime of the Africans, are ominous. Thoughtful men dare not close their eyes to the elements of this inflammatory situation. The existence of present conditions will not be a paralytic longevity, unless Anglo-Saxon history is reversed. Neither education nor the sanctuary, it is believed, will ever remove African racial peculiari- ties here. The white and the black races can not blend. The difference between them is not merely a difference in color. It is of very small importance in the race question. The distinctive race qualities of the Africans are not only unique, but fix the gulf between the Africans and the Anglo-Saxons. Upon these qualities rests the history of this race, and these qualities call aloud for their exodus, their colonization. It is mercy, humanity, and justice to them.

Dr. E. T. Winkler relates in the *International Review*, that at the National Emigration Convention of Colored People, held at Cleveland, Ohio, in August, 1854, Dr. M. R. Delany, a negro of pure blood, who was then recognized as one of the most cultivated and distinguished representatives of his people, and who subsequently received the rank of major in the service of the United States, presented a paper on the *Political Destiny of the Colored Race*, which was adopted by the Convention without modification. The following extracts from this authoritative document are worthy of attention:

"Our friends in this and other countries, anxious for our elevation, have for years been erroneously urging us *to lose our identity as a distinct race, declaring that we were the same as other people. The truth is, we are not identical with the Anglo-Saxon, or any other race of the Caucasian, or pure white, type of the human family;* and *the sooner we know and acknowledge the truth, the better for ovrselves and our posterity.* The English, French, Irish, German, Italian, Turk, Persian, Greek, Jew, and all other races, have their native or inherent peculiarities, and why not our race? We are not willing, therefore, at all times and under all circumstances, to be moulded into various shapes of eccentricity to suit the conveniences and caprices of every kind of people. We are not more suitable to everybpdy than everybody is to us; therefore, *no more like other peo-*

ple than others are like us. We have inherent traits, attributes, so
to speak, and *native characteristics, peculiar to our race, whether of
pure or mixed blood;* AND ALL THAT IS REQUIRED OF US IS TO
CULTIVATE THESE, AND DEVELOP THEM IN THEIR PURITY. . . .
They [our fathers] admitted themselves to be inferiors ; we barely
acknowledge the whites as equals, perhaps not in every particular."

This extract is taken from the *Life of Major
M. R. Delany.*

To cultivate these " inherent traits " and " native
characteristics," peculiar to the race, and " develop
them in their purity," demands separation. It cannot be done on American soil.

Dr. Winkler adds :

" Twenty years ago (1854) the Cleveland Convention directed the
African exodus to Central and South America and the West Indies ;
and to-day (1874) Mexico fronts these wandering tribes as the land
of promise and the seat of power. There they may rest, amid such
conditions of climate, soil, and company as suit their constitution,
their habits, and their instincts. There they will feel at home, as
they bask in the sun, and feast upon the spontaneous fruits of the
tropics." *

Since then, the great Congo Basin of Africa has
been opened. This is the native land of the Hamites.†

" In the opinion of some of the eminent scientists of the world,
the Congo Basin will become the granary of the world. Vegetation
of all kinds thrives most luxuriantly, as many as three crops a year of
some kinds of vegetables coming to maturity. Coffee grows wild."

Can the negroes go without help? It is fair, it
is but common justice to this people, that the
nation that enslaved them should not only aid them

---

* *International Review*, Vol. I., No. 5, pp. 591–594.
† New York *Times*, Feb. 14, 1889.

7

in selecting their future home or homes, but transport them to their homes, and provide them with the necessaries of life during the first year of their new residence.

A thoughtful writer from Georgia has shown in the *Times-Democrat* of New Orleans, of May 23, 1893, that the entire negro population of the United States—9,000,000—can be transported to Africa in thirty years, at a cost of $25 per capita, or a total of $225,000,000. To this sum he adds $525,000,000 to start them in their new home with food supplies, clothing, and necessary implements of husbandry. This makes a grand total of $750,000,000, and this vast sum can be raised at a cost of 1½ per cent. on the assessed valuation of our property. According to this plan, 300,000 could be transported annually. The sooner the initiatory steps for the exodus of the negroes are taken, the better will it be for both races.

The advantages of such an exodus of the negroes will be manifold.

1. It will relieve the whole country of its embarrassed condition. The racial qualities of the Africans threaten the peace of the country every day. It is the only plan by which a war of races can be averted in the near future.

2. As fast as they leave, a vigorous white population will take their place. The same enterprise and industry attending the influx of population into Texas and Florida will characterize the South.

3. The negroes from the Southern States will be better prepared to work out their destiny in their

new home than those of Hayti and the British colonies of the West India Islands. Their close touch with the Anglo-Saxon people, the educational and religious influence, the industry and enterprise of the land, ought to fit African leaders for independent national life. If ever the negroes can be fitted for self-government, they have had splendid opportunity for such preparation, North and South, during the past thirty years. This may be the way of Providence concerning the sons of Ham.

4. The gradual exodus plan, whether it covers twenty or thirty years, would annually throw new and vigorous life into the new African home and government.

5. If Christian negroes, ministers of the gospel particularly, have the zeal and the missionary spirit of their white brethren, they will embrace this plan to carry the gospel message to their kindred of the Dark Continent. Through them Africa can be Christianized. More ought to be done for Africa by a large number of negro ministers of the gospel in one year than has thus far been accomplished in fifty years.

6. It solves the negro problem. The exodus of this people puts forever at rest this vexed question. Without it, there is no peace for the South; its development is checked; its prosperity is lame and sickly; misunderstanding of the negroes between the North and the South will continue; violence and lawlessness will hardly cease; the negro's idleness will continue to paralyze agricultural industry; and the alarming increase of crime and vice among

this people will hasten the day of a pitiless war of races.

In these pages the Africans have frequently been referred to as negroes. The term has been used in no sense to express anything that is degrading. Under the term "colored population" are included negroes, mulattoes, quadroons, octoroons, Chinese, Japanese, and Indians. Negroes designate all those of African descent.

We have described this people as a daily witness of their life on the farm, in the village, and in the town, for a period of twenty-eight years. Neither ill will nor prejudice has been our motive. We have befriended them in their educational work and in their religious work. We have defended them in times of violence. We are not conscious that there is a negro, living or dead, whom we have knowingly wronged in any sense whatsoever, and this is the statement of candor and truth.

Our plea to-day is—as it has ever been our plea —as long as the negroes remain among us, show them kindness—genuine kindness—and in full measure. Deal fairly and honestly with them. Help them educationally, religiously, and industrially. Help them with good counsel. Organized efforts may improve their morals. Industrial schools, not makeshifts, but such as shall do what the name implies, may do much. The common schools, so far as they relate to this people, and so far as these agencies can be judged by the fruit they have borne, are not satisfactory. They have removed illiteracy in a degree. The beneficiaries have not been in-

spired to make their lives useful, but rather to shun
and despise honest toil. Make these schools something better than mere mechanical agents to impart
so much knowledge. Lessons in punctuality, clean-
liness, honesty, industry, and the like, would be invaluable to this race. Make these schools morally
disciplinary. Knowledge should show the path to
virtue. Make the common schools efficient agents
to energize moral principle. Dead perfunctory
hearing of lessons is a waste of time and money.

In dealing with the race problem, and until it is
solved, no duty is more solemnly binding upon the
Southern people, and joined to every interest, than
obedience to constituted legal authority. Defective
laws are better than no laws. A bad government is
better than anarchy. To render obedience to " the
powers that be," to sustain the authorities, to let
the law take its course, are the dictates of reason.
A lawless land, where every man can take his grievances, real or imaginary, into his own hands, is an
accursed land. There can be no safety to life or
property where this spirit prevails. Mob law is
hateful in every way. It is subversive of justice.
It is an adder, always stinging its deluded victims.
It converts right into wrong. It damages the par-
ticipant ; to him it is a personal injury. It is cruel
in all its features. Under such a rule innocence has
no protection. To-day it strikes the negro ; to-
morrow it threatens the white man. It is ruinous
to the country. It shames our Christianity. Such
a law is a cheat and a delusion. It proposes to correct crime with crime, and so it forms a league with

guilt. It has done infinite harm, and reformed nothing. Distress and trouble have invariably come home to its blind partisans.

"Righteousness exalteth a nation," not violence. Strengthen the right by every influence that can give it power. Wrong in every form must be brought into disrepute. The perjurer wickedly insults the God in whose hand his breath is, severs the bond that binds truth to the throne of justice, and destroys the confidence that holds society together. The assassin assumes the prerogative of God, and loads his memory with a crime that gnaws to the core. Every lawless act has its penal consequences. No crime exalts, but degrades. All guilt lowers the man before the court of his own soul. Wrong is commissioned with curses; right is dowered with blessings to mankind. Right knows neither rich nor poor, neither white nor black.

To do the right is the path of wisdom and virtue. The best interests of the individual and the country depend upon it. Here is hope; here is order; here is security. Happy are the people who love and honor the laws of the land. Every evasion, infraction, or subterfuge affecting the purpose or the execution of law is a public injury. Right embodied in statutes, and these firmly and impartially enforced, are essential to peace and prosperity.

INDEX.

A.

Acreage, farm, increase of, 103.

Acres, number of, in England, owned by 11,000 persons, 154.

Acres, number of, in England, Wales, Scotland, and Ireland, 154.

Acres, three-fourths of an, to each of 27,000,000 Englishmen, 155.

Africa, Rev. W. H. Sheppard favors, 254.

Africans, aspiring portion of, 205.

Agencies to wrest the land from the people, 158.

Agents, all the, used in production, entitled to their just share, 185.

Agricultural States, twenty-nine, under mortgages, 153.

Agriculture, report of the Commissioner of, 244.

Alabama, credit system in, 72, 82.

Alabama, negro crimes in 1890, 232.

Ancestor of the negroes, 203.

Anglo-Saxon free men, their galling yoke, 49.

Anglo-Saxons a dominant race, 255.

Anglo-Saxons rule North and South, 8.

Area, land, in the Southern States, 134.

Arithmetic, too much in lien laws, 51.

Arkansas, credit system in, 72, 77.

Atkinson, Mr. Edward, on cotton production, 246.

Attorney-General of Texas on lands granted to corporations, 160.

Australian negro, a type of negroes, 203.

Avoirdupois, a pound equals twelve ounces, 50.

B.

Bacon, pounds of, sold by one merchant in fifteen years, 128.

Balance sheet of losses, 128.

Balances of merchants in November and December, 18.

Bankruptcy, first step to, 20.

Barbadoes, prosperity ended with emancipation, 117.

Baubles, effect on negroes, 6.

Baxendale, Joseph, maxims of, 95.

Bengalee, the character of, 175.

Bills, railroad land grant, 140, 141.

Blacks in the United States, 204.

Blacks, the, of Jamaica, will not work, 116.

Blakely, Mr., speculator in warrants, 65.

Boss, effect of the boss idea on the negroes, 41.

"Breeding, brains, or bullion" control society, 182.

Business conducted on credit, ruinous to the masses, 168.

Business, everybody's, to do right, 178.

Business, its scope and meaning, 165.

Business, the prettiest in the world, 47.

Business, the term degraded in its use, 165.

C.

Caffres, type of negroes, 203.

Caperton, James, merchant, on prices, 65.

Capital of credit merchant, gains on, 80.

Capital, when a Nero, is a tyrant, 185.

Carelessness not the basis of prosperity, 19.

Cash and credit prices, table of, 92.

Cash basis, when attainable, 92.

Cash business, a necessity for the masses, 35

Cash merchant, experience of, 30.

Cash prices of certain articles, 29.

Cattle, number of, in 1860 and 1890, 125.

Cause, a, of the farmer's troubles, 22.

Causes, general and special, of depression, 34.

Cereals in 1860, Table I., 99.

Cereals in 1889, Table II., 100.

Characters, leading, in "Uncle Tom's Cabin," 207.

Cheat, the successful, soon became rich, 168.

Christianity must give sanction to laws, 184.

Church, colored, draws rent from 180 farmers, 153.

Churches, negro, in Pike County, Miss., 233.

Civilization, the, of the Huguenot, in danger, 231.

Clarion-Ledger, opinion of, on lien laws, 90.

Class, the industrious, sustains the towns, 197.

Classes, four industrial classes in Southern towns, 188.

Cleveland, the convention, conclusion of, in 1854, 257.

Climate, no effect of, on white men, 246.

Coffee, production of, during era of freedom, 115.

Coffee, production of, in Hayti in 1789, 114.

Collar, a, around the neck of the Anglo-Saxon, 168.

Colonization of the negroes best for both races, 255.

Comparison in land area between the South and the German Empire, 134.

Competition, healthy, in trade, dead, 60.

Condition of farmers in 1890, 132.

Condition of Hamitic labor, a serious matter, 238.

Confidence, basis of, 13.

Congo Basin of Africa, productiveness of, 257.

Connecticut, negro crimes in, 1834 and 1880, 228, 229.

Content, torpid, of Dominica, 249.

Continent, the Dark, what has been done for, 218.

Copartnership, the joint, 23.

Copartnership with sorrow, 50.

Corn acreage, short, 63.

Corn, the negro will not raise, 109.

Cotton, bulk of, in Mississippi raised on the hills, 246.

Cotton, can white men raise, 244.

Cotton crop cornered, effect of, 55.

Cotton crop, value of, 66.

Cotton crop, value of, in 1870 and 1879, 120.

Cotton growing urged, 57.

Cotton, increase of, in its use, 60.

Cotton plant, 48.

Cotton produced now in three negro parishes of Louisiana, 246.

Cotton production, by black and white in Pike County, Miss., 233.

Cotton, production of, during era of freedom, 114.

Cotton, production of, in Hayti, in 1789, 114.

Cotton, purchaser of, determined eight months before it is made, 74.

Cotton raised by whites in 1883, 1884, and 1885, 245.

Cotton raised in ten States by black and white, 245.

Cotton, 70 per cent. raised by white men, 246.

Cotton, the world's demand from 1893 to 1899, 63.

Counsels, the, of an old book, 173.

Counterfeit, the, damages the true, 196.

Country, the, is the town's workshop, 191.

Course, common school, importance of defining, 192.

Covenant, the, 23.

Credit business, fruit of, in twenty-eight years, 95.

Credit, doctrine of, 12.

Credit, his line of, and cotton growing, 57.

Credit prices, 20 to 100 per cent. above market value, 84.

Credit system, a step to lien laws, 46.

Credit system, indefiniteness of, 15, 16.

Credit system, opinion by Raymond *Gazette*, 74.

Credit system, pernicious effects, 12.

"Cretians, the, are always liars," 175.

Crop, one commercial, policy of, 130.

Credit system introduced, 10, 11.

Cultivation of the soil in Dominica growing less, 249.

Cultivation of the soil in Dominica, less annually, 117.

Cultivators, white, of cotton, increasing, 245.

Customers, good, pay bad debts, 66.

D.

Damage, the, of too many studies, 193.

Debtor bound to the creditor, 17.

Debts, bad, who pays them, 24.

Debts in 1865, 10.

Debts in Jamaica, 116.

Decoy ducks, variety of, 42.

Deficiency in corn and oats, 103.

Depredations, negro, causes leading to, 45.

Desolation in the South in 1865, 1.

Despotism of fear on negroes, 4.

Destiny of the colored race, by Dr. M. R. Delany, 256.

Difference in grain crops and population, 101.

Disabilities, political, on black, effect of, 249.

Disadvantages of the Southern farmer, 2.

Discount placed on all services by lien laws, 51.

Disease, too large a population in towns, proof of, 188.

Disparity in the crime record, 225.

Distinction, moral, defaced, 165.

Distress, negroes in, how regarded, 3.

Disturbances, causes leading to, 32.

Dollars, two million, saved on cash basis, 95.

Dominica, rich soil of, 117.

Drawbridge executes a mortgage, 21.

Drew, Samuel, on remedy for hard times, 67.

Dumas, Alexander, to find a man, 67.

Duty as related to consequences, 179.

E.

Easygo, Mr., terms on which bought, 61.

Economy, what it could have done, 27.

Education in towns, 191.

Education of negroes, result of, in Northern States, 224.

Effect of negative characters on society, 177.

Effect of night meetings on negroes in some cases, 5.

Effect of the negroes on the English West Indies, 212.

Effect of the negroes upon the country, 212.

Effect of town schools upon the country, 196.

Encouragement offered by the white people, 6.

England's farm tenantry, condition of, 154.

English, the, in the West Indies, melting away, 116.

Enrolment, school, in three

Northern States and three Southern States, 213.

Epitaph on the life of Mr. Hacker, 171.

Estate, superb, sold under the hammer, 62.

Estate, the American landed, 135.

Estates, humbler, hopeless prospect of the, 62.

Estates in Jamaica offered for sale, 116.

Everett, Mr., on negro crimes in Massachusetts in 1833; 228.

Evils, great, in their relation to peace, 180.

Evils in society, how checked or exterminated, 178.

Example, pernicious, of an influential man, 198.

Exchange, the science of, its prominence, 166.

Excuses, crowding life with, 190.

Expenditure, school, per capita, Table B, 214.

Expenditure, school, per cent. on valuation of property, 214.

Expense bill that could be saved, 66.

Expensiveness of the credit business, 80.

Exports of Hayti, highest annual, since 1790, 115.

Exports of Hayti in 1789 and 1790, 115.

F.

Failure of four months' schools, cause of, 194.

Failures in business are not all honest, 173.

Farm, every, a feeder to the town, 189.

Farmers, American, their position to society, 166.

Farmers embarrassed by merchant farmers, 41.

Farmers, general condition of, 31.

Farmers, how they fared under existing methods, 169.

Farmers, the Southern, their hard lot, 2.

Farm-life favorable to virtue, 166, 167.

Farms cultivated by owners in 1880, 145.

Farms, effect of credit system on, 152.

Farms, merchant, how worked, and effect, 39, 40.

Farms, number and size, gains as to ownership, 150.

Farms, number and size, in 1860 and 1880, 148.

Farms, number and size, in three groups, 149.

Farms, number and size of, in each class, 147.

Farms, number and size of, in ten States in 1880, 145.

Farms, number and size of, in ten States in 1860, 144.

Farms rented for money, Table IV., 146.

Farms rented for share of product, Table V., 146.

Farms, tenure of, in ten States, in 1880, 147.

Farms, who own them, 151.

Fences, cost of, in ten States, 131.

Fertilizers, cost of, in ten States, 131.

Fitzurse, Dick, the son of Riskall, 169.

Florida, credit system in, 82, 83.

Florida, immigration into, 246.

Florida, land in, owned by foreigners, 143.

Flour, value of, 28.

Food products, annual loss of, in Mississippi, 129.

Foot-ball, the, the negroes, of superior races, 201.

Forces, the moral, of society, of supreme importance, 182.

Forces, the uplifting and the down grade, of the negroes, 209.

Foreclosures of mortgages, 10.

" Forty acres and a mule," 4.

Freedmen, the effect of their ignorance, 2.

Freedom, stimulus of, no incentive to the negro, 117.

Freeholders, their danger, 21.

Froude, James Anthony, quoted, 116.

Froude, Mr., on the two races in the English West Indies, 249.

Funerals, negro, attendance on, 3.

G.

Gains, cash basis, table of, 93.

Gains, on a cash basis, on 10,000 bales of cotton, 94.

Galveston News on land held by aliens, 160.

Gambling in negro labor, 3.

Georgia, credit system in, 83.

Gorget, significant inscription on, 168.

Government of a dozen, sign of decay, 200.

Grady, Henry W., effects of wealth, 54.

Grants, land, to build railroads, 141, 142.

Grasp, beyond, of many farmers, buying on time, 69.

Grenada, scene of desolation in, 116.

Groove, farmers and merchants have dropped into, 79.

Grundy, Mrs., opinion of, 50.

Guinea negroes, qualities of, 205.

Guinea, the type of negroes in the South, 203.

"Gurth," no real, in the South, 168.

H.

Hacker, Mr., an honest man, 170.

Ham, four types of, in Africa, 203.

Hamites, the past, a dreary waste, 203 ; prospects of the educated, 241 ; prospects of the race, 248.

Hammond, Harry, Esq., on credit system, 84.

Hammond, J. H., United States Senator, prediction by, 250.

Harlem, merchant, view of the situation, 24.

Haygood, farmer, cash and credit prices, 65.

Hayti, production of in 1789, 114 ; productions during era of freedom, 114, 115.

Hill, Hon. B. H., ruined by speculators, 59.

Hogg, Governor, of Texas, on land corporations, 162.

Holland, Dr. J. G., on silence, 180.

Home, live at, 63.

Homeless in the land of their birth, 10.

Honesty no substitute for meanness, 170.

Honesty relegated to an inferior position, 48.

Honor prostituted, 176.

Horses, number of, in 1860 and 1890, 126.

Hostility, no cause for, between classes, 32.

Hottentots, type of negroes, 203.

I.

Idea, the retaliatory, in the conduct of men, 172.

Idleness not a virtuous commodity, 190.

Ignorance, as to size of debts, 17.

Ignorance, negro, effect of, 6.

Immigration, white, into Florida, 246.

Immigration, white, into Texas, 246.

Inches, twenty, equal a yard, 172.

Income of 200,000 Englishmen, 156.

Indefiniteness of our school work, 196.

Indefiniteness of the credit system, 15, 16.

Indians forced westward, 248.

Indifference of towns respecting farm labor, 190.

Industry, principal, of Southern towns, 187.

Influence, evil, of the system of advances, 82.

Influence, for the negro, extraneous, 202.

Influence, moral, of the towns, 197.

Ingalls, J. J., Senator, on the destiny of the negroes, 251.

Intelligence of the Iolofs and Caffres, 205.

Iolofs, a type of negroes, 203.

Irby, Senator, on the causes of unrest in the South, 73.

Irresponsibility, false claim of, 176.

Island of Dominica, torpid content of, 249.

J.

Jamaica, debt and taxation of, in 1887, 116.

Jamaica, productions of, in 1834, 1860, and 1867, 115.

Jefferson, Thomas, predictions by, concerning negroes, 251.

Joshua, no, among the negroes, 201.

Judiciary, report of common, relative to negroes, 229.

Justice, the administration of, effect of the doctrine of irresponsibility on, 181.

L.

Labor, depreciation of, in value, 236.

Labor, free negro, a failure in three lands, 117.

Labor, how regarded by negroes, in 1874, 211.

Labor, in general, may act the tyrant, 185.

Labor, need of, on farms compared with need of roads, 189.

Labor, negro, effect of merchant farms on, 41, 42, 43.

Labor, negro, unsupervised, cause of trouble, 87.

Labor, supervision of negro, necessary, 244.

Land, available and unavailable, 136.

Land corporations in Texas, 161, 162.

Land, farm, owned by merchants, 38.

Land, farm, total in acres, 136.

Land in Florida owned by foreigners, 143.

Land in Texas owned by one syndicate, 142.

Land, large bodies of, few left, 75.

Land, Mississippi, owned by English syndicate, 143.

Land monopoly, danger toward, 151.

Land owned by aliens, locality of, 139.

Land, railroad, 140.

Land spoliation, the danger of, 159.

Landlords, England's, 157.

Laws, the best, how evolved, 190.

Lawyers, success of, 31.

Lessons in industry, value of, 209.

Liberia favored as a home for the negroes by Bishop Grant, 254.

Lie, a, is a confession of weakness, 175.

Lies, a catalogue of, 176.

Lien laws, general effect of, 36.

Lien laws in relation to negroes on merchant farms, 41.

Lien laws, opinion concerning, by *Clarion-Ledger*, 90.

Lien serf, the, Harry Yellowly, 168.

Liens, cost to record, 91.

Liens, number, in eleven counties of South Carolina, 85.

Life, no, isolated, 199.

Life on farms, conducive to morality, 166, 167.

Lincoln County, Mississippi, mulattoes at institute, 207.

Lincoln, Mr., opinion of, concerning the negroes, 251.

Live-stock in 1860 and 1890, Tables I., II., and III., 125, 126.

Loss, annual, for current supplies, 79.

Loss, average, for each county in the Southern States, 79.

Loss in animals, Southern States, 124.

Loss on cotton in 1867 and 1868, 59.

Losses, balance sheet of, 128.

Louisiana, credit system in, 76.

Lucia, St., the chief complaints in, 116.

M.

Macaulay, on debts, 17.

MacVicar, Rev. Dr., on licentiousness of negroes, 231.

Management, wild, 20.

Man, the selfish, makes the world useful to himself, 180.

Man, the true, makes himself useful to the world, 180.

Mann, Horace, quoted, 188.

Mark, the fatal cross, on liens, 172.

Marlborough, character of, 183.

Massachusetts, negro crimes in, 1833, 228.

Matthews, William, 54.

Mechanics make a living, 31.

Memories, bitter, 43, 44.

Men, bad, in every organization, 167.

Men expressing convictions, few, 177.

Men, five hundred, tied up, 48.

Men, many distinguished, raised on farms, 166.

Men of convictions, many, 176.

Men, professional, fate of, if all were Nabal Hackers, 171.

Merchant, cash, experience of, 30.

Merchant, standing and service, 166.

Meriwether, Mr. Lee, on mortgages, 153.

"Might is right," the bad doctrine, 169.

Milch cows, number of, in 1860 and 1890, 125.

Millionaires in the South, 54.

Mississippi, credit system in, 72, 76.

Mississippi, land in, owned by English syndicate, 143.

Mississippi, negro crimes in, 1890, 232.

Moderation, selfish, mistaken for purest integrity, 181.

"Money, big, in nigger trade," 171.

Money, had more after the failure than before, 174.

Money, two plans to make, 46.

Morals and wealth, value of, to society, 182.

Morals, industrial, committee on, in order, 191.

Morals in politics, opinion of, by high official, 158.

Morals in public men, demand of, 183.

Morals, negro, in Dominica and Jamaica, 210.

Mortgage indebtedness, cost to ascertain, 91.

Mulattoes in the United States, 204.

Mulattoes, per cent., in each section of the United States, 205.

Mulattoes, qualities of, 205.

Mules, number of, in 1860 and 1890, 126.

N.

Negrillo, a type of negroes, 203.

Negroes, treatment of, by master and stranger, 3 ; their labor, a gambling commodity, 3; whims of, 3 ; fascination for political meetings, 3 ; three do as much work as one formerly, 111 ; quality of their work, 111 ; negro farm labor decreasing, 112; their number in Hayti in 1789, 113 ; in English West Indies, in 1834, 115; their passive nature, 201 ; a bone of contention, 202 ; achievements of, 202 ; aboriginal type in five lands, 203 ; description of, 203; in what they have made progress, 207, 208 ; effect of racial qualities, 213 ; what the South has done for their education, 215, 216 ; contribution for, by organized benevolence, 217 ; by the Southern States, 217 ; number in six Northern States, Table D, 219; number of convicts in these States, Table E, 220 ; number in six Southern States, Table F, 220 ; convicts in six Southern States, Table G, 221 ; number of convicts per 100,000 inhabitants in six Northern States, Table H, 221 ; number convicts per 100,000 inhabitants in six Southern States, Table I, 222 ; criminal record of, in Northern States, 223 ; criminal record of in Southern States, 225 ; general crime record, 226 ; trials in inferior courts, 227 ; crimes against each other, 227 ; crimes in Massachusetts in 1833, 228 ; crimes in Connecticut in 1834, 228 ; crimes in Connecticut in 1880, 229 ; crimes in Ohio in 1835, 229 ; in Ohio, 1880, Table H, 221 ; crimes of, in Vermont, 1830, 229 ; transformation in the life, from 1860 to 1890, 230 ; Southern towns embarrassed by their vices, 230; degradation of, 231 ; treatment of the "one crime," 231 ; testimony by Rev. Dr. MacVicar, 231; crimes in Alabama in 1890, 232 ; in Mississippi in 1890, 232 ; in Pike County, Miss., 1893, 232 ; status of this race in Pike County, Miss., 233, 234 ; cost of crime and education in Pike County, Miss., 234 ; church members in Mississippi, 235 ; cost of education in Mississippi, 235 ; value of the work of the younger generation, 237 ; race not self-sustaining, 238; non-productive class, Tables A, B, and C, 238, 239 ; working class, Table D, 240 ; prospect of the educated Hamites, 241 ; labor of, in English West Indies, 249 ; number of, in Dominica, 249 ; in St. Vincent, 249 ; door to advancement of, closed in the North, 252 ; "must go to the wall," 253 ; number in asylums, 253 ; government aid necessary to colonize them, 257 ; cost to colonize, 258 ; advantages of colonization, 258, 259 ; a plea for fair dealing, 260, 261, 262.

North Carolina, credit system in, 85, 86.

Nudity and rags, sign of, 188.

O.

Object of towns, 187.

Octoroons in the United States, 204.

Officers of the State make a living, 31.

Ohio, negro crimes in, 221, 229.

Opinion, concurrent, concerning furnishing merchants, 79.

Opinions, public, how produced, 178.

Ounces, twelve, equal a pound, 172.

Outlook, the, blue for the farmer, 21.

Overproduction of cotton, cause of, 56.

Ownership, alien, in land, 138, 139.

Ownership in land by syndicates, 139.

Ownership, land, 136, 137.

Ownership, railroad, in land, 137, 138.

Ox, the, thou shalt not muzzle, 169.

P.

Papuan, a type of negroes, 203.

Parade, too much, in our school work, 193.

Parishes, three, in Louisiana, cotton produced in, 246.

Pay, poor, to educated men, 197.

Pen-mark, no, of a pure Hamite, 202.

People, five hundred, in town, without money, 188.

Percentage, the, that farmers cannot pay, 169.

Perils threatening the American estate, 158.

Perjury, its effect on society, 25, 174.

Persons engaged in agriculture, Table VI., 106; classified,

Table VII., 110; value of negro work on the farm, Table VIII., 110.

Physicians make a moderate living, 31.

Picayune, the New Orleans, on concentrating wealth, 56.

Pike County, Miss., negro crimes, 1893, 232.

Plaint, the monotonous, 132.

Plan, the credit system, too dangerous, 68.

Policy, the selfish, had no remedy, 89.

Population, increase in ten Southern States, 97; white, three periods, Table IV., 104; colored, three periods, Table V., 105; surplus in, in Southern towns, 188; school, in three Northern and three Southern States, 213; in Pike County, Miss., 232; of England, 154.

Pork cornered, 55.

Poverty of Southern farmers, 62.

Poverty of Southern people in 1865, 9.

Preparation for dishonest failures, 173.

Presidents of the United States, fifteen came from farms, 166.

Price of cotton and old debts, 53.

Price of cotton, fluctuations in, 58.

Price of provisions, 58.

Prices, credit, from 1865 to 1893, 70, 71, 73, 93.

Productions in Jamaica, three periods, 115.

18

Productions on six square miles, 191.

Productiveness, Congo Basin, Africa, 257.

Products, agricultural, of 1860 and 1880, Table III., 102.

Products, food, decrease of, in Southern States, 97.

Progress, how measured, 54.

Progress of the negroes, 207, 208.

Property, effect of negro licentiousness on, in Connecticut, 229.

Properties, fine, in the market in Jamaica, 116.

Prosperity, general, not in the country, 32.

Prosperity in Barbadoes ended with emancipation, 117.

Prosperity, material, not the supreme object, 198.

Prosperity of furnishing merchants, 62.

Prudence, value of, 178, 179.

Q.

Quadroons in the United States, 204.

Qualities of the negroes, 210.

Qualities, the racial, of the negroes, ruinous effect of, 213.

Quality, the industrial, of the negroes, opposed to progress, 241.

Quicksand, the man in the, 68.

R.

Race question, the, demands attention, 247.

Races in the English West Indies will not blend, 249.

Races, unlike, cannot live in harmony, 248.

Railroad land owned by foreign capitalists, 142.

Railroads, miles of, in the United States, 141.

Raymond *Gazette* on the credit system, 74.

Reasons for deportation of negroes, by Bishop Turner, 255.

Reconstruction period in the South, lessons of, 253.

Reënslavement, effect of report on negroes, 4.

Reflections, bitter, traced to credit business, 21.

Reformation, how produced, 81.

Relations between black and white, 235.

Religious meetings by negroes, 4, 5.

Remedies against land speculation, 164.

Remuneration of capital on farms, 33.

Rental drawn from English farms, 154.

Residence of blacks and mulattoes in the United States, 204.

Right and wrong not contingent on knowledge, 171.

Risks of the farmers, 34.

Roads, good, value of, 189.

Roads in Dominica, 249.

Ruskin on the condition of the poor in England, 157.

S.

Salary of 177 clergymen in England, 156.

Saying, a favorite, of Mr. Hacker, 170.

Schedule, tax, effect of idleness on, 189.

Schools, common, in towns, who support them, 193.

Schools, high, need of, 196.

Schools, public, in Pike County, Miss., for negroes, 233.

Schools, the four months of the country, follow the town, 194.

Self-denial, what it can do, 50.

Selfishness, the dominant, read in the desolation of homes, 171.

Selma *Times*, Ala., how to get out of debt, 75.

Separation, the path of safety, 253.

Services, all, discount placed on, by lien laws, 51.

Share plan of working, a favorite, 37.

Sheep, number of, in 1860 and 1890, 125.

Sherman, Wade, a negro, management of, 59.

Shylocks, their opportunity, 9.

Signatures, false, 50.

Situation, inflammatory elements of the, 255.

Situation, the, in 1893, 86.

Situation, the, in the South, an invitation to crookedness in business, 167.

Slavery, negro, dead forever, 6.

Slaves, eight hundred, do my bidding, 48.

Slaves in the English West Indies paid for, 115.

Smiles, Samuel, on high profits, 16.

Smith, Prof. Eugene Allen, on credit system, 82.

South, the, cannot be made a Hayti, 7.

South, the condition of, in 1865, 1.

South Carolina, credit system in, 84.

South-land, the, Shylock's eye is on, 152.

Speculation, era of, in the South, 57.

Speculators, their feast day after the war, 9.

Splendor, guilty, inquiry as to the cause, 167.

Statistics as to valuation of property in 1880, 26.

Stephens, Alexander H., quoted, 115.

Struggle, the, the English of Jamaica tired of, 116.

Studies in common schools, too many, 192.

Sugar, production of, during era of freedom, 114.

Sugar, production of, in Hayti in 1789, 114.

Sugar struck from the custom house lists in 1821, 114.

Surface land in ten States, 135.

Swearing, false, 25.

Swine, number of, in 1860 and 1890, 125.

Sympathy, the need of, between farmer and merchant, 69.

System, negro tenant, one form of, 87.

System, the oppression, broader than losses, 62.

T.

Talfourd, Judge, on sympathy, 69.

Temple, Sir William, considered self first, 180.

Testimony as to high prices and credit system in Alabama, 72 ; in Mississippi, 72 ; in Texas, 72 ; in Arkansas, 72 ; in Louisiana, 76 ; in Mississippi, 76 ; in Tennessee, 77 ; in Arkansas, 77 ; in Texas, 78 ; in Alabama, 82 ; in Florida, 82, 83 ; in Georgia, 83 ; in South Carolina, 84, 85 ; in North Carolina, 85, 86.

Texas land granted to corporations, 161.

Texas, land in, owned by one syndicate, 142.

Texas, white labor placed, at the head of cotton States, 246.

Thievery, negro, the cause of violence, 46.

Thrall, the, of Wagter Brothers, 169.

Times, hard, not surprising, 20.

Town, a, full of unemployed labor, no benefit to, 189.

Town, the, a political centre, 199.

Towns, ambition of, 188.

Townships in Southern States that lost population, 189.

Transactions, scurvy, what must be done to make them look fair and honest, 174.

Transactions, unscrupulous, cause of, 50.

Trusting, blind, required, 19.

Turner, Colonel, flimsy reflection of, at the gallows, 183.

Type of negroes that furnish leaders, 206.

U.

Uncle Tom's Cabin, leading characters in, 207.

Unrest, cause of, in the South, 73.

V.

Valuation of property in 1880, 26.

Value of farms, no progress in, Table IX., 118.

Value of farms, ten Northern States, Table X., 119.

Value of two cotton crops, 108.

Value, production of, 14.

Values, farm, cause of their reduction, 113.

Vermont, negro crimes in, 1830, 229.

Vice, men connive at, 181.

Vincent, St., prosperity of, 249.

Virtue, the one vicarious, on record, 171.

Voorhees, Senator D. W., on condition of England's farm tenantry, 154.

Votes, how cast by negroes, 4.

W.

Wage plan disliked by the negroes, 36.

" Wamba," no real, in the Southland, 168.

Warrants, school and bridge, price of, 65.

Wealth and morals, value of, to society, 182.

Wealth, great, a menace, 54.

Wealth, guilty, an infamous load, 172.

Wealth of the nation, 31,100 people own two-thirds, 184.

Wealth, when a blessing, 184.

Wheat crop cornered by one man, 55.

White Cap-ism, occasion of one form of, 86, 87.

White cultivators of cotton increasing, 245.

White labor in Texas, effect of, 246.

Whites in English West Indies drifting into ruin, 250.

Whites leaving Dominica, 249.

Winkler, Rev. Dr. E. J., opinion of, concerning the negroes, 211.

Work, better, in common schools, the need of, 195.

Work of negroes, character of the, 243.

Work of white man, character of the, 242.

Work-people, treatment of, in a Massachusetts factory, 54.

World, The, on land spoliation, 159.

Y.

Yard, a, equals 25 inches, 50.

Yellowly, Harry, the son of Hardfate, 168.

Yoke, Rehoboam's, is heavy, 170.